Instructor's Manual with Tests and Transparency Masters

6th Edition

# ORGANIZATIONAL BEHAVIOR
# AN EXPERIENTIAL APPROACH

# Instructor's Manual with Tests and Transparency Masters
Joyce S. Osland
Mary Anne Rainey

## 6th Edition

# ORGANIZATIONAL BEHAVIOR AN EXPERIENTIAL APPROACH

**David A. Kolb**
*Case Western Reserve University*

**Joyce S. Osland**
*University of Portland*

**Irwin M. Rubin**
*Temenos, Inc.*

PRENTICE HALL, Englewood Cliffs, New Jersey 07632

Project manager: Amy Hinton
Acquisitions editor: Natalie Anderson
Associate editor: Lisamarie Brassini
Manufacturing buyer: Ken Clinton

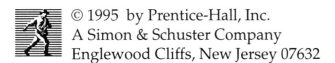 © 1995 by Prentice-Hall, Inc.
A Simon & Schuster Company
Englewood Cliffs, New Jersey 07632

All rights reserved. No part of this book may be
reproduced, in any form or by any means,
without permission in writing from the publisher.

Printed in the United States of America

10  9  8  7  6  5  4  3  2  1

ISBN 0-13-158171-6

Prentice-Hall International (UK) Limited, *London*
Prentice-Hall of Australia Pty. Limited, *Sydney*
Prentice-Hall Canada Inc., *Toronto*
Prentice-Hall Hispanoamericana, S.A., *Mexico*
Prentice-Hall of India Private Limited, *New Delhi*
Prentice-Hall of Japan, Inc., *Tokyo*
Simon & Schuster Asia Pte. Ltd., *Singapore*
Editora Prentice-Hall do Brasil, Ltda., *Rio de Janeiro*

# CONTENTS

Introduction

## Part I
## UNDERSTANDING YOURSELF AND OTHER PEOPLE AT WORK

| | | |
|---|---|---|
| 1. | The Psychological Contract and Organizational Socialization | 1 |
| 2. | Theories of Managing People | 9 |
| 3. | Individual and Organizational Learning | 15 |
| 4. | Individual Motivation and Organizational Behavior | 22 |
| 5. | Values and Ethics | 28 |
| 6. | Personal Growth, Career Development, and Work Stress | 33 |

## PART II
## CREATING EFFECTIVE WORK RELATIONSHIPS

| | | |
|---|---|---|
| 7. | Interpersonal Communication | 39 |
| 8. | Interpersonal Perception and Attribution | 47 |
| 9. | Group Dynamics and Self-Managed Work Teams | 53 |
| 10. | Managerial Problem Solving | 61 |
| 11. | Intergroup Conflict and Negotiation | 69 |
| 12. | Managing Diversity | 76 |

## PART III
## LEADERSHIP AND MANAGEMENT

| | | |
|---|---|---|
| 13. | Leadership | 83 |
| 14. | Leadership and Organizational Culture | 90 |
| 15. | Leadership and Decision Making | 97 |
| 16. | Leadership, Power and Influence | 105 |
| 17. | Empowerment and Coaching | 111 |
| 18. | Performance Appraisal | 117 |

## PART IV
## MANAGING EFFECTIVE ORGANIZATIONS

| | | |
|---|---|---|
| 19. | Organizational Analysis | 122 |
| 20. | Organization Design | 126 |
| 21. | Job Design and Job Involvement | 132 |
| 22. | Managing Change | 138 |

## APPENDICES

| | | |
|---|---|---|
| Appendix A: | Sample Short-session Course Design | 145 |
| Appendix B: | Sample Long-session Syllabus | 149 |
| Appendix C: | Peer Evaluation Form | 155 |
| Appendix D: | Annotated Bibliography on Cooperative Learning and Writing | 156 |
| Appendix E: | Mid-Course Evaluation Form | 162 |
| Appendix F: | The Personal Application Assignment (PAA) | 164 |
| Appendix G: | What We Look For When Grading Personal Application Assignments | 180 |
| Appendix H: | Example Personal Application Assignments | 182 |
| Appendix I: | Course Objectives | 187 |
| Appendix J: | Name Bingo | 188 |
| Appendix K: | How to Succeed in Organizational Behavior by Really Trying | 189 |
| Appendix L: | Performance Appraisal Role Plays | 190 |

## TRANSPARENCY MASTERS

| | |
|---|---|
| 1-0 | Characteristics of Organizational Behavior |
| 1-1 | Model for Managing Psychological Contracts |
| 2-0 | Young Lady |
| 2-1 | Old Lady |
| 2-2 | Old Lady/Young Lady |
| 2-3 | Quinn's Competing Values Model of Leadership |
| 2-4 | The Positive and Negative Zones |
| 3-0 | David Kolb's Experiential Learning Model |
| 3-1 | Learning Style Type Grid |
| 4-0 | David McClelland's Motive Theory |
| 4-1 | Expectancy Theory |
| 5-0 | Three Levels of Moral Development According to Kohlberg |
| 6-0 | Tripod of Life Plan Perspectives |
| 6-1 | Transactional Model of Career Stress |
| 7-0 | Model of Communication |
| 7-1 | Arc of Distortion |
| 7-2 | Categories of Behavior Characteristics of Supportive and Defensive Climates in Small Groups |
| 8-0 | Johari Window |
| 8-1 | Count the Squares |
| 9-0 | The Punctuated Equilibrium Model of Group Development |
| 9-1 | "Pure Types" of Emotional Behavior in Organizations |
| 9-2 | Symptoms of Groupthink |
| 9-3 | Remedies for Groupthink |
| 10-0 | Problem Solving as a Dialectic Process |
| 10-1 | The Learning Model and the Problem-Solving Process |
| 11-0 | Five Conflict-Handling Orientations |
| 12-0 | Geert Hofstede's Four Value Dimensions of National Culture |
| 13-0 | Continuum of Leadership Behavior |
| 13-1 | Continuum of Manager/Non-Manager Behavior |
| 13-2 | The Path Goal Theory |
| 14-0 | The Five Phases of Growth |
| 15-0 | Decision Process Flow Chart |
| 16-0 | Definition of Influence Tactics |
| 16-1 | Influence Styles |
| 17-0 | Effective and Ineffective Feedback |
| 18-0 | General Beliefs About Performance Appraisal |
| 19-0 | Components of an Open System |
| 19-1 | The Open System View of Organizations |
| 20-0 | Functional Form of Organization |
| 20-1 | Product or Service Form of Organization |
| 20-2 | Matrix Form of Organization |
| 21-0 | Job Characteristics Enrichment Model |
| 22-0 | The Process of Planned Change |

# INTRODUCTION

Thank you for choosing our textbooks: *Organizational Behavior: An Experiential Approach*, which we refer to as the workbook, and its companion volume, *The Organizational Behavior Reader*. We hope that teaching this course will be as pleasurable and rewarding for you and your students as it has been for us. We continue revising these books year after year because we strongly believe an experiential approach is the most effective way to teach this material and create a productive learning environment.

In addition to major revisions in the textbooks, this instructor's manual explains in greater detail how we teach the course and avoid or handle potential tricky bits. Professors always put their individual stamp upon this course. Many of them are kind enough to share their innovations with us, which we then incorporate into the texts or the manual. Please take the suggestions in this manual in the spirit we offer them -- not as the "one best way" to teach these classes but merely lessons professors have learned over the years that you may find helpful.

**Please note that the exercises in chapters 13 and 22 require materials that you will need to gather or prepare beforehand. Furthermore, the facilitator instructions for the exercise in chapter 13 are found only in the Instructor's Manual.** With a few exceptions that are noted in the beginning of each chapter in the instructor's manual, the other chapters contain all the materials and instructions you will need for the group exercises.

## I. About The Sixth Edition

Two decades have passed since the two original authors of the textbook started what they believed was an experiment in teaching the beginning Organizational Behavior course at the Sloan School of Management, MIT. That beginning resulted in six editions of these textbooks.

We have made major revisions in the workbook and the reader, in response to both developments in the field and feedback from professors who use these books. Major changes include new chapters on ethics and leadership, an expanded organizational culture chapter, and the addition of material on organizational learning, self-managed work teams, stress, and negotiation to existing chapters. The workbook format remains the same, but the text includes recent research findings and more information related to managing both diversity and international differences. The *Reader* includes numerous new articles that capture current thinking in the field.

## II. Overall Intent of the Text

Our stated intent in writing the workbook is to provide students of management with a course that engages not just their intellect, but their behaviors and feelings as well, so that they may actually experience in the classroom many of the issues associated with organizational life. In doing this, students work toward a second goal: learning how to learn from experience. The experiential learning model found in the third chapter explains the authors' assumptions about this type of learning; please read this chapter before beginning to structure your course. You may also wish to read David Kolb's book, *Experiential Learning*, (Englewood Cliffs, NJ: Prentice-Hall, 1984).

The chapters are designed to take the student through the experiential learning cycle -- concrete experience, reflective observation, abstract conceptualization, and active experimentation. The chapters begin with a **Vignette** that emphasizes the practical importance of the topic. The **Pre-meeting Preparation** not only outlines the "homework" for each session, but also attempts to ground students in their own experience and encourages them to focus upon what they want to learn. The ubiquitous question "What are the significant learning points from the readings?" nudges students to analyze what they've read and come prepared to integrate those points with the experiential exercise. The **Topic Introduction** presents what we see as the essential content information. Each chapter has an experiential exercise, described in **Procedure for Group Exercise**, that includes both instructions and debriefing questions. The **Follow up** either elaborates upon what occurred in the exercise or contributes additional content material. The **Learning Points** summarize the key points and **Tips for Managers** provide practical advice. Each chapter ends with the **Personal Application Assignment** which helps students analyze a personal incident by guiding them through the entire learning cycle.

### III. Role of the Instructor

Experiential learning requires a very different role for the instructor than the standard lecture or seminar format. It helps to think of yourself as a coach who should be modeling good supervisory or managerial behavior. Each chapter includes an exercise (role play, simulation, case) that is designed to involve all students in a variety of ways. The teacher's role becomes less one of purveying information and more one of managing the class and classroom as a learning organization. Some units require you to do very little other than keep track of time, a chore you may wish to delegate anyway. There are many times when the instructor should play an unobtrusive role and let the students take the major responsibility for the learning that goes on. The primary task of instructors is to develop a good climate for learning; this means modeling respect, curiosity, and a non-judgmental attitude. Some of the most common interventions that instructors make are: bringing a discussion back on track, ensuring that students are not avoiding or overlooking certain types of behavior, and clarifying points about research findings. With the exception of the opening lecturette, the instructor contributes knowledge on an "as needed" basis and always attempts to let the students get there first.

Given the experiential nature of the course, it's a great advantage if instructors can "read" group and individual behavior and skillfully handle whatever situations arise. Occasionally, they must gently help students see the negative effects of their behavior on other people. If you want to develop these process skills, it helps to observe an experienced instructor or read more about group facilitation. When you first begin teaching this course, you often come up with your best responses to questions and what occurs in class as you are driving home ("What I really should have said was..."). You just have to trust that all that revisionist history and delayed brilliance in the car will eventually find its way into the classroom. Students learn from the exercises and each other, in spite of our fumbles.

Because of the emphasis placed upon self-awareness in this course, students often come to instructors or teaching assistants with questions about personal issues relating to the course topics. It's neither necessary nor advisable to set yourself up as a therapist, but if you develop an open environment and demonstrate a willingness to be helpful, students are more likely to voice important concerns or issues, either in class or afterwards. There are many opportunities to use coaching or counseling skills when you teach this course, which students seem to appreciate.

Students, especially undergraduates, sometimes ask the instructor for permission to behave in a particular way during a simulation ("Can we ...?"). You don't want to become the arbiter or authority figure in this way. Therefore, simply tell them that as long as they follow the rules established for the simulation, they can do whatever comes naturally. There is no predetermined right or wrong behavior in a simulation; we try to learn from whatever behavior emerges.

When instructors debrief a session, the emphasis is upon what students have learned. The art of debriefing lies in finding a happy medium between a meandering laissez-faire approach at one extreme and, at the other, pushing students to see a point that only the instructor thinks is important. We are open and enthusiastic about whatever students key in on and find important; not only is this the essence of experiential learning, but it is also what makes it possible to teach this course year after year without becoming bored. As an instructor, you never know what will happen with different groups of students and there is always something to learn from them. However, we also go into a debriefing session prepared for things that could and even should emerge. This preparation comes from past teaching experience, our stated goals for the chapter, and from observing what's occurring during the group exercise. After students mention a key concept, we try to highlight it ("Let's analyze this a bit more. Why did your group react like this? Is that what typically happens in a work setting?"). We have tried to create debriefing questions that will elicit good discussions after each exercise. However, if by the end of the debriefing, students have not mentioned something that is an important OB concept, we ask another prompt question to get at it. Nevertheless, instructors should avoid asking questions in a way that causes students to feel as if they are guessing an obscure answer that the instructor is looking for but won't tell.

The role of the instructor is to teach students to think like an organizational behavior expert. This means modeling and explaining your own approach to situations and how you perceive them. It also means asking questions in class (and on exams if you use them) that will elicit this type of critical thinking.

We suggest that you take a few minutes at the end of each class to set the stage for the next session by briefly telling students about the articles they will be assigned in the *Reader* and explaining the premeeting preparation for the next chapter.

### IV. Ways of Organizing

Sequencing. The four sections of the workbook progresses from the level of the individual to the level of the organization in its environment:

    Part I    Understanding Yourself and Other People at
              Work
    Part II   Creating Effective Work Groups
    Part III  Leadership and Management
    Part IV   Managing Effective Organizations

We think the order of the chapters promotes group development and personal growth. In addition, later chapters build upon concepts and skills covered earlier in the course. The initial chapters focus upon different mental maps in order to help students see and appreciate individual differences. This sets the stage for different ways of viewing behavior. The second section, Creating Effective Work Relationships, begins with basic interpersonal skills that are a prerequisite for subsequent chapters like conflict management and performance appraisal. We encourage instructors to modify the sequence of chapters in whatever order best fits their particular objectives and circumstances. For example, some professors prefer to cover Career Development and Stress Management at the end of the course. Others, especially those who teach in schools that emphasize macro courses, begin with the last section because topics like organizational analysis and design are more similar to what students have received in other courses. Regardless of the order you choose, we do however recommend that you begin with the first chapter, "The Psychological Contract and Organizational Socialization," followed by either Chapter Two, "Theories of Managing People," or Chapter Three, "Individual and Organizational Learning." The first chapter sets the stage for experiential learning and focuses upon the process of joining an organization where it is most relevant. The second chapter describes the evolution of management thought and provides a conceptual ground from which to build. The third chapter establishes the learning methodology for the course and helps students understand some of the ways individual differences will be accepted and used. If you wish to use Chapter Two later on in the course, or to omit it, we suggest you begin with Chapter One, followed by Chapter Three. This ensures a good beginning to the course.

<u>Chapter Times and Flexibility</u>. The chapters in the text are designed for 2-hour class sessions but can be easily adjusted to shorter or longer class sessions. The transition is usually a simple one of splitting the unit up for shorter sessions or expanding the times listed for longer sessions. In each unit, there are limited times for each step and the time if often tight. These times are not cast in stone; they are merely guidelines.

One-hour class sessions constitute the greatest challenge because some exercises are so lengthy that the debriefing time may be too limited to gain the maximum learning. One solution is to leave out certain steps in the exercises; another is to have students bring their written reactions and answers to the debriefing questions to the next class. We have included sample course designs in the appendix for both short (A) and longer (B) class periods. It is not impossible to use this course in a 50-60 minute format, but it is easier if the sessions are at least 80 minutes in length.

The debriefing time is the most important portion of the class, so avoid scrimping on debriefing time. You may not be able to cover all aspects of an exercise and you certainly don't have to use all the debriefing questions, but make sure students have the opportunity to reflect upon what they learned and pull these lessons together. Otherwise, instructors could leave themselves open to charges that experiential learning is just "fun and games."

**Saturday Sessions**. We strongly recommend including a longer Saturday session in your course design. The expanded time format permits more comprehensive examination of a particular chapter and a synergistic presentation of several chapters. These sessions are like a workshop and students appear more relaxed in these sessions and welcome the change of pace they bring.

Saturday sessions can be used in various ways. Some professors have one 8-hour session near the beginning of the course to help students become acquainted with their learning group and move quickly through the beginning stages of group formation. Students "bond" much more rapidly in a Saturday session than they do in class. Make sure you do Chapter 3 on learning either before the Saturday session or as the first event. Others have two four-hour sessions -- one in the beginning of the course for these reasons mentioned previously and one towards the end. One of the authors incorporates outdoor challenge course activities into these Saturday sessions, which students see as the highlight of the course. The hours in the Saturday sessions replace regularly scheduled class meeting times, which means that the course usually ends early, another advantage in the eyes of students.

To avoid scheduling problems, it works best if the Saturday sessions are listed in the course descriptions provided at the time of registration. This way students realize what is involved and can clear their own schedules ahead of time. When it is not possible to set the date as part of the course description, professors can ask the students if they agree to a Saturday class and give them three dates from which to choose. In our experience, students have always been willing to attend a Saturday class, even though it meant juggling work schedules, etc.

Learning Teams. Learning teams or groups are one of the most important features of the course because they provide an opportunity for students to work in a successful team, receive feedback on their behavior, and learn to get along with people who may be quite different from them. Since students work in the same group throughout the course, they come to value the belonging and friendship these groups provide. In some schools, the organizational behavior course is strongly recommended for entering MBA students because it helps them quickly form relationships with other students. It is not uncommon for both undergraduate and MBA students to remark that their learning group was the most successful group experience they have ever had. Chapter Three contains advice on forming the learning teams.

## V. Evaluation Methods

<u>The Personal Application Assignment</u>. Some professors have difficulty with the issue of grading in experiential courses that are ideally driven more by student learning than the professor's evaluation requirements. For example, grading class participation may introduce a power and authority dynamic into the exercises that could potentially have a negative effect on the interaction. However, some form of systematic feedback is an essential element in the learning process. The grading assignment that is most in keeping with the philosophy of the course are PAA's (personal application assignments), because they model both the learning cycle and organizational behavior thinking. PAA's allow students to write on topics that are relevant to them and provide them with a framework they can use throughout their career when they face problematic situations. Some instructors use the brief PAA format found at the end of each chapter while others require longer versions. Examples of the longer PAA format are included in the appendix, along with instructions, entitled "The Personal Application Assignment" which we hand out to students along with the Grading Criteria ("What We Look For When We Grade...") found in the appendix.

Other professors prefer a less structured approach to this assignment and use them as homework assignments. For example:

> "Each week following our in-class experiences each student will write a 3-5 page paper called a PAA. These PAAs will be your way of reflecting and commenting on the class experience and applying some personal interest or experience of yours to the class lesson. Each PAA should:

a. summarize what you learned from the in-class exercise(s) including your opinions, feelings, and thoughts;
b. demonstrate some of the knowledge gained from the articles in the reader;
c. show how you experienced in the past or plan to apply the acquired knowledge to a real situation of your own;
d. demonstrate what you learned about yourself from partaking in the exercise; and
e. demonstrate wit, humor and be delightful to read."

When we grade the PAA's, we take a developmental approach that both models good coaching and demonstrates how an organizational behavior person thinks.

With MBA students, we require four PAA's unless they opt for a take-home mid-term and final or a learning journal. Students respond well to being given a choice in the way they are evaluated.

Undergraduates have less life experience and sometimes have difficulty finding PAA topics. Therefore, we require one or two PAA's for undergraduates in addition to other evaluation methods.

Exam Questions. The instructor's manual includes various types of exam or review questions that cover material from both the workbook and the reader. We use these questions almost exclusively with undergraduates. Some of the questions merely test whether students have learned the key points; others are geared more towards applying knowledge. We also ask students to contribute exam questions, which they put on the board at the beginning of each class. We would caution you against the exclusive use of multiple choice tests because this test format is not entirely compatible with the overall philosophy of the course.

Term Papers. Students have the option of writing a personal analysis of their role as a manager (a journal can be used to record and keep track of their daily activities) and/or an analysis of an organization, following the format outlined in Chapter 19, Organizational Analysis.

Thought Pieces. These are short 1-2 page reactions to the readings or what has occurred in class. They are an excellent device for understanding where students are. Requiring that these thought pieces by sent via E-mail promotes Internet use and allows the professor to make an immediate quick response. This has been particularly effective with international students who feel more comfortable with this medium than speaking up in class.

With undergraduates who need to develop critical thinking skills, we sometimes require a certain number of reaction pieces on reader articles. Students are asked to summarize the gist of the article in the first one or two paragraphs and follow up with their own reaction to the article and a real-life example of this concept.

Journals. Journals are a good way to see how students are responding and learning from the course. Some professors use the brief PAA forms at the end of each chapter, while others simply have students describe their reactions and learning from each class. It's a good idea to vary the journal assignment so that it does not become stale. For more information on using journals, please see Toby Fulwiler, *The Journal Book* (Portsmouth, NH: Boynton/Cook 1987).

Group Projects. Group projects provide an opportunity for students to practice group dynamics and learn from their experience. The major complaint about group projects, both in class and at the workplace, is that some members do not carry their share of the workload. For this reason, we aim for both individual accountability and a group grade. The percentage of the group grade that an individual receives is determined by peer evaluations. We have feedback sessions on group projects so that students have the opportunity to learn from and improve their performance as a group member.

With MBA students, one possible assignment is to ask that each learning group present, in the most creative way possible, what they see as the common threads or integrating themes found throughout the course (appreciation of differences, contingency theory, analyzing the situation before choosing a certain behavior, management as a developmental approach, etc.). This assignment helps them integrate the material and by the time each group has made their presentation, the learning has been strongly reinforced. Their presentations are made in the last class session, which then takes on the air of a celebration.

Group projects with undergraduates can be designed to expose them to OB issues in real organizations; they involve interviews, surveys and analyses of local businesses or a university process or department that is trying to make improvements. For example, one class researched and made improvements on course registration in the business school, teaching the need for continuous improvement in processes.

Another effective use of group projects is to have groups take the responsibility for leading a class session or a portion of the class. For example, groups can be assigned to investigate and report on outstanding companies that can be used as benchmarks in the area of career development, managing diversity, performance appraisal, etc.

Peer Evaluation. A small percentage of the grade can be determined by the students' learning group. We have them assign 0-5 points to the students' class preparation (reading and homework assignments) and in-class contributions and participation in the group exercises. Please see the Peer Evaluation Form in Appendix C, which also includes a section on group project contributions. We warn students to take these evaluations very seriously and to keep their personal feelings (positive or negative) about other students from biasing their evaluations. It's a good idea to check these forms while the students are still in class to make sure they have filled them out correctly.

## VI. Participation

One of the advantages of beginning the course with the group exercise in Chapter One is that it models participation and gets students involved and talking right away. If your first classes are more lecture than group work, it is more difficult to break out of this mold. Active participation is seldom a difficulty at the MBA level; indeed, the greater problem may be tactfully managing people who talk too much and bore the other students or make it difficult to complete the exercises without rushing.

Encouraging participation may be more of a challenge at the undergraduate level or with international students who are less comfortable with English as a second language and with this type of classroom expectations. One way to get undergraduates talking is to have them write on the board at the beginning of class a significant point from the readings and a question. Undergraduates may be more likely to speak up if they have been asked to do a "quick-write" response to the exercise before a general debriefing. We recommend cooperative learning techniques, especially for classes that have difficulty participating. If you only have time to read one book on this subject, try D.W. Johnson & R.T. Johnson's *Learning Together and Alone: Cooperative, Competitive, and Individualistic Learning* (Englewood Cliffs, NJ: Prentice-Hall, 1987). There is an annotated bibliography in Appendix D that includes recommended resources on both cooperative learning and writing.

## VII. Mid-course Evaluation

It's always helpful to utilize a mid-course evaluation form, like the one shown in Appendix E. This allows you to see what students are thinking and, if there are problems to be rectified, you will have time to do so before the course is finished. This models the lesson from Sherwood and Glidewell's Pinch Model (Chapter 1) to look for "pinches" before they become "crunch points."

## VII. Teaching Assistants

If you have the luxury of teaching assistants, you could consider following the method Dave Kolb used with great success for teaching doctoral students how to teach. He had two-three teaching assistants for a class of 45 MBA students. Kolb met with the teaching assistants before every class to debrief and evaluate the last session and plan the upcoming session. Each teaching assistant was assigned two-three learning groups; during the group exercise they would observe these groups, answer their questions and occasionally make a process intervention. They graded the PAA's written by their learning group members; Kolb would check their grading in the beginning of the course to make sure it was consistent. The TA's eventually assumed some of the teaching responsibilities --

the lecturette, the debriefing, or the design of a new exercise. This was a wonderful learning experience.

## VIII. Format of the Manual

For each chapter, you will find:

-Materials needed
-Learning objectives
-A sample design for a two-hour session
-Setting the stage -- suggestions about beginning the class
   and the lecturette
-Issues to consider in leading the experiential exercise
-Transparency Masters (at the end of the manual)
-Exam or review questions from both the workbook and reader
-Reader articles that can be used with the workbook chapter
   Rather than listing additional resources, we direct
   your attention to the chapter bibliographies which
   contain the sources we find most important.

Instructor's Manual with Tests and Transparency Masters

6th Edition

# ORGANIZATIONAL BEHAVIOR AN EXPERIENTIAL APPROACH

# Chapter 1
# THE PSYCHOLOGICAL CONTRACT AND ORGANIZATIONAL SOCIALIZATION

**Materials Needed**: Name tags or name tents and chairs or desks for representatives in the front of the class. Some instructors hand out Appendix K, "How To Succeed in Organizational Behavior by Really Trying" in this session.

**Objectives**: After completing this chapter, students should be able to:

A. Define the terms "psychological contract" and the "self-fulfilling prophecy" and explain their importance.
B. Describe the external influences that affect expectations.
C. Describe predictions about the workplace in the year 2000.
D. Explain the "pinch model."
E. Make a psychological contract with the instructor.
F. List the characteristics of the field of organizational behavior.

## Sample Design

|  |  |
|---|---|
| 6:00 - 6:25 | Icebreaker and Introduction |
| 6:25 - 6:45 | Students prepare to be interviewed in groups |
| 6:45 - 7:05 | Instructor interviews students |
| 7:05 - 7:15 | Students prepare to interview instructor |
| 7:15 - 7:40 | Students interview instructor |
| 7:40 - 8:00 | Summary and Debriefing (Pinch Model) |

## Setting the Stage -- Lecturette

To save time, instructors can have both syllabus and name tags or tents available as students enter the classroom.

Our first concern is helping students enter a new situation so they feel comfortable enough to participate. Therefore, we begin with a 15-minute ice-breaker, usually Name Bingo (see appendix J) which is adapted for each class. This exercise works well because it provides students with a task and an excuse to approach people they don't know. In the process, they learn more about the other students and also begin learning names. It also serves a frame-breaking purpose and signals to students that they have entered a different type of course where the traditional expectations do not apply. The person who has gathered the most signatures wins a prize (bag of Goldfish or something else students see that there is a purpose behind the instructor's actions, which builds credibility.

The next step is providing enough information to let students know what organizational behavior is and your objectives for the course (WHAT), its benefit to students and organizations (WHY), the methodology used in the course (HOW), and when special Saturday sessions will be held if that's applicable (WHEN). For the "what" section, we use the "Characteristics of Organizational Behavior" section, p. 16 (see transparency T1-0) and "Course Objectives," p. 17 of the workbook. We put the objectives on a transparency (see Appendix I) that we show the students again at the last class session as a check that we did indeed do what we set out to accomplish. Instructors, like good managers, have a motivational role, and enthusiasm for one's subject is crucial. In discussing the "why" aspect, they can tell students why it's important to study organizational behavior in whatever way is most persuasive to students. The "how" part should be a quick description of experiential learning and why it's appropriate for this course. You can either explain your role at this point or during the interview process.

We quickly define the psychological contract and explain the self-fulfilling prophecy and the effect of expectations upon behavior. Read the instructions on page 11 to the class and begin the exercise.

## Issues to Consider in Leading the Experiential Exercise

A. This unit is designed to let students get to know you and exchange expectations. By encouraging them to think about what they want out of the course, they are more likely to take responsibility for their own learning. It's useful to think about your answers to the interviewer questions ahead of time. Try to put yourself in their place and envision the key issues for them. If your syllabus is clear and detailed, you can avoid devoting all the interview time to the mechanics of grades, paper length, etc.

B. The key issue is the initial negotiation of a psychological contract between you and the class, which legitimizes the renegotiation of that contract during the course as either you or the students feel what Sherwood and Glidewell call a "pinch." (See Chapter 1 in the workbook and Transparency 1.1 for the Pinch Model.) This is not intended to be just a simulation of how the socialization process might take place in a real organization. Rather, it is designed to be a real contracting activity that clarifies how you and your students are going to work together in the real organization of the class for the entire term. It is a genuine attempt to avoid "a cold slap in the face" (see Chapter 1 vignette) where expectations are transgressed and parties to a relationship eventually become psychologically disconnected from each other.

C. Your own behavior in this class may strike many students as rather surprising. They are likely to be unaccustomed to interacting with professors in this way. Consequently, you may well find some signs of disbelief, e.g., sighs, cynical looks. This is the first sign of a "pinch" in that some of their implicit expectations are undoubtedly being violated. You should try to be sensitive to these signs and confront them as much as possible in this session. In doing so, you will be modeling a very important norm of openness and directness which should elicit comparable behavior on their part. This also makes it easier for people to raise their own "pinches" with classmates or with you later on in the course. Incidentally, we've never had students complain about serious pinches; having a vehicle in place for dealing with problems is merely a safeguard.

D. The questions that you ask the students will be of your own choosing. Unless you instruct them otherwise, they can concentrate on the four general areas outlined in the workbook when preparing to be interviewed by you. We suggest you take notes on their responses (or have a teaching assistant take notes). You can also put their goals on a transparency that can be reviewed along with the course objectives in the last class session when you evaluate the course.

The following issues may arise in regard to the workbook student interview questions:
1. <u>Goals</u>. Within the larger framework of the learning goals established by you and in the text, what specific things do people want to get out of the course? There will be different responses and they will, for the most part, be reasonable ones. Occasionally students will ask why we bother seeking their input if the syllabus is already laid out. One response is to note that although organizations always have both goals and constraints, they must also integrate individual goals. Another response is to mention that an understanding of student goals helps the instructor know what types of examples to use in class and how much emphasis to place in different areas. If possible, the instructor can also make some modifications in the syllabus. One of the authors teaches an extra class if there is widespread interest in a subject not included in the syllabus.

2. <u>Attitudes and Reservations</u>. These questions allow students (especially those who are simply taking the course as a requirement) to examine their feelings about their new association with what is often regarded as the "soft-touchy-feely," less-rational area of either organizational behavior or the business school curriculum. Students are

usually struggling more with the stereotypes about the discipline rather than with a prejudice that they themselves hold. You can stress the importance of both the hard and soft subjects or approaches and provide examples of the latter. We'd avoid getting into an argument with students or pushing your own point of view too strongly. The intent with these questions is to get the issue out in the open and acknowledge their concerns so that the focus can be on learning.

If there are fears about experiential learning, they often concern being forced to do role plays or disclose more of themselves than they want. We reassure students that participation in role plays in front of the entire class is strictly voluntary (and fairly rare in most courses). Other role plays occur in their learning groups with everyone participating, so no one feels under much performance pressure. Concerning self disclosure, we point out that no one is ever pressured to talk about themselves and this is not a T-group atmosphere. Nevertheless, it is true that the more they invest in the course and the more they open themselves up to examining their own behavior and receiving feedback from others, the more they will learn in the course. They themselves will determine their receptivity and openness without pressure from others. We point out that this course is like a laboratory. It's a safe place to see how your behavior affects others and vice versa and to make mistakes and learn from them. Better to learn these things in a course among people whom most students come to see as friends than at work.

Students who have little or no work experience sometimes worry that this is a serious constraint in a course like this. You can honestly reassure them that lack of experience has never proved to be a major drawback. Even if they cannot contribute work examples or lessons, they can participate in the class exercises and tease out the learning from them as well as other students. This particular concern usually vanishes after the first few classes. It helps that the PAAs can be written on incidents that have taken place outside a work setting.

3. <u>Resources</u>. With this question, we are modeling our belief that adults bring skills and expertise to the classroom that can benefit everyone. This allows students to establish themselves as people with knowledge to contribute. It also alerts the instructor that there are extremely capable students in the class who can be used as a resource or who may be likely to "compete" with the instructor. You can defuse the latter situation by sincerely welcoming their expertise ("I'm glad to hear we have someone in the class with experience in that area.") and requesting their opinions in class ("Sam, you've had

experience with self-managed work teams. What do you think are the main difficulties with implementing them?").

4. <u>Reputation</u>. This is a good opportunity to learn about your reputation as a teacher or a department, although you are more likely to hear the positive side than the negative. If you seem open, they will mention negative things they have heard. This gives you a chance to explain or to note that you have made changes in assignments, etc. Sometimes, it can be an impetus to change your ways.

5. <u>Ground Rules</u>. We've found that asking this question in the beginning of both courses and seminars eliminates most negative behaviors and gives the participants a sense of ownership over the environment we are creating. If someone exhibits a behavior that was talked about here, another student is likely to point that out to the offender, saving the instructor from taking on the role of authoritarian. If the students fail to mention it, the instructor can refer back to the ground rules in a low key manner. If you happen upon an especially unruly group, you can post the ground rules on the wall or provide each student with a copy.

E. The students also have the opportunity to interview you. You can set the stage here and signal what type of questions you are willing to take. Students seem to appreciate being able to question instructors about their background and life. They typically ask us about our educational history, work experience, family, hobbies, biggest work mistake or success, life goals, etc. Afterwards they always comment that they like having this understanding of our personal context. However, if you are a very private person, you may wish to limit them to the questions pertaining to the course like those in the workbook.

This will probably be such a new experience for them that you may see a whole range of behaviors, from currying favor to outright hostility (a rare occurrence, but it's good to be prepared). How you deal with these behaviors is, of course, a function of your own personal style and teaching style. Being honest about your feelings ("I feel as if I'm under attack" or "I feel as if I'm being seduced") usually helps to clear the air and allows the entire group to share the problem and hopefully, the solution to it as well. **The most important thing to remember here is that your behavior should model the behaviors (openness, respect, non-defensive reaction, curiosity) that will set a solid foundation for the rest of the course.**

The reference in the book to self-fulfilling prophecy and the role of expectations is a perfect opportunity to tie in your own high expectations of the students. If you like, you can hand out "How to Succeed in Organizational Behavior by Really Trying" (Appendix K) either at the first or the second class session.

F. The **debriefing** question, "What differences do you see when you compare this method to the traditional way other courses begin?", models how we will examine the results of behavior throughout the rest of the course. Students often comment that it's easier to participate in a course that begins using an exercise like this and that they feel more motivated to work as a result of the interviews. This provides an opportunity to bring up the "decision to join versus decision to participate" concept, which is exemplified in the different goals students give for taking the course.

G. We ask for examples about broken psychological contracts in real life as a lead-in to the Sherwood-Glidewell Model, which we present after the debriefing.

H. We finish the class by going over the learning points and the tips for managers. **Make sure you explain to students how to use the workbook.** For every chapter, they read the objectives and opening vignette and do the pre-meeting preparation. Their before-class assignments are always in the pre-meeting preparation instructions, rather than in the syllabus.

**Transparency Masters**

1-0        Characteristics of Organizational Behavior
1-1        Model for Managing Psychological Contracts

**Exam and Review Questions**

1. The psychological contract
   a.   is a written notarized document
   *b.  defines a dynamic, changing relationship
   c.   is irrevocable
   d.   states only the employers' expectations

2. Which two classes of decisions do individuals make when approaching a new organization?
   *a.  The decision to join and the decision to participate
   b.   The decision to be socialized and the decision to participate
   c.   The decision to join and the decision to cooperate
   d.   The decision to join and the decision to be socialized

3. Give an example of the self-fulfilling prophecy.

4.  What's the difference between a psychological contract and an employment contract?

Answer: Psychological contracts, unlike employment contracts, are usually not written and are often not even explicit. Psychological contracts focus upon a dynamic relationship that defines the employee's psychological involvement with their employer.

5.  The (Pinch Model) describes the process by which psychological contracts are established, disrupted, and renegotiated.

6.  What percentage of the work force will be made up of white males by the year 2000?
    a.   54%
    b.   23%
    *c.  39%
    d.   15%

7.  Why is continuous learning important for employees?

Answer: Employees need to manage their own careers since companies have moved to "just-in-time" work forces. Given the rapid rate of change, employees will have different jobs in different careers and will need to train themselves to keep from becoming obsolete.

8.  What do broken psychological contracts result in?

Answer: disillusionment, lower employee satisfaction, lower productivity, increased desire to leave the company


READER QUESTIONS:

**"The Impact of Changing Values on Organizational Life -- The Latest Update," Richard E. Boyatzis and Florence Skelly**

9.  What are two ways in which values impact organizational life?

Answer: 1) joining and staying; 2) giving your all -- determines effort; or 3) may cause intergenerational conflict

10. "Growth through materialism" is a characteristic theme of which generation, according to Boyatzis and Skelly?
    *a.  late 1940's to early 1960's
    b.   mid-1960's to late 1970's
    c.   late 1970's to 1980's
    d.   1990's

11. "Social pragmatism" is a characteristic theme of which generation, according to Boyatzis and Skelly?
    a. late 1940's to early 1960's
    b. mid-1960's to late 1970's
    c. late 1970's to 1980's
    *d. 1990's

12. According to Schlesinger's alternating periods (in Boyatzis and Skelly), what stage is the United States currently in? Justify your answer with examples. (essay)

**"The Paradox of Corporate Culture: Reconciling Ourselves to Socialization," Richard Pascale**

13. (Socialization) is the systematic means by which firms bring new members into their culture.

14. What's the purpose of humility inducing experiences in the process of socialization?

Answer: Precipitates self-questioning of prior behavior, beliefs, and values. A lowering of individual self-comfort and self-complacency promotes openness toward accepting the organization's norms and values.

15. Which of the following is not a step in the socialization process?
    a. careful selection of entry level candidates
    b. consistent role models
    c. reinforcing folklore
    *d. appreciation of diversity

**Reader Articles**

1. "The Impact of Changing Values on Organizational Life -- The Latest Update," Richard E. Boyatzis and Florence Skelly.
2. "The Paradox of Corporate Culture: Reconciling Ourselves to Socialization," Richard Pascale.

# Chapter 2
# THEORIES OF MANAGING PEOPLE

**Materials Needed**: Transparency of old lady/young lady.

**Objectives**: By the end of the chapter, students should be able to:

A. Describe six theories of management and their "ideal" manager.
B. Explain why it's important to identify their personal theories about management and organizational behavior.
C. Describe their personal theory of management.
D. Identify the managerial skills they need in today's environment.

**Sample Design**

| | |
|---|---|
| 6:00 - 6:30 | Lecture: Theory X and Y |
| | Evolution of Management Thought |
| | Quinn's Competing Values Theory |
| 6:30 - 7:00 | Groups prepare speeches and select speaker |
| 7:00 - 7:30 | Manager Of The Year speeches |
| 7:30 - 8:00 | Summary and debriefing |

**Setting the Stage -- Lecturette**

This is the first of four chapters that are integrated by the idea of mental maps (management theories, learning styles, motivation, and values) that leads to an understanding of individual differences. If you wish, you can ease into mental maps by using a perception figure that contains two images, like the old lady/young lady (see the Transparency Masters T2-0). One of the authors modifies this figure to make two other transparencies, one that emphasizes the young lady and another one that emphasizes the old lady. She has half the class shut their eyes and shows the other half the young lady. Then she asks the latter group to shut their eyes and shows the other half of the class the old lady. Next, she shows everyone the combined figure and asks them what they see; some students will have trouble seeing the second image. This leads into a discussion of the difficulty of seeing another image once one has already been perceived. (This figure is so popular that you may be better off digging up one that is less well known.) It also indicates the need for humility when arguing with people who see things from a different perspective or mental map.

Theory X and Y are examples of different mental maps about human nature. We go over the theory and their scores on the test and comment on cultural differences relating to this theory. The majority of U.S. students that we have seen in recent years categorize themselves as Theory Y, so you can bring the theory home to them and provoke an interesting discussion by asking them if they think their fellow students are Theory Y or X concerning their studies. What would a Theory X and Y student look like? How do you manage people, some of whom fall into both categories or somewhere in between?

If you want to go over the evolution of management thought, you can involve the students by putting these categories on the blackboard: 1) theory, 2) historical time, 3) social climate, and 4) concept of the "ideal manager." Then we ask them to fill in the blanks for scientific management, administrative theory, human relations, open systems, contingency management, and Quinn's theory.

Another technique we sometimes use to introduce Quinn's theory is to ask the students, "What's the best way to manage people?" As students contribute their ideas, the instructor places them into the appropriate columns which are not labelled until the end of the exercise. Often, there is a preponderance of items in one category, e.g., human relations.

We give a brief recap of Quinn's theory, using the two transparency masters (T2-3 and T2-4) and emphasizing its usefulness to a manager. We make the point that our theory determines what we see. (Incidentally, there is a questionnaire on page 128 of Quinn's book, *Beyond Rational Management*, that you may want to use with MBA students.)

Another type of mental map that works well with this chapter is the structural, human resource, political, and symbolic framework found in Bolman and Deal's *Reframing Organizations* (Jossey-Bass, 1991).

## Issues to Consider in Leading the Experiential Exercise

A. Divide the students into groups of approximately five people; consider how many speeches this will mean in the time you have available before you determine the number of people per group. Too many speeches in a row can become boring. Before students select a group member to give the speech, remind them that your goal is to have everyone participate during the course; encourage them to share the opportunity to get speaking practice in class.
B. When the groups are ready to begin their speeches, explain the coding scheme. It may help to show them the Quinn's Competing Values Model of Leadership (T2-3) again.

C. For shorter classes, you can do the theory one day and the speeches the next. Be careful though about having too many lecture classes in the beginning of the course, because this sets a norm of passivity that does not promote experiential learning and participation. For this reason, we included the suggestions on how to make the lecturette more interactive.

D. Barker's video on Paradigms or Mintzberg's video on The Manager's Job: Folklore and Fact could be used in this session.

**Transparency Masters**

2.0 Old Lady/Young Lady
2.3 Quinn's Competing Values Model of Leadership
2.4 The Positive and Negative Zones

**Exam or Review Questions**

1. The socio-historical context of a strong union movement, distrust for businessmen, decreased immigration, and scarce labor served as the backdrop for
   a. Scientific management
   *b. Human Relations School
   c. Administrative Theory
   d. Open Systems Theory

2. The contention that our decisions are limited by the amount of variables our brains can handle, the time available, and our reasoning powers is known as
   *a. bounded rationality
   b. maximization
   c. entropy
   d. interdependence

3. The 1920's solution to the nepotism, favoritism, and unprofessional behavior found in organizations at the time was
   *a. bureaucracy
   b. systems theory
   c. span of control
   d. scientific management

4. What is the basic premise of contingency theory.

Answer:
There is no one best way to manage in every situation. Managers must find the appropriate method to match a given situation.

5. Write a narrative that contains examples of both Theory X and Theory Y behavior. (essay)


READER QUESTIONS:

**"The Manager's Job: Folklore and Fact" by Mintzberg**

6. Which of the following does Mintzberg describe as "folklore" about managerial work?
   a. managerial work is characterized by brevity, variety and discontinuity
   *b. managerial work is a science and a profession
   c. managerial work involves performing rituals and ceremonies
   d. managerial work involves performing regular duties

7. According to Mintzberg, managers seem to cherish
   *a. gossip, hearsay, and speculation
   b. periodicals
   c. large databases
   d. routine staff reports

**"Mastering Competing Values: An Integrated Approach to Management" by Robert E. Quinn**

8. How do "Master Managers" differ from other managers, according to Quinn?

Answer: Master managers look at situations from various perspectives and have learned to balance competing values. They use whichever theory is most appropriate for a given situation.

9. The stage of evolution of mastery marked by the emergence of effortless performance is
   a. the competence stage
   *b. the proficiency stage
   c. the novice stage
   d. the expert stage

10. Using Quinn's theory of competing values, which management theory does each person in the following example hold?

Ellen    = _____

Carlos    = _____

Anne      = _____

Tom       = _____

There is a problem at the factory. The production figures are way down and employees are grumbling. You have been asked to attend a problem solving meeting with the managers. **Ellen** thinks the best solution is to set clear production goals and carefully delegate tasks. **Carlos** thinks management should talk to employees to find out what is bothering them and then do team building with the key employees. **Anne** suggests that it's time to put their house in order by coming up with tighter procedures and information systems. **Tom** is advocating an expansion program because he thinks that the market is favorable and the challenge will pull everyone together.

11. According to Quinn, what are the major characteristics of each of the four management theories in the competing values model? Provide examples for each management theory. (essay)

**"The Human Side of Management" by Douglas McGregor**

12. The "human side" of enterprise relies heavily on
    a. external control
    b. shared beliefs
    c. reward and punishment
    *d. self-control

13. Advocates of Theory X believe that worker behavior is the consequence of
    a. managerial policy and practice
    *b. the worker's inherent nature
    c. organizational culture
    d. industrial organizations

14. Your friend Joe works at a grocery store; he's been complaining bitterly about his job and his boss. Since he knows you are becoming an expert on organizational behavior, he has come to you for advice. He tells you that his boss is constantly looking over Joe's shoulder and telling him what to do next, even when it's obvious. The boss threatens all the employees that he will fire them if they do anything wrong, and he's always sneaking around trying to catch them in the act. Joe asked if he could learn how to do some of the ordering for his department; his boss replied that Joe is paid good money to do the job he already has and that

should be good enough for Joe. Joe was excited about a new customer service program that corporate headquarters wanted to implement. However, he overheard the boss tell his supervisor they could forget implementing this program in Joe's store because the employees were lazy and incapable of adapting to change. Joe sees himself as highly responsible and dedicated and wishes the boss trusted him more.

What OB concept could you use to explain to Joe what's going on here? _____

Answer: Boss has a theory X orientation while Joe appears to have Theory Y values.

## **Reader Articles**

1. "The Manager's Job: Folklore and Fact" by Henry Mintzberg
2. "Mastering Competing Values: An Integrated Approach to Management" by Robert E. Quinn
3. "The Human Side of Management" by Douglas McGregor

# Chapter 3
## INDIVIDUAL AND ORGANIZATIONAL LEARNING

**Materials Needed:** Masking Tape to make a grid on the floor of the classroom or in an adjacent space.

**Objectives** By the end of the chapter, students should be able to:

A.  Describe the model of adult learning.
B.  Identify individual learning styles.
C.  Improve the learning organization in this course by sharing learning objectives, available resources for learning, and learning environment preferences.
D.  Understand the importance of continuous learning.

**Setting the Stage - Lecturette**

To set the stage for the experiential exercise, we try to link the importance of learning in materials already covered in the course. For example, much of what we've read or studied so far has some relationship to learning. Mintzberg stated that managers have to learn about the job of managing and be introspective. Quinn's article mentioned that people need to learn how to become a master manager and part of that is learning to identify your own theory of management. The vignette about Shell explained how one company tried to accelerate learning and mentioned the research they did which concluded that organizations that don't learn simply don't survive. Companies that can adapt quickly to changing rules have a competitive advantage. All of this brings us to today's topic, which is how people learn. No one can teach students everything they will need to know in their career, but we can teach them how to learn -- our purpose in this session.

We know that adults learn differently than children. Aside from Kolb's theory, we ask students what other ideas they have about how adults learn.

We cover the following points in the lecturette:
- Lewin's model
- the two paradoxical axes (concrete-abstract, active-passive), using transparency T3-0
- the four words that sum up what is happening at each of the four points (feeling, watching, thinking, doing)
- because of individual differences people tend to put more emphasis upon a particular mode
- How do the students think that comes about? personality, education, family, career, current job/life situation, psychological type

- we ask students to look at the profiles on page 51 to see where they stand compared to others who have taken the LSI and describe each of the four learning modes
- help them locate their style on the graph on page 53 and explain the four learning styles.
- Remind students that this instrument measures their perception of the way they learn. Each question in the instrument relates to feeling, watching, thinking, or doing. Do their scores make sense when they compare them to the learning experience they described in the premeeting preparation? How people learn the computer is a good way to point up differences in learning styles.
- The LSI is useful to point out individual differences but shouldn't be used to stereotype people.

There is invariably one student who scores his or her instrument incorrectly. Therefore, we use the transparency (T3-1) of the Learning Style Type Grid to graph an example for the whole class. To check whether they have done this step correctly, they can refer back to the Profile Norms on pg. 51 to see where their scores were highest. In most cases, you can predict the style from that chart.

When students have a score that is very close to the junction of the axes, this indicates that they have a balanced learning style. Their scores were fairly similar on all four modes.

A common question is whether your learning style can change over time. A particular type of educational program or job, as well as a concerted self-improvement effort, can develop a learning mode and change your score.

**Issues to Consider in Leading the Experiential Exercise**

A. Make sure the students understand that no one style is better than the others. The LSI gives individuals some data about which aspects of the learning cycle they may prefer or be good at. For most individuals, however, this approach will vary somewhat from situation to situation. By locating themselves on the LSI grid and discussing their self-assessment with others of similar learning style, individuals get additional data to assess their approach to learning. Finally, future course experiences in the heterogeneous student learning groups will provide additional data about learning styles.

B. Point out that the LSI is not a perfectly predictive instrument. You may wish to raise concerns in the discussion at the end of the like-style group reports about the use and validity of "pen-and-paper" tests describing individual differences. For example, what are some instances where tests such as the LSI might be useful? What are the instances where it might not be recommended? What are the dangers in the use of such tests? The LSI has its critics. Nevertheless, it has a great deal of face validity and many students find it to be a very useful theory.

C. The interesting aspect of this process is that people often act out their learning styles during the discussions. Some will focus on abstract conceptualization issues, e.g., validity of the theory, evaluation of the instrument, what is the "right" score. Others with an active experimentation bent might seize on issues of pragmatic usefulness, e.g., how can the theory or test be used to help a manager? The concrete experiencers may struggle to identify and deal with the feelings they are having, while the reflective observers might be doing just that -- sitting back and observing. The accommodators usually finish their discussion questions before the other groups and remark upon that.

D. After the groups have presented the results of their discussions, the instructor can direct their attention to the chart on page 65 to see if there is anything that needs to be added. The excess and deficiency categories on this chart explain what happens when there are too few or too many of a particular learning type in an organization, i.e., it refers to organizational rather than individual excess or deficiency. The point here is that students understand that each style has strengths and weaknesses and groups benefit from having people with different learning styles. Students like to hear real life examples of learning style differences and how people learn to monitor their own style-related behavior.

E. One of the most important steps in the course is the **formation of learning groups** that occurs during this session. Some criteria are stated at the top of page 61, but you can also ask students to determine the criteria themselves. We tell students to go back to the grid and stand in their learning style quadrant. Then we announce that no groups are completely formed until everyone is satisfied with the group they are in. Some instructors warn students not to choose a group based on either friendship or personal attraction. These groups have difficulty getting members to pull their weight or they spend so much time flirting that their grades suffer.

Instructors should consider carefully how many groups they want to have. Too many groups means that too much time will be devoted to repetitious group report-outs during the debriefing section. (If you have extremely large classes, you may want to modify the debriefing instructions to focus more on individual contributions, so each group does not have to speak. It is possible to teach this course with casts-of-thousands style classes; 300 students is the highest we've heard of. One of the authors taught a 100+ student class by delegating the responsibility for group exercises to students on a rotating basis, meeting with them before each class, and evaluating their facilitation efforts.) On the other hand, if your learning groups are too large, students won't have enough opportunity to talk. Eight is probably the maximum number and six or seven is the ideal number. You may also want to take attendance patterns at your school into consideration. If groups are too small, absent members can limit the group's ability to do the exercises.

F. The newly formed groups need time to introduce themselves and do the Creating a Learning Community exercise on page 61. It is not necessary to reconvene the class afterwards if you think the groups can profit more from using this time on their own. With undergraduates who will be doing group projects together, we ask them to establish their ground rules for working together and report these back to the entire class for cross-fertilization purposes.

G. In shorter class sessions, instructors may wish to form the learning groups in a separate class session. If the instructor is using a Saturday session, this can also be done in the beginning of such a session. Make sure you have people in their permanent groups for a Saturday session because the groups develop and "form" so extensively on this occasion that students will not want to change their allegiance to another group. Later on in the course, it does no harm to modify the group formation for specific exercises (e.g., having them number off by four to create the four groups necessary for a specific exercise). It is good to let students see how other groups or students function later in the course; in the beginning days of their learning groups, it is best to keep them in their own learning groups.

H. The end of this session or the beginning of the next one is a good time to explain the PAA assignment in greater depth.

**Transparency Masters**
3-0   David Kolb's Experiential Learning Model
3-1   Learning Style Type Grid

**Exam and Review Questions**

1. In the vignette, "Institutional Learning and Survival," the organizational learning process is described as
   *a.   hearing, digesting, confirmation, action
    b.   diverger, assimilator, converger, experimentation
    c.   planning, controlling, organizing, commanding
    d.   goal setting, action, review

2. Kolb's model of adult learning emphasizes
   a. learning as a linear process
   b. generalized and teacher-directed learning
   *c. the relevance of learning in our daily lives and work
   d. concepts before experience

3. Excellent ability in organizing relations into a meaningful "gestalt" is characteristic of a(n)
   a. accommodator
   b. assimilator
   c. converger
   *d. diverger

4. Gloria's boss, George, is good at inductive reasoning, creating theoretical models, and planning. Therefore, you think that his learning style is the (assimilator) style.

   The strengths of Gloria's learning style are learning by trial and error, getting things done, and risk taking. She has the (accommodator) style.

   Given their different learning styles, what difficulties might Gloria and her boss have in working together?

Answer: George may want to take more time planning whereas Gloria may want to leap into action and prefer a trial and error method. George may find Gloria to be pushy. Gloria may be uncomfortable if George focuses more on ideas than on people issues, and vice versa.

5. What's the difference between adaptive and generative learning? Provide an example of each in your answer.

Answer: Adaptive learning (single loop learning) focuses on coping -- solving problems in the current way of doing things. Generative learning (double loop learning) focuses on creating -- continuous experimentation and feedback in an ongoing analysis of how organizations define and solve problems. The latter involves questioning our assumptions about the way we work. Examples are ...

6. An espoused theory, according to Argyris, is
   a. a theory that guides our behavior
   b. a theory that has been held for a long time
   *c. a theory that we say we believe
   d. a theory that underlines the need for balance

7. Defensive routines prevent people from questioning their
   *a. assumptions
   b. values

        c.   self concept
        d.   learning style

READER QUESTIONS:

**"R&D Organizations as Learning Systems" by Barbara Carlsson, Peter Keane, and J. Bruce Martin**

8.   Experiments suggest that key steps on the progress of R&D projects follow
      a.   a linear sequence through the problem solving model
      b.   a counter-clockwise sequence through Kolb's learning model
   *c.   a clockwise sequence through Kolb's learning model
      d.   a random sequence through Kolb's learning model

9.   When organizations are viewed as learning systems, the project manager's role can be seen as one of
      a.   planning, organizing, directing and controlling
      b.   delegating authority
      c.   creating new ideas
   *d.   providing leadership in the learning process

**"The Leader's New Work: Building Learning Organizations" by Peter M. Senge**

10.  Explain Senge's "Principle of Creative Tension" and provide an example. (essay)

11.  According to Senge, what is the new work of leaders? (essay)

12.  Which of the following is not one of the roles of leaders in Senge's concept of learning organizations?
      a.   designers
      b.   teachers
   *c.   heroes
      d.   stewards

13.  Based upon the readings, what is a learning organization and how does it function? What are the advantages of a learning organization? How would you evaluate your own organization as a learning organization? (essay)

**"Building a Learning Organization" by David A. Garvin**

14.  What are the building blocks of a learning organization according to Garvin?

Answer: systemic problem solving, experimentation, learning from past experience, learning from others

15. What conditions are necessary to build a learning organization, according to Garvin?
    a.   financial stability, learning councils, e-mail
    *b.  time, open boundaries, learning forums
    c.   employee involvement groups, mature staff, leader as steward
    d.   creative tension, meetings, diversity

**Reader Articles**

1. "R&D Organizations as Learning Systems" by Barbara Carlsson, Peter Keane, and J. Bruce Martin
2. "The Leader's New Work: Building Learning Organizations" by Peter M. Senge
3. "Building a Learning Organization" by David A. Garvin

# Chapter 4
## INDIVIDUAL AND ORGANIZATIONAL MOTIVATION

**Materials Needed:** None.

**Objectives:** By the end of this chapter, students should be able to:

A. Explain several theories of motivation.
B. Understand McClelland's three basic social motives and how they are defined.
C. Gain insight into your own motive patterns.
D. Explain how managers can direct individual motivation and behavior in organizations.

**Setting the Stage -- Lecturette**

One way to begin a discussion of motivation is to ask what happens when people win the lottery -- do they quit their jobs or continue working? Approximately 80% continue at work, which can lead into the discussion of what meaning work has for people. What needs does it meet, beyond money for basic subsistence?

Our lecturettes usually begin with a definition of motivation and reemphasize that it is not something you do to other people. However, good managers and team members understand what motivates the people they work with and create an environment in which individual motivation is aligned with company goals and rewards. We distinguish between content and process theories and cover the key theoretical points of Maslow, Herzberg and McClelland. We use the transparency (T4-0), "David McClelland's Motive Theory." **Be careful not to present some of the three needs as more desirable than the others because this can bias the scoring and cause students to worry about their motive patterns**. Finally, we ask students to figure out how these three theories relate to each other so they can integrate these ideas and remember the theories more readily. We present the process theories <u>after</u> the group exercise.

Another technique to get them thinking about manifestations of McClelland's theory is to have students guess at behaviors related to motivation research results. What type of sports do people with a dominant need in the three motives tend to play (*n*-Pow = football; *n*-Ach = cross country, tennis, golf; *n*-Aff = volleyball)? What type of books would they be likely to read (*n*-Pow = Ludlum type mysteries, books that focus on glamour; *n*-Ach = science fiction, Agatha Christie type mysteries where the reader works to figure out "Who done it;" $n$-Aff = romance)?

McClelland's theory of motives is another type of mental maps -- they reflect our preoccupations and the way we see the world.

**Issues to Consider in Leading the Experiential Exercise**

A. The T.A.T. is used as the diagnostic stimulus to let students gain some insight into their own motives and see how differently people respond to the same stimulus. We tell students that our diagnoses will not be as accurate as those made by trained coders in laboratory conditions; we use the T.A.T. as a pedagogical tool for learning about the research on motivation and for stimulating thought about one's own motive patterns. The instructor should make sure that this distinction is made between research and pedagogy and that students understand that this is not being used as a clinical instrument to give them final answers about their motive patterns. The themes that are identified in the stories may be rightfully seen as indicators of motive directions, but the scoring system used here is a simplified one. Students can continue examining their own behavior to better understand their motive pattern.

B. Read the coding criteria out loud to the students. Make sure they understand that you only code actual words, not assumptions or interpretations. This is an exercise in content analysis, not interpretation.

C. Offer your services if they come upon a story or sentence they find difficult to code ("Let me know if you find something that stumps you.") Walk around and listen unobtrusively to the groups at work. This allows you to see whether they are coding accurately and following instructions and, more importantly, you can see interesting events that should be included in the debriefing section. If they don't mention these things in the debriefing of their own volition, you can gently prompt them by saying something like, "Would you mind telling us what happened in your group when you were discussing the second picture?"

D. Some students will be worried about their motive patterns and what it means. While it is true that managers should encourage $n$-Ach behavior in the workplace, instructors should not convey the idea that people whose dominant needs are either affiliation or power are less valuable. Students may also worry if their stories have no power imagery and they want to be managers. You may need to reassure them that we find successful people with all types of motive patterns. Some are merely more comfortable in certain jobs due to their motive pattern. Others find they have to make a special effort to focus on things that do not naturally grab their attention (i.e., the manager low in affiliation who finds himself in an organizational culture or business that values warm, personal relationships and has to schedule in time to make the rounds and talk to employees).

E. In **debriefing**, students often mention how surprising it is that people can come up with such disparate stories for the same picture. This fits right into the mental map analogy and idea that we are "programmed" differently when it comes to motives. Good managers learn to identify the motive patterns of the people they work with. Why is this important? This is a good place for real-life examples, e.g., letting a colleague with a high need for power make the final presentation. How can we figure out motive patterns without administering a test like the TAT?

F. If you as a professor were trying to elicit $n$-Ach in the classroom, what would you do? Incidentally, don't forget to act like a good manager and tell the class when they're doing well. Students usually work very hard in this course so we compliment them individually and as a group whenever we remember and catch them doing things that warrant reinforcement, like good preparation, getting down to task quickly, respect for others, etc.

G. In a long session, we present the process theories (expectancy theory, equity theory, reinforcement theory, and goal setting) after the exercise, using the $T = M \times E \times R$ theory as a link. The transparency on expectancy theory (T4-1) is taken from the *Reader* article and seems to be the easiest way for students to understand this theory. We ask students to analyze their own motivation for this course, using expectancy theory. One way to demonstrate reinforcement theory is to throw candy to students who speak in class. This usually results in a debate about the theory and a timely discussion on class participation.

H. With shorter class sessions, the process theories are presented in a follow-up class. It works well to ask students to identify all the things managers can do to encourage high performance and a motivated work force. This helps them integrate the practical implications from all the different theories. For this reason, some instructors schedule Chapter 21 on job design to follow the motivation chapter.

**Transparency Masters**
4-0   David McClelland's Motive Theory
4-1   Expectancy Theory

**Exam and Review Questions**

1. Maslow argues that human motivation can be viewed in a
    a. horizontal fashion
    *b. hierarchical fashion
    c. loop
    d. schematic diagram

2. The two factors that comprise Herzberg's theory of motivation are "motivators" and
    a. intrinsic factors
    b. job enrichment factors
    c. content theory
    *d. hygiene factors

3. According to McClelland, a high need for achievement seems absolutely necessary for
    *a. entrepreneurs
    b. social workers
    c. managers
    d. supervisors

4. Which of the following is <u>not</u> a characteristic of high need for achievement
    a. like to set their own goals
    *b. like to own prestige belongings
    c. tend to avoid either extremely difficult or extremely easy goals
    d. prefer tasks that provide immediate feedback on their performance

5. Fill in the blanks
    positive face of *n*-affiliation = <u>(interest)</u>
    negative face of *n*-affiliation = <u>(assurance)</u>
    positive face of *n*-power = <u>(socialized)</u>
    negative face of *n*-power = <u>(personalized)</u>

6. In the behavioral formula T = M x E x R, E refers to
    a. environment
    b. strength of expected motive
    *c. expectation of rewards for motivated action
    d. evaluation of reward value

7. <u>(Equity Theory)</u> maintains that employee motivation is affected by the perceived fairness of what people contribute and receive.

8. When people learn to use behaviors that are rewarded and to suppress behaviors that are punished, this is an example of
    *a. social reinforcement theory
    b. expectancy theory
    c. equity theory
    d. goal setting

9. McClelland has developed ways of measuring and defining three human motives that direct our behavior. Name, define, explain, and give examples of each of these motives. Explain how they are measured in people. (essay)

10. What is the difference between positive and negative need for power? Discuss the factors that make up these different faces of power and provide examples of both faces. (essay)

11. What is the difference between the positive and negative faces of need for affiliation? Provide examples. (essay)

12. You have taken over a company that has a poorly motivated work force. Describe all the tools or actions that a manager can use to improve motivation and achieve a high performance workplace. (essay)

READER QUESTIONS:

**"Work Motivation: Theory and Practice" by Katzell and Thompson**

13. People are motivated to perform well when there have been positive consequences of good performance is an example of
    a. motive/need theory
    b. goal theory
    *c. reinforcement theory
    d. sociotechnical system theory

14. What is the basic proposition of goal theory?

Answer: People perform better if goals are defined that are difficult, specific, and attractive.

15. Which of the following is not a characteristic of people with high self-efficacy?
    *a. success is due to external factors
    b. higher performance standards
    c. greater willingness to put effort into challenging tasks
    d. expectations of better performance

**"Motivation: A Diagnostic Approach" by Nadler and Lawler**

16. According to expectancy theory, a person's motivation is a function of the following:

    a. _____ to performance expectancies
    b. Performance to _____ expectancies
    c. Perceived _____ of outcome

17. Take two different students in this course -- one who was motivated to study for this exam and one who was not -- and thoroughly explain their motivation or lack thereof using expectancy theory. (There is no need to name names.)

**"That Urge to Achieve" by McClelland**

18. McClelland states that high achievement motivation is
    a. an inherited condition
    b. learned at school
    *c. learned from parents
    d. partly inherited and partly nurtured

19. Which of the following is not one of the goals of McClelland's training to increase n-Ach?
    a. teach participants to think, talk, act like a person with high n-Ach.
    *b. acceptance of one's destiny
    c. goal setting
    d. self awareness

**Reader Articles**

1. "Work Motivation: Theory and Practice" by Raymond A. Katzell and Donna E. Thompson
2. "Motivation: A Diagnostic Approach" by David Nadler and Edward Lawler III.
3. "That Urge to Achieve" by David McClelland

# Chapter 5
# VALUES AND ETHICS

**Materials Needed:** None.

**Objectives:** By the end of this chapter, students should be able to:

A. Describe how organizations foster unethical behavior.
B. Explain how organizations can promote ethical behavior.
C. Define ethics and values.
D. Better articulate their own values.
E. Distinguish between ethical and non-ethical values.
F. Explain and recognize the stages of moral reasoning.
G. Describe four different ethical models.

**Sample Design**
6:00 - 6:25      Lecturette
6:25 - 7:00      Read case individually and come to group consensus (Step 1 & 2)
7:00 - 7:20      Learning groups identify the values in their discussion and determine what stages of moral development are reflected in group and individual decisions. (Step 3 & 4)
7:20 - 8:00      General debriefing (Step 5)

**Setting the Stage -- Lecturette**

The purpose of this chapter is to get students thinking about their own values and introduce them to the basic principles of ethics so they can discuss ethical problems. In the lecturette, we highlight the need for ethical behavior in business and present the basic themes in the topic introduction. After a brief overview of Rokeach's model, we discuss the students' scores on the Rokeach instrument in the premeeting preparation. By a show of hands, we see the dominant value orientations in the class.

We present Kohlberg's theory, using the transparency "Three Levels of Moral Development According to Kohlberg" (T5-0), and make sure that students understand each level. We give them samples of moral reasoning and ask what level they represent. We ask students to summarize the research findings on Kohlberg's theory. Kohlberg's theory has come under attack, and you may wish to read some of the criticisms and counterdefenses for yourself so you can respond to student questions. We included Kolhberg's theory in the workbook after consulting with several ethics scholars who say some of the criticisms have been answered and who believe that it is still the best theory we have at present.

**Issues to Consider in Leading the Experiential Exercise**

A. **We apologize but there may be a mistake in the order of the Procedure for Group Meeting, depending upon which printing your textbooks are in. Do not let students read Figure 5-3 until after the learning groups have discussed the case. They should read Figure 5-3 at Step 4, not before they read the extended case. If your textbooks are out of order, tell them to ignore that figure until the appropriate time.**

B. Try to avoid judgmental arguments in this session. Moralistic students are sometimes offended by "expedient" decisions whereas worldly students may look down upon the "idealism" of other students. The emphasis has to be upon understanding the different approaches, the values that drive them, and their consequences.

C. We recommend you read James Weber and Sharon Green's "Principled Moral Reasoning: Is it a Viable Approach?" *Journal of Business Ethics*, 10 (1991), p. 328 because it concerns teaching ethics to business students. According to their research, most sophomore undergraduate students (77%) reason below stage 4, so we should not give them the impression that they should be more advanced than they are. As with any developmental theory, there is a concern that people will want to be at the top rather than the bottom of the scale. Instructors should be sensitive to this issue.

D. When you come to question #5 on page 117, you can ask students to do a quick-write about what Roger should have said to the partner. Then ask for volunteers to role play what they would say in Roger's shoes. Afterwards, create with students a list of suggestions that might work -- "avoid a moralistic tone, get the partner to problem solve with Roger, etc.".

E. Allow students to read the four models of ethics.

F. With a shorter class session, teach values on one day and use the ethics case on another.

G. Undergraduates sometimes have difficulty looking beyond short-term expediency to the long-term consequences of unethical behavior (diminished reputation, loss of business, termination, etc.). They may also mistakenly assume that everyone cheats to get ahead in business. To give students a dose of reality, some instructors take students to prison where they interview white collar criminals. Whenever you have business people as speakers, ask them about business ethics.

H. One of The Massey Triad videos on values can be used with a values class, although there is some overlap with the Boyatzis and Skelly article. The Enterprise Trust videos on companies that have been rewarded for their social consciousness are very good.

**Transparency Masters**

5-0  Three Levels of Moral Development According to Kohlberg

**Exam and Review Questions**

1. (Values)  are core beliefs or desires that guide or motivate attitudes and actions.

2. Which of the following is not a characteristic of companies in which unethical practices are likely:
    a. sole focus on profit and intense competition
    b. top management gives only lip service to ethical behavior
    *c. top management sets up clear policies and adequate controls
    d. insensitivity to customer's best interests

3. Why do ethical practices pay off in the long run?

Answer: trusting relationships and well-satisfied customers are the basis of repeat business.

4. Terminal values
    a. fall into two categories: moral and competence
    b. are preferable modes of behavior
    c. are the means to achieving one's instrumental values
    *d. are desirable end states of existence or the goals people want to acomplish in their lifetime.

5. What are ethics based upon?

Answer: moral duties and virtues arising from principles about right and wrong.

6. Which of the following is an ethical value?
    *a. responsibility
    b. ambition
    c. personal security
    d. materialism

7. Kohlberg's theory of moral development consists of three levels
    a. self-motivated, confirmed, principled
    *b. self-centered, conformity, principled
    c. self-importance, conscious, principled
    d. self-serving, congruence, principled

8. If a person believes you should not cheat on income taxes because you might be put in jail, what level of moral reasoning is this?
   a. Stage three - interpersonal accord, conformity
   b. Stage Five - social contract
   c. Stage four - social accord
   *d. Stage one - obedience and punishment

9. The workbook identifies four models of ethics. Identify, define, and explain each model. Provide examples that show how the models are different from one another. (essay)

READER QUESTIONS:

**"America's Problems and Needed Reforms: Confronting the Ethic of Personal Advantage" by Terence R. Mitchell and William G. Scott**

10. Which of the following is not one of the values that comprises Mitchell and Scott's "ethic of personal advantage?"
    a. concern for environmental issues
    b. short-term rather than long-term perspective
    c. emphasis on individual over the community
    d. focus on ends rather than means

11. What reforms do Mitchell and Scott recommend to counteract the ethic of personal advantage?

Answer:
a) changing values through moral development
b) reward ethical behavior and punish unethical behavior in the legal arena
c) reform organizational governance and due process

**"Changing Unethical Organizational Behavior" by Richard P. Neilsen**

12. According to Nielsen, how does organizational culture affect ethical behavior within an organization? (essay)

13. According to Nielsen, what are the limitations of the intervention strategies an individual can use to change unethical organizational behavior?

Answer:
a. individual can be wrong about the organization's actions
b. relationships can be damaged
c. organization can be hurt unnecessarily

    d.    strategies can encourage "might makes right" climate

14. Identify and describe four of the intervention strategies an individual can employ to change unethical behavior. Provide an example of each one. (essay)

**Reader Articles**

1. "America's Problems and Needed Reforms: Confronting the Ethic of Personal Advantage" by Terence R. Mitchell and William G. Scott
2. "Changing Unethical Organizational Behavior" by Richard P. Neilsen

# Chapter 6
## PERSONAL GROWTH, CAREER DEVELOPMENT, AND WORK STRESS

**Materials Needed**: Some instructors prefer flip chart paper and markers to the Life Line page in the workbook page 146. Otherwise, no additional materials are needed.

**Objectives**: When this chapter is completed, students should be able to

A. Describe the characteristics of adult development.
B. Explain Levinson's concept of life structures.
C. List the different career anchors and their significance.
D. Describe the functions that mentors perform.
E. Identify trends in career management and planning.
F. Explain the transactional model of career stress.
G. Assess your current life-career situation and develop a plan for the future.

**Sample Design**
6:00 - 6:20    Lecturette
6:20 - 7:40    Self-assessment and Life Planning Exercise
7:40 - 8:00    Debriefing and lecturette on stress

**Setting the Stage -- Lecturette**

Some instructors prefer to use this chapter at the end of the course when students know each other extremely well and are looking ahead to the future. When instructors use this chapter in the sixth session (after people settle down a bit and have some familiarity with each other), it helps students set goals relevant to the course and can focus their learning. It also allows them to understand each other much better. If you use it in the sixth session, you can check up on their achievement plan progress at the end of the course if you wish.

The purpose of the chapter is to model for students the self-assessment and career planning process and help them identify the aspects that are important for them in planning a balanced, satisfying life. This chapter is extremely useful for some students and not at all useful for others; the determining factor seems to be the student's <u>felt need</u> for life planning at the time. For this reason one of the authors assigns this unit (including the trio work called for in the career planning exercise) as an outside project -- sometimes required, sometimes as an option among several term paper type projects.

We begin the lecture by writing Eisenhower's quotation on the blackboard, "A plan is nothing; planning is everything," and go on to discuss the importance of career planning. There is a great deal of career-related anxiety among students; the trick here is to emphasize the need to be proactive about one's career without depressing students unduly about the job market. We do a brief overview of the adult development theories in the Topic Introduction, focusing on developmental challenges. We ask the MBA students if these theories seem valid, given their own life experience.

Next, we briefly cover career anchors, balancing dual careers, and mentoring in as interactive a fashion as possible. There is a survey instrument in Schein's book, *Career Dynamics*, that you could use with students if you want to do some self-assessment in this area.

The changes in career planning, particularly the shift to employee responsibility for career development and life planning as a continuous process, provide a lead-in to the exercise. We show the transparency (T6-0), "Tripod of Life Plan Perspectives," and note that the premeeting preparation exercise contains aspects of both the present and the future. The class exercises complement the premeeting preparation and are similar to the exercises used in career planning workshops.

**Issues to Consider in Leading the Experiential Exercise**

A. Tell the students to search for themes as they listen to the people in their trios talk about themselves and their history. Career counselors help people to identify these career anchors and interests; students in learning groups come to know each other so well that, if they are perceptive, they can pick up these themes. For example, one student complained that she had no career and no goals, just a series of jobs. However, when she described her work history, the other students noted that she had always accepted jobs that involved setting up new programs and left when the routine aspect of the job became intolerable. As a result, she decided to capitalize on her creative and entrepreneurial skills.

B. If you have former homemakers or international students without much formal job experience, they may need individual reassurance that their experience as volunteers, Scout leaders, Sunday school teachers, domestic engineers, serious hobbyists, etc., is not insignificant and should be analyzed.

C. The life line exercise is often used in the beginning of team-building workshops to help people understand each other's personal contexts. People tend to appreciate others more after hearing their life history with its ups and downs.

D. We mention the importance of goal-setting and publicly sharing one's goals before asking students to share the goals they set in the premeeting preparation exercise with their trio in Step 5.

E. This exercise has no formal general debriefing questions at the end. You can ask for their reactions to the exercises if you wish ("Were the exercises helpful?" "What did you learn from doing this?")

F. We segue to the topic of stress as shown in the beginning of the Follow-Up section (the effect of cultural differences regarding destiny on career planning and the stress that abounds in restructured economies). Next, we define stress and describe the stress response. We walk them through the "Transactional Model of Career Stress" transparency (T6-1). We note the costs of excessive work stress and, if time permits, ask students how they reduce and manage stress.

**Transparency Masters**
6-0  Tripod of Life Plan Perspectives
6-1  Transactional Model of Career Stress


**Exam and Review Questions**

1.  Levinson refers to the pattern or design of a person's life as
    a.   developmental boundaries
    *b.  life structures
    c.   stage themes
    d.   developmental challenges

2.  According to Levinson, major life transitions occur about the ages of
    a.   12, 21, and 40
    b.   6, 8, 22, and 40
    c.   13, 30, and 40
    *d.  30, 40, and 50

3.  According to *Workforce 2000*, Americans can expect to change jobs
    a.   three times
    b.   five times
    c.   seven times
    *d.  ten or more times

4.  Which of the following is not one of the syndromes formed early in life to create the career anchors that guide and constrain people's careers?

35

a. attitudinal
*b. interests
c. motivational
d. values

5. Why is it so important to set career goals?

Answer: Those who set goals are more likely to achieve them.

6. A __(mentor)__ is a senior person within the organization who assumes responsibility for a junior person.

7. According to research findings, what are the advantages of being mentored?

Answer: more promotions, higher pay, higher job satisfaction

8. __(Stress)__ is defined as the nonspecific response of an organism to demands that tax or exceed its resources.

9. Which of the following is not a coping mechanism?
a. direct action
b. cognitive reappraisal
c. symptom management
*d. general adaptive syndrome (GAS)

10. Type A behavior is always associated with greater susceptibility to stress-caused heart disease.
____ True __X__ False Why?

Answer: Type A correlates with stress-induced heart disease when it is accompanied by quickness to anger, mistrust, and suspicion. When "workaholics" are not hostile, they are not prone to greater stress.

11. People with external locus of control perceive situations to be more stressful than people with internal locus of control. __X__ True ____ False Why?

Answer: External locus of control signifies a belief that one's life is controlled by outside forces; internal locus of control means that people control their own destiny. Having some degree of control in a situation reduces stress.

READER QUESTIONS:

**"On the Realization of Human Potential: A Path with a Heart" by Herbert A. Shepard**

12. A "path with a heart"
a. promotes conformity

     b.    emphasizes human similarities
     c.    encourages people to offset the boredom of their jobs with hobbies and outside interests they love
  *d.    encourages uniqueness

13. Which of the following institutions does Shepard identify as the most immediate custodian of society's standards and dogma?
     a.    the church
  *b.    parents
     c.    schools
     d.    work organizations

14. What does Shepard call the "worthwhile life" indicator that emphasizes feeling good about your relationships?
  *a.    resonance
     b.    tone
     c.    perspective
     d.    social support

**"Career Gridlock: Baby Boomers Hit the Wall" by Douglas T. Hall and Judith Richter**

15. Which of the following is <u>not</u> one of the distinctive values of Hall and Richter's baby boomers?
     a.    sense of freedom to act on values
     b.    strong concern for basic values
  *c.    focus on community
     d.    need for autonomy and questioning authority

16. What do Hall and Richter mean when they write about replacing a promotion culture with a psychological success culture? Why is this necessary? Evaluate the culture of your organization in these terms. (essay)

**"Organizational Stress" by Robert L. Kahn and Philippe Byosiere**

17. Selye believed that all stressors are undesirable.
     \_\_\_\_ True   <u>X</u>  False  Why?

<u>Answer</u>: This is false because Selye distinguished between good stress (eustress) with its challenges and bad stress (distress).

18. Physiological responses to stress are
     a.    anxiety, burnout
     b.    absenteeism, turnover
     c.    circulatory and respiratory problems
  *d.    heart rate, blood pressure

19. Using Kahn and Byosiere's article, analyze the stressors and stress responses in your organization. (essay)

**Reader Articles**

1. "On the Realization of Human Potential: A Path with a Heart" by Herbert Shepard.
2. "Career Gridlock: Baby Boomers Hit the Wall" by Douglas T. Hall and Judith Richter
3. "Organizational Stress" by Robert L. Kahn and Philippe Byosiere

Note: Depending upon the printing, there may be an error in the Tips for Managers, pg. 155. The "Ignore" that begins the second point is superfluous.

# Chapter 7
## INTERPERSONAL COMMUNICATION

**Materials Needed**: None.

**Objectives:** By the end of this chapter, students should be able to:

A. Understand the model of communication.
B. List common sources of distortion.
C. Identify gender differences in communication.
D. Describe and recognize the five response styles.
E. Explain how to create a climate that encourages nondefensive communication.
F. Recognize assertive communication and utilize I-statements.
G. Improve their listening skills.

**Sample Design**

| | |
|---|---|
| 6:00 - 6:40 | Lecturette on interpersonal communication |
| 6:40 - 7:40 | Active Listening Exercise |
| 7:40 - 8:00 | Debriefing and I-statements |

**Setting the Stage -- Lecturette**

The purpose of this chapter is to give students a basic grounding in interpersonal communication. Consequently, this chapter is best used after several class sessions, but before the chapters on Interpersonal Perception and Attribution, Inter-group Conflict and Negotiation, Performance Appraisal, and Power and Influence. If you are following the chapter order in the workbook, you can explain to students at this point that we have completed the beginning topics that focused upon mental maps and individual differences and are embarking upon the skill-building portion of the course. The Communication chapter lays the groundwork for the remaining chapters in Part II.

The lecturette we use (crafted by a gifted professor, Gail Ambuske) begins with an explanation of why communication is such an important skill for both managers and employees. We define communication as mutual understanding and warn students that communication doesn't happen until the message has been accurately received. Sometimes we use the "Arc of Distortion" transparency (T7-1) at this point and mention that many communications result in partial misunderstanding.

We use the "Communication Model" transparency (T7-0) and launch into the barriers or distortions in the communication process. We begin by asking students why two people might encode a message differently. This leads to a discussion of the individual differences that affect encoding and decoding. We also cover or elicit from the students the remaining barriers: individual differences in encoding and decoding, noise, defensiveness, self-esteem, gender differences, lack of clarity, emotions, and poor listening skills.

At this point, we go over the Communication Climate Inventory in the pre-meeting preparation and Gibb's model that underlies it (transparency T7-2, "Categories of Behavior Characteristics of Supportive and Defensive Climates in Small Groups ").

We emphasize the fact that meaning lies in people, not words and quote Mehrabian and Weiner's findings that only 7% of meaning comes from words, 55% from facial expressions and posture, and 38% from vocal intonation and inflection. We give an example of a discrepancy between words and posture. We also ask for a student volunteer with dramatic aspirations to read us a sentence ("Why did you come to this meeting?"), accenting different words with each reading to demonstrate the importance of inflection.

After briefly explaining the response styles, we ask for another volunteer who is instructed to initiate a conversation with the instructor, always using the same sentence ("I think I lost the bid" for MBA's and "I think I failed the midterm" for undergraduates). The instructor uses one of the response styles and the rest of the class identifies the response style. We do this in part because it's fun, but mainly because students need practice hearing and recognizing the styles. Instructors can reinforce this learning throughout the course by asking, "What kind of response style was that?". We mention that the only response style that does not involve a one-up, one-down relationship is the understanding response, which introduces the topic of active listening. We explain the importance of active listening and refer back to the Model of Communication and the role of active listening in the feedback loop.

We distinguish between normal and active listening, using the analogy of a worn-out marriage where the couple read their newspapers at the dinner table versus the total attention that characterizes the courtship phase. We explain why it's easy to divert your attention from speakers (brain's over capacity to process words) and the competitive nature of many U.S. conversations. People hear a topic and run it through their mental computer, searching for what they will say when the speaker finally stops talking. It's easy to come up with real-life examples of this type of conversation.

# Issues to Consider in Leading the Experiential Exercise

A.  To begin the exercise, we recommend either using a training video on active listening, or explaining the components of active listening and giving a demonstration with a willing student volunteer. The skill-building exercise works best if they can see what active listening looks like. If we have a student who is trained in customer relations, we ask them if they want to do the demonstration; otherwise, the instructor does it. Then we use the observer criteria to evaluate the active listener. Sometimes instructors make mistakes when they demonstrate a skill. If this occurs, an admission of error ("I could have done a better job with reflecting possible implications; what else could I have said there?") is a good example for students and reinforces the laboratory nature of the course.

B.  Since the feeling part of the message is often the most difficult, make sure students understand why it is necessary to key in on feelings. The instructor can provide examples of communications that lacked congruence and their consequences.

C.  Make sure that students can distinguish between "inviting further contributions" and the probing response style. In active listening, we invite further contributions when we don't yet have enough information to understand what the speaker is saying. Our motivation is merely to gain full understanding, not satisfy our curiosity or catechize the speaker.

D.  If you want to let students choose a controversial topic of discussion rather than use the scenarios in the workbook, spend a few minutes asking them to identify hot topics which you then write on the blackboard. They do not have to find a topic on which partners are on opposite sides, since it could take too long to find one. Warn them not to spend too much time settling on a topic, because the topic is less important than practicing the skill.

E.  The role playing stimuli are designed to be very realistic and require that students be themselves rather than "making believe."

F.  Warn the students who will be speaking that they should pause to let the active listeners paraphrase their meaning before an overwhelming number of sentences has gone by. Remind students that the feedback/discussion phases of the exercise provide yet another opportunity to practice active listening.

G.  For many students, the most difficult part of active listening is suppressing their own opinions. Caution them beforehand that this is not a dialogue or an argument; the listener's task is simply to understand and feedback the message they received to ensure it was transmitted accurately and fully. Walk around the room and listen to their communication. If it is not obvious who is the listener and who is the talker, you can politely interrupt and ask the observers what is occurring. See if the observers can pinpoint the problem before you advise the active listener (empowerment strategy).

H. In initial efforts at active listening, students usually focus primarily on paraphrasing literal content, sometimes in a stilted or even mocking way. Reflecting expressed feelings is harder for them and may presuppose a certain level of trust and rapport, which is why we do this chapter at this point in the course. Some students are not used to tuning into either feelings or non-verbal cues, and they will need extra help with this. We have run into younger students who cannot distinguish between thoughts and feelings; they mistakenly assume that a sentence that begins with "I feel" is automatically a feeling.

I. In the **debriefing**, a student will invariably say that they feel somewhat silly when they paraphrase. The instructor can explain that we all feel a bit silly when we are practicing a new skill and that it may feel forced in the beginning. However, people who are good at active listening and use it appropriately have a great advantage both in the workplace and at home. The trick is learning to use it naturally and almost unconsciously. Students should be seeing examples of naturally-occurring active listening in the classroom when instructors check to make sure that they really understand student questions and comments.

Typical reactions that are mentioned in the debriefing are that it was nice to be "heard" and that active listening was much more difficult and exhausting than it looks. The latter reason is why therapists and interviewers are careful not to over-schedule their days. Ask students when active listening should be used (when people are angry or troubled, negotiating, selling, handling complaints, or uncertain whether or not they have accurately received the message). You can ask students to practice active listening at home and work during the week and report on their efforts at the next class.

J. At the end of the class, we go over assertive communication and Figure 7-1 and I-statements. It is surprising how many undergraduates write PAAs on negative situations with bosses whom they never confronted; they simply became less motivated and eventually quit the job. Therefore, it may be more important to emphasize this with younger students and devote more time to this issue.

We use real examples of I-statements from the class ("When you come to class late...") to model that it is possible to give feedback in a non-threatening way. Then we ask students to write down an I-statement for a personal situation where they need to give someone feedback. We ask for volunteers to read these out loud and correct them as a group. It takes some practice for people to master I-statements. In collectivist cultures, people are uncomfortable owning the feeling part of the I-statement; they prefer to say "we" or to leave the feelings out altogether. You may want to ask international students whether they could use this format in their country. Students often ask if I-statements always result in getting people to change their behavior and, of course, they do not. Some people are remarkably intransigent and it takes much more than an I-statement to do the trick. Nevertheless, learning to give feedback in this manner is an especially valuable skill for supervisors, managers, and team members. As you know, young supervisors often have difficulty reprimanding or giving feedback in an appropriate manner.

We also touch upon the importance of seeing communication within a historical context and not merely as individual statements. Covey's idea of an Emotional Bank Account, described in the Follow-up section, highlights the significance of the relational context.

K. In shorter class sessions, present all the content in the first session and do the active listening exercise in the next.

**Transparency Masters**
7-0  Model of Communication
7-1  Arc of Distortion
7-2  Categories of Behavior Characteristics of Supportive and Defensive Climates in Small Groups

**Exam and Review Questions**

1. According to the research results presented in the vignette, "Do you Have What it Takes?", the variable that is the best predictor of managerial success is
   a. intelligence
   b. educational background
   *c. communication skills
   d. decision making skills

2. Draw the Model of Communication.

3. Why do we say that meaning lies in people, rather than words?

Answer: Because people decode messages in their own unique way; thus, words have different meaning for different people. Furthermore, words account for only 7% of the meaning in communications.

4. The type of response that communicates that the listener has positioned him or herself on the same level as the speaker is
   a. the supportive response
   b. the evaluative response
   c. the interpretive response
   *d. the understanding response

5. The arc of distortion is best described as
   *a. the difference between what the speaker intended to communicate and what the speaker communicated unintentionally
   b. the difference between what the speaker communicated and what the receiver wants to hear
   c. meaning lies in people, not words
   d. the difference between communication feedback and noise interference

6. Which of the response styles is the most common?
   a. the supportive response
   *b. the evaluative response
   c. the interpretive response
   d. the understanding response
   e. the probing response

7. Name four possible sources of distortion in the communication process.

Answer: individual differences in encoding and decoding, noise, defensiveness, self-esteem, gender differences, lack of clarity, emotions, and poor listening skills.

8. _(Assertiveness)_ is the ability to communicate clearly and directly what you need or want from another person in a way that does not deny or infringe upon the other's rights.

9. Give an active listening response, using as many components as possible, to this harried-looking, tense employee. Kathy: "I didn't get the bid in on time. I think I have ruined our chances of getting the Nike advertising account and I'll probably lose my job because of it!"

   Your response:

10. Ben ran into his dorm room shouting that he'd just gotten caught cheating on an exam, and he thought he'd be kicked out of school. His roommate, Michael,

responded, "How could you do such a stupid thing?  Wait until your parents hear about this!"
a. What type of response is this, according to Rogers? _(evaluative)_
b. Ben then punched Michael.  What was it about Michael's response that caused Ben to hit him?

<u>Answer</u>:  This was a one-up type of response with no empathy or understanding.  This response just made Ben feel worse.

c. As Michael was rubbing his sore chin, he regretted not putting more effort into learning active listening.  What should he have said to Ben?  (Make sure your response includes the major components of active listening.)

11. One of the members of your study group, Joshua, never prepares for class and doesn't seem to take the in-class exercises very seriously.  He's always talking about things that have nothing to do with the class.  You feel that this is holding your group back and getting in the way of your own learning in the course.  You don't want to make him angry, but you think it's time to give Joshua some feedback on his course performance in the hope that he will change his behavior.

    Compose an I-statement that would be appropriate for this situation **AND** label each of the three components of your I-statement.

COMPONENT
LABELS:

YOUR ACTUAL
WORDS TO
JOSHUA:


<u>READER QUESTIONS</u>:
**"Active Listening" by Carl Rogers and Richard E. Farson**

12. The active listener
    *a. allows the speaker to say what's on his or her mind and makes sure the message is understood
    b. probes for more facts
    c. tries to make the speaker feel good about herself
    d. focuses only on the content of the speaker's message

13. Rogers and Farson identify the two components of a message as <u>content</u> and
    a. definition

      *b.   feeling
       c.   facts
       d.   structure

**"Communication: The Use of Time, Space and Things by Anthony G. Athos**

14. How does culture affect the way we communicate? Include examples in your explanation. (essay)

15. Which of the following is <u>not</u> identified by Athos as an American dimension of space?
    a.   in is better than out
    b.   higher is better than lower
    c.   more is better than less
    *d.  public is better than private

**"Defensive Communication" by Jack R. Gibb**

16. Fill in the missing descriptions of Gibb's defensive and nondefensive climates.

    | DEFENSIVE | vs. | NONDEFENSIVE |
    |---|---|---|
    | evaluative | | _____ |
    | controlling | | _____ |
    | certainty | | _____ |
    | _____ | | equality |
    | _____ | | spontaneous |
    | _____ | | empathy |

17. One way to avoid provoking defensive communication is by
    a.   controlling the situation rather than assuming a problem solving orientation
    *b.  being provisional rather than certain
    c.   being neutral rather than showing empathy
    d.   being evaluative rather than descriptive

**Reader Articles**

1. "Active Listening" by Carl Rogers and Richard E. Farson
2. "Communication: The Use of Time, Space and Things by Anthony G. Athos
3. "Defensive Communication" by Jack R. Gibb

# Chapter 8
## INTERPERSONAL PERCEPTION AND ATTRIBUTION

**Materials Needed**: None.

**Objectives** By the end of this chapter, students should be able to:

A. Define perception and explain the perceptual process.
B. Identify the sources of misinterpretation in cross-cultural interactions.
C. Understand both the benefits and the drawbacks of the perceptual process.
D. Recognize common perceptual errors.
E. Describe the Johari Window.
F. Explain attribution theory.
G. Understand the relevance of perception and attribution for managers.

**Sample Design**

| | |
|---|---|
| 6:00 - 6:30 | Lecturette on interpersonal perception and the Johari Window |
| 6:30 - 7:40 | Perception Exercise |
| 7:40 - 8:00 | Debriefing and attributions |

**Setting the Stage -- Lecturette**

The purpose of this chapter is to familiarize students with perception, their own schemas, and how others see them. While we would not use the group exercise with a work group, it is very effective with learning groups that know and trust one another. For this reason, the chapter occurs when it does in the sequence. Some instructors who have never used this exercise find it threatening, but we have used it for years without any difficulty. In fact, most students really like the exercise and find it both enlightening and entertaining. People are very curious about how others see them.

We begin the lecturette by noting that perception was mentioned in the previous chapter as a barrier or potential distortion in the communication process. Many instructors begin the lecture with a perceptual exercise, like the old lady/young lady illustration in this chapter (T2-0, 2-1, 2-2) or the "Count the Squares" transparency (T8-1). Instructions for using the old lady/young lady are contained in Chapter 2 of the instructor's manual. When using the Count the Squares transparency, one instructor asks, "How many squares are there?". Students first count alone and without discussion with others. All the different totals are recorded on the blackboard. Individuals are asked to show the rest of the class how they arrived at their total.

With both these exercises, we emphasize that all the perceptions are partially correct at the same time that they are partially incorrect. Students are reminded that with the help of others, many of them were able to view the same situation in more than one way; without that help we are likely to assume that what we perceive is what is actually there. Perception is another example of individual differences and yet another way in which we perceive the world in different ways.

We define perception and ask students how the perceptual process works. In the ensuing discussion, we make sure that the following points are covered: selective attention and the internal and external factors that influence what we attend to; the concept of figure and ground; organizing into schemas; evaluation or inference; sources of misinterpretation in cross cultural interaction; and stereotyping. In sum, because of perception, we don't hear or see everything we should; we only pay attention to a part of what we hear; then we usually take that and interpret it subjectively, rather than objectively. Furthermore, stereotyping is always a danger.

However, perception performs a useful function by limiting information, selecting what input we will attend to, organizing and classifying input. If you want to show students a visual demonstration of perception, you can ask them to position their thumb and index finger in front of their eye, as if it were the lens of a camera. Instruct them to keep your entire body inside that frame and then walk from one end of the room to another, so that they will have to move their fingers to keep you within that frame. What the naked eye sees is a person becoming bigger and smaller; the perceptual process stabilizes that input and gives us the message that the person's size is really constant.

Next we cover the common perceptual distortions: halo effect, central tendency, contrast effects, projection, and self-fulfilling perceptual defenses. We explain the Johari Window, using the transparency (T8-0), as an information processing model.

NOTE: As described in the reader article, Jay Hall has an instrument that measures how much people self disclose and seek and offer feedback. It is copyrighted by Teleometrics International, 1755 Woodstead Court, The Woodlands, TX 77380/ tel.(713)367-0060.

## Issues to Consider in Leading the Experiential Exercise

A. When introducing this exercise, we mention that it may look silly but if taken seriously it is a good opportunity to see how other people see you and to become more aware of your own perceptual schema.

B. The exercise instructions are very complete. The only addition we make is to give an example, using a learning group, of how the process works (e.g., "In this group, say Sam decides he wants to go first, so Julie reads off all the things she has written down about Sam, and then Martha does the same thing and so on until we have gone around the entire group. Then Sam reads the words he used to describe himself.") We advise students to request feedback by asking why a person came up with a particular word if they are curious but to accept that the person may not always be able to explain their impression.

C. If there is an extremely difficult person in the class, you may want to observe what happens during his or her turn. We've never seen this exercise blow up, but better safe than sorry.

D. Some groups may finish before others. If that occurs, have them work ahead on the group discussion questions. Knock out these questions for groups that are very slow. If some groups have more members than others, they will finish at different times.

E. In the **debriefing**, students often mention that they were not comfortable giving negative impressions and they were astonished there was so much agreement (to the extent of several people choosing the same words in several categories) about some people. People who disclose little about themselves are often surprised at the impressions they create. We mention that self disclosure is a bell-shaped curve -- too much frightens others off; too little leads others to "project" their own attributions on the "mystery" person.

F. After the debriefing, we quickly cover attribution theory, as presented in the Follow-up section, and the Tips for Managers about how to manage perceptions at work.

**Transparency Masters**

8-0  Johari Window
8-1  Count the Squares

**Exam and Review Questions**

1. That portion of the Johari Window characterized by information known by the self and unknown to the other is
   a. unknown
   *b. facade
   c. blindspot
   d. arena

2. To move from the facade portion of the Johari Window to the arena portion requires
   a. receiving feedback from others
   b. giving feedback to others
   *c. disclosing information about oneself
   d. hiding information about oneself

3. Give an example that explains how internal factors affect what we perceive.

4. __(Selective attention)__ means that people perceive only some of the stimuli that is actually present.

5. __(Schemas)__ are cognitive frameworks that represent organized knowledge about a given concept, event or type of stimulus.

6. Which of the following is not a source of misinterpretation in cross-cultural interactions
   a. subconscious cultural blinders
   b. lack of cultural self-awareness
   *c. contrast effects
   d. projected similarity

7. What is the definition of stereotyping?

Answer: Attributing behavior or attitudes to a person on the basis of the group or category to which the person belongs.

8. List and explain three perceptual distortions that can bias the evaluation process.

Answer:
a. stereotyping = attributing behavior or attitudes to a person on the basis of the group or category to which the person belongs
b. halo effect = our perception of another is dominated by only one trait
c. central tendency = avoiding extreme judgments and rating everything as average
d. contrast effects = evaluations are affected by comparisons with other people we have recently encountered who are better or worse in terms of this characteristic
e. projection = tendency to attribute one's own attitudes or feelings to another person

f. self-fulfilling perceptual defenses = screens that block out what we do not wish to see and allow through stimuli that we wish to see

9. Good communication is most likely to occur when which of the four quadrants is the largest?
   a. unknown
   b. facade
   c. blindspot
   *d. arena

10. According to attribution theory, what is the difference between an internal cause and an external cause?

Answer:
Internal causes have to do with personal characteristics (lazy, irresponsible, undisciplined) whereas external causes are outside reasons for the person's behavior (overwork, lack of job clarity, etc.).

11. If many subordinates agree that a particular boss does not know how to delegate, this is an example of
    *a. consensus
    b. distinctiveness
    c. fundamental attribution error
    d. consistency

12. What is the definition of the self-serving bias?

Answer:
when people attribute success to personal internal factors (intelligence, initiative), but attribute failure to external factors (tough competition, poor leadership).


READER QUESTIONS:
**"Communication Revisited" by Jay Hall**

13. Behavior designed to laterally enlarge the arena portion and reduce the blindspot portion of the Johari Window is
    a. the exposure process
    b. the attribution process
    c. the self-disclosure process
    *d. the feedback process

14. Hall states that the most significant determinant of the quality of relationships is
    a. personal values
    b. cultural aspects of the organization
    *c. interpersonal styles of the parties involved
    d. organizational roles

**"The Thinking Organization: How Patterns of Thought Determine Organizational Culture" by Evelyn Pitre and Henry P. Sims, Jr.**

15. Executives build __(prototypes)__ of good and bad performers (person schema) that they use to select or appraise employees, according to Pitre and Sims.

16. An __(event schema)__ allows a person to act automatically in a given circumstance like an interview or meeting, freeing him or her of unnecessary cognitive burdens.

17. What are the four types of schemas described in the Pitre and Sims article?

Answer: person, event, role, and self.

18. What is the relationship, according to Pitre and Sims, between patterns of thought and organizational change? How can a manager utilize this knowledge when trying to change an organization? (essay)

**Reader Articles**

1. "Communication Revisited" by Jay Hall
2. "The Thinking Organization: How Patterns of Thought Determine Organizational Culture" by Evelyn Pitre and Henry P. Sims, Jr.

## Chapter 9
## GROUP DYNAMICS AND SELF-MANAGED WORK TEAMS

**Materials Needed**: Two concentric circles of chairs for each pair of groups. Flip charts and markers are optional.

**Objectives:** By the end of this chapter, students should be able to:

A. Identify what organizational requirements must be in place to set the stage for successful work teams
B. Describe two models of group development
C. Distinguish between group content and group process
D. Explain and diagnose group process behaviors that either help or hinder group effectiveness
E. Describe and recognize group roles
F. Combine the role of a participant in task accomplishment with the role of an observer of group process

**Sample Design**

6:00 - 6:15     Lecturette on self-managed work teams and group dynamics
6:15 - 7:30     Inner-Outer Exercise and subgroup analysis
7:30 - 8:00     Subgroup presentations and debriefing

**Setting the Stage -- Lecturette**

Although we are fans of the Desert Survival and Lost at Sea type exercises, we have found that many students have already been exposed to them. Therefore we chose a different group exercise that we hope you will like as well as or better than Lost at Sea. It sounds complex but works extremely well. This is an excellent way to begin a Saturday session in the beginning of the course. With undergraduates, we do this exercise sitting on the floor of a lounge.

We remind students at this point that OB has three levels of analysis -- individual, group, and organizational -- and we are focusing for the first time on the group level with this chapter. Our purpose here is to sensitize students to group process issues so they can learn to pay attention to both process and content dynamics in groups.

We try to keep the lecturette in this session as brief as possible to reserve more time for the exercise. We cover the growth of self-managed work teams, their characteristics, and what they need to be successful (common purpose, specific goals, supportive context in the form of top management, organizational culture, and policies that promote and support teamwork, skilled supervisors and team members). We present the two theories of group development presented in the workbook. We explain the difference between task and process and quickly run through the process issues that should be observed in groups -- communication, decision-making, task, and maintenance behavior. If time is short, we wait to talk about self-oriented behavior and norms during the exercise. Some instructors introduce the exercise by saying that students will finish this exercise with a whole new perspective on group functioning.

## Issues to Consider in Leading the Experiential Exercise

A. Beforehand, instructors need to decide how many groups they wish to run in this session. You can simply join two learning groups together to make a pair of groups; that has the advantage of showing how an established group functions. If you have an odd number of learning groups and a small class, you can have people number off and form new groups. This will be more of a stranger group since they will not have the history of the learning groups. There are pros and cons to both methods; just make sure the paired groups are as equal as possible in size. The ideal size for each group is 6-10.

B. The first time you try this exercise you may want to stick to the instructions -- 4 rounds of 4 minutes' duration which adds up to 36 minutes. In the future, you can modify it slightly according to your particular situation. Reducing the rounds to three minutes doesn't seem to make much difference in the outcome, although it may make the groups feel more stressed if they have trouble coming to agreements. Larger groups need more time than smaller groups. Don't short-change the subgroup analysis afterwards; if you're rushed for time, make the rounds shorter or eliminate a round. The consultation period is crucial and should not be jettisoned.

C. Put a schedule on the board that explains the rounds and the times:
```
Introduction
Round One
    Group A          four minutes
    Group B          four minutes
Round Two
    Group A          four minutes
    Group B          four minutes
Round Three
    Group A          four minutes
    Group B          four minutes
Consultation        four minutes of mutual feedback
Round Four
    Group A          four minutes
    Group B          four minutes
```

If the chairs are not already in place, you may want to draw an inner and outer circle of chairs on the board so they can visualize it more readily.

D.   Also write this on the board beforehand:

The two tasks are:
1. Be the most effective group you can
2. Create a list of the ten characteristics of effective groups and rank order it.

E.   Ask if anyone has ever done this exercise before. If so, are they willing to be observers? Ask for other volunteer observers so you have two for each pair of groups. If you have a choice, select students who are perceptive. Tell them to read the observer instructions on page 230.

F.   The timing of the rounds is important. It works best with a watch that can be set to beep when time is up. I usually delegate that job to a student in one of the groups who has a fancier watch than mine. Just make sure the timekeeper is immediately resetting the alarm and keeping time fairly for both groups. As soon as the alarm goes off, the groups quickly change places and the inner group begins work without waiting for the instructor to give them the go-ahead. This works better than waiting till they are all seated and ready to begin timing.

G.   **Don't tell them they can use the flip chart or blackboard**, but you can have a flip chart in the room and see if using it occurs to them. If they ask for permission, say something low-key like "It's up to you." How they decide to keep track of their ideas will affect their group process. Some groups use the flip chart, which allows everyone to see what's happening; other groups have one person who records the list and may assume ownership of it. It is more difficult to keep people involved with the latter method. In other groups, everyone keeps a copy of the list, but that is not very efficient. In the debriefing section, ask what effect their record-keeping had on group dynamics. They may also mention that they mistakenly assumed they could not use the flip chart or blackboard, rather than testing how proactive they could be. Occasionally a student will suggest using the flip chart, only to be told by another student that it's against the rules! Groups and teams often accept boundaries without testing them, which hampers their creativity and effectiveness.

H.   Make sure the observers understand how to use the Observer Chart. Each observer is responsible for only one subgroup. It's a good idea for them to switch locations occasionally so they can observe from a different perspective. Their job is extremely important. Most groups profit a great deal from this feedback. For example, in one group the observer noticed that a male student only made eye contact with the other U.S. males, ignoring the women and international students unless they spoke. He was grateful for the feedback and worked to be more inclusive. In many groups, this feedback allows them to discuss who's talking too much and too little and to identify the consequences of these behaviors.

I. Although the rules prohibit talking among members of the outer circle, some people will want to continue working on their list. Politely remind them that their job is to silently observe.

J. When it comes time for the consultation round, reiterate that the person in the inner circle should turn around and consult with the person directly behind. This pair has four minutes that they should divide so both of them have an opportunity to give and receive feedback.

K. Note how much time each group devotes towards talking about or trying to be the best group they can be. Pay attention to whether the groups utilize the feedback they received during the consultation phase. If they don't, ask them why in the debriefing section.

L. When you reach Step 6, briefly go over the four tasks, either before or after you have divided the students into four heterogeneous groups. It's important that each subgroup has members from all the inner-outer groups. You can flesh out these concepts. For example, self-oriented behavior is an example of an individual goal that may be operating in a group. We use the analogy with "membership" of the person who joins a country club but is still not accepted. You can remind students of the "norms" they set in the first class about what was effective behavior in this course. Encourage them to provide specific examples in their presentations ("When so-and-so did such-and-such...")

M. Observe the discussion in each subgroup to see if they need help. If there was an autocratic leader who steamrollered his or her group, this person could come in for direct personal criticism by the leadership subgroup. This exercise usually provides a vivid comparison in leadership styles. Sit with them and ask how they are planning to present their findings ("How will you say that? How can you couch it so that person doesn't go home feeling like dogmeat but will consider changing his or her style?"). Encourage them to focus on the pros and cons of different leadership styles. They will have to name names but it can be done respectfully. When this group presents their findings, be prepared to support leaders who caused resentment. Make sure their side of it is heard as well as their frustration at being criticized. One of the best lessons that comes out of this exercise is the vulnerability of autocratic leaders and how to avoid this situation. Ask group members why they did not speak up at the time if they were unhappy with the way things were going and make the point that everyone shares the responsibility for effective group process, not just the leaders. This also demonstrates that silence does not always signify satisfaction or support.

N. When the subgroup on goals has finished presenting, ask the groups how much time they devoted to the two assigned tasks. Usually a tiny percentage or no time at all is dedicated to the process goal (be the best group you can) and the task (ranking a list) receives all the attention. Why is that? They often answer that due to time constraints, the list was more important and they simply assumed they were already doing the other task or else they ignored it. Make the point that we always have time constraints of one sort or another, but a failure to discuss group process can also lead to wasted time. The failure to discuss the consultation feedback is another example of ignoring process issues. What could the groups have done to address the first assigned goal?

O. After the subgroup presentations, the groups revert to their exercise configuration so that the observers can present their feedback. Some instructors switch the order here to go directly to the general debriefing questions, Step 9, p. 230 and then do the observer feedback.

**Transparency Masters**

9-0 The Punctuated Equilibrium Model of Group Development
9-1 "Pure Types" of Emotional Behavior in Organizations
9-2 Symptoms of Groupthink
9-3 Remedies for Groupthink

**Exam and Review Questions**

1. When a group is focusing on its stated goal or task, this is an example of group
   a. process
   b. communication
   *c. content
   d. values

2. Self-oriented behavior tends to be more prevalent
   a. towards the end of the group
   b. when the group is focusing on task
   c. midway into the life of the group
   *d. when a new member joins an established group

3. (Norms) are unwritten, often explicit, rules that define the behavior and attitudes of group members.

4. Becoming overwhelmed by love or hate is a threat to
   a. the friendly helper
   b. the tough battler
   c. the gatekeeper
   *d. the logical thinker

5. What are the necessary conditions for self-managed work teams to succeed?

Answer: Supportive top management, organizational culture and policies that promote teamwork, teams with a common purpose and specific goals, and supervisors and team members who have the necessary skills to make teams function.

6. Which stage in the Five Stage Model of group development is described as "members confront the issue of how much individuality they must relinquish to belong to the group"?
   a. forming
   *b. storming
   c. norming
   d. performing
   e. adjourning

7. According to the Punctuated Equilibrium model of group development, a group can be expected to be most productive
   a. when they first begin to meet
   b. when they recommit themselves to their original direction
   *c. after a midpoint transition
   d. when they reach the performing stage

8. What is the difference between group task/content and group process? Give an example of both group task and group process from a class exercise.

Answer: Task is "what" the group does (their assignment), whereas process is "how" they work together. Process is concerned with issues like leadership, communication, decision-making, and norms. Examples =

READER QUESTIONS:
**"Groupthink Reconsidered" by Glen Whyte**

9. How does groupthink affect group decision making?

Answer: Members of cohesive groups are so busy striving for unanimity that this overrides their motivation to realistically appraise alternative courses of action. Therefore, they reach consensus upon a poor decision because the group failed to voice both ideas and controversy.

10. Name four symptoms of groupthink.

Answer: illusion of invulnerability, illusion of morality, rationalization, stereotyping, self-censorship, illusion of unanimity, direct pressure on dissidents, and reliance upon self-appointed mindguards.

11. According to the aspiration-level concept mentioned in Whyte's article, risk preference is more accurately viewed as
    a. risk aversion
    b. risk seeking
    *c. a mixture of risk seeking when individuals choose between losses and risk aversion when individuals choose between gains.
    d. weaker in group decisions than individual ones

12. As reported in Whyte's article, what are two products of group interaction?

Answer: uniformity pressures and group polarization

13. __(Group polarization)__ refers to an increase in the extremity of the point of view initially dominant in the group.

14. Whyte's argument is that bad decisions result from
    a. groupthink alone
    b. people who seek risk
    c. people who are averse to risk
    *d. how a group frames the decision and then makes choices

**"Work Teams: Applications and Effectiveness" by Eric Sundstrom, Kenneth P. DeMeuse, and David Futrell**

15. According to the article on work teams, a cockpit crew is an example of
    a. low differentiation and high external integration
    b. low differentiation and low external integration
    c. high differentiation and low external integration
    *d. high differentiation and high external integration

16. Which of the following is not one of the work team categories?
    a. advice and involvement
    b. production and service
    *c. social action
    d. projects and development
    e. action and negotiation

17. __(Differentiation)__ is the degree of specialization, independence, and autonomy of a work team in relation to other work teams.

18. Cohesive groups are more productive than non-cohesive groups. _____ True __x__ False  Why?

**Answer**: Cohesion doesn't determine productivity. A cohesive group can be highly unproductive. Productivity has more to do with group norms.

## Reader Articles

1. "Groupthink Reconsidered" by Glen Whyte
2. "Work Teams: Applications and Effectiveness" by Eric Sundstrom, Kenneth P. DeMeuse, and David Futrell

## Chapter 10
## MANAGERIAL PROBLEM SOLVING

**Materials Needed**: None.

**Objectives:** By the end of this chapter, students should be able to:

A. Explain the four stages of managerial problem solving.
B. Describe the red/green modes of problem solving.
C. Explain the different roles a manager plays during problem solving.
D. Discuss the link between learning styles and problem-solving.
E. Identify what problem-solving stage a group is in and have some ideas about how to facilitate a group's progress.

**Sample Design**

| | |
|---|---|
| 6:00 - 6:30 | Lecturette on problem management |
| 6:30 - 7:10 | Cardiotronics Case |
| 7:10 - 7:30 | Group Review |
| 7:30 - 7:45 | Summary Reports |
| 7:45 - 8:00 | Debriefing |

**Setting the Stage -- Lecturette**

The purpose of this chapter is to teach students a problem solving model that is more complete than the usual models. We emphasize the importance of a shared problem solving model for team members (regardless of what model is used) so that everyone is "on the same page" at the same time. The Total Quality movement has given a major boost to team problem solving.

We bring in some of the points from Basadur's article in the *Reader*, e.g., what companies do to encourage problem identification and solution. We also include some information on creativity and its role in problem solving.

We ask students to identify counterproductive steps in problem-solving that they have observed (denying the problem, ignoring problems, blaming others or blaming oneself, getting too many or not enough people involved in the solution, etc.) so that they ground themselves in their past experiences and we can start compiling a list of characteristics of effective problem solving efforts.

Next we carefully run through Kolb's problem solving model, using the transparency (T10-0), and try to make it as simple as possible for them, using examples at each stage. We suggest they think of the green mode as diverging to gather information and ideas and the red mode as converging on a decision that allows the group to proceed to the next stage. Whenever possible, we take a problem that all students are familiar with and apply the model to it.

## Issues to Consider in Leading the Experiential Exercise

A. Your greatest potential problem with this chapter is students who have not done their homework and prepared the case (i.e., come up with a list of questions that Marion could ask at each stage of the problem solving process). Our purpose in the premeeting assignment is to give students practice in facilitating problem solving. To make sure students are prepared, you could ask them to write up the pre-meeting preparation to hand in, and collect it at the end of class.

The following are examples of the type of questions that can be asked in each stage of the process.

1. **Situation Analysis**

    Valuing/Exploration
    a. What do you think about the situation?
    b. How do you feel about it?
    c. What's the real problem?
    d. Is there something else we should be looking at first?
    e. What do you hope is the outcome?
    f. What's really important in this situation?
    g. What other problems does this one relate to?
    h. Let's see if we can draw a problem tree.
    i. What values are involved in this situation?

    Priority Setting
    a. What's the most important problem that, if resolved, would cause other things to fall into place? Why?
    b. What do others in the organization think about this?
    c. What would other parts of the organization say is the most important problem?
    d. Do we all agree that this is the key problem that needs to be solved?

2. **Causal Analysis**

    Information Gathering

a. Let's try to put our biases aside and take an objective look at the situation. What do we know about it?
b. What do we need to know before we can really define the problem?
c. Who else should we talk to?

Problem Definition
a. Do we have enough information to put together a model of the problem or to define the problem?
b. What's our model of what's causing this problem or situation? Can we draw it?
c. What factors caused it?
d. What else contributes to it?
e. What factors affect how we go about solving it?

3. **Solution Analysis**

Idea Getting
a. Let's brainstorm possible solutions to the problem but let's not evaluate them until the ideas are all out.

Decision-Making
a. Are we ready to evaluate these suggestions?
b. What criteria should our solution meet?
c. Which of these solutions meets all the criteria?
d. Are there any unintended consequences of this solution?

4. **Implementation Analysis**

Participation
a. Who would be affected by the implementation of this solution?
b. How can we involve them?
c. Who else should be involved in implementing this?
d. Who has the most at stake or the most energy to get this accomplished?

Planning
a. In the actual planning process, who does what and when?
b. What tasks need to be done? In what order?
c. What deadlines are we facing?
d. Who will do what?
e. How shall we evaluate the implementation and the solution?
f. Is everybody satisfied with our decision and our plan?

B. Read the instructions to the students for the group meeting exercise and the tips on role playing on page 255.

All the names in the case are more or less unisex. Caution students **not** to read the role play instructions for others. The role play is very realistic. Emphasize that role players should be themselves as much as possible while being faithful to their role instructions; students should not view this as an opportunity to be the "employee from hell." Whenever we do role plays of managers, we mention that we don't expect people to perform perfectly as a manager -- we do expect everyone to learn from their behavior.

C. If there are more than six members in your groups, ask for volunteers who can observe the groups using the Cardiotronics Case Review form on page 257. Observers can contribute a great deal to this exercise.

D. The instructor should also observe what is occurring in the groups so he or she can better facilitate the **debriefing**.

E. Marion's role is a difficult one because the person playing this role makes himself or herself vulnerable to criticism and even blame. We note the difficulty of this role and try to support the "Marion's" while still letting them hear the feedback on their performance. One of the authors adds in another step to this exercise before the general debriefing session; she asks each group to list what Marion did that helped the group and what he or she could improve upon. This is usually very valuable feedback for the person playing Marion and it also sets a positive tone for the general debriefing.

If in the debriefing, it looks as if a group is excessively blaming Marion, the instructor can shift the focus of the discussion. You can always ask why group members did not speak up, reinforcing the lesson that everyone in a group is responsible for how the group functions and not just the leader. The instructor can also note the positive things students did during the debriefing session. We seldom see this type of blaming problem because the groups usually develop a strong sense of liking and loyalty among their members.

F. These are five frequent solutions listed in order of effectiveness:

1. **Transfer the problem to someone else** - "ask management to build another assembly unit or ask for pay bonuses or automated equipment."

2. **Fire Joel** - a weak solution that offers only marginal value since Jerry is almost as slow as Joel. Can you continue firing the slowest members?

3. **Help Joel** - a moderate solution since some labor agreements don't allow management to order workers to help each other keep up.

4. **Rotate workers at regular intervals through all jobs** - this way the line moves at the average speed of all workers rather than the speed of the slowest workers. This is an ideal solution that takes account of all information given in the case (desire of some to work faster, boredom, etc.)

5. **Let each worker make the entire board** - a good solution that would allow for greater motivation and less boredom, **but** it depends upon the feasibility of reorganizing the assembly line equipment into individual stations.

G. When you go over the Cardiotronics Case Review, page 257, you can help students think of examples of behavior, like those shown below, that are consistent with the problem solving model. The most value comes from going over the first four items below, which indicates the importance of getting off to the right start in problem solving.

**Valuing:** *What issues did you discuss here?*
Values = a) age discrimination "How do we treat older employees?"; b) work ethic values such as "Is it okay for employees to be working under capacity?"
Opportunities = could we better utilize all workers and make the job more satisfying to those who are underutilized?

**Priority Setting**: *What was the most important problem for your group?* Getting from 36 to 40 units is the correct problem

**Information Gathering**: *What type of information were you looking for?* "What is keeping the team from making 40 units a day?" is the best focus here.

**Problem Definition**: *How did your group define the problem?* It's an employee utilization problem and a work flow imbalance.

**Idea Getting**: *What possible solutions did you come up with?*

**Decision-making**: *What solution did you choose?*

**Participation**: *Who needed to be involved to implement this?*

**Planning**: *What plan did you come up with?*

H. In the debriefing, this case usually demonstrates the need for "green mode" information gathering to correctly define the problem and arrive at creative solutions. Younger students often see Joel as the problem and focus their energies on getting rid of him. They can be very insulting to Joel, which raises the issue of age discrimination and how we treat loyal employees who might be slowing down. If the students who play Joel are treated badly in some groups, the instructor can ask them how they felt during the role play. Thus, this case also demonstrates that individuals are often blamed for problems that are better viewed as system problems. We tell students that it is important to find "what, not who, is the problem." (Even in the rare instance when an individual, rather than a systemic problem, appears to be the sole cause of a problem, there is nothing to be gained by identifying him or her as "the problem." Doing so only provokes resistance and bad feelings and generates no energy to improve the situation. Even if you were planning to fire such a person immediately, face-saving is an important consideration.)

I. The instructor may wish to go over the common obstacles to effective group problem solving, presented in Tips for Managers, page 263.

J. After the debriefing is complete, the instructor can review the relationship between learning styles and the problem solving model, which is covered in the Follow-up section and presented on the transparency (T10-1), "The Learning Model and the Problem-Solving Process."

**Transparency Masters**

10-0 Problem Solving as a Dialectic Process
10-1 The Learning Model and the Problem-Solving Process

**Exam and Review Questions**

1. Which of the following is <u>not</u> a premise of Kolb's problem-solving model?
    a. learning from experience
    b. mind over matter
    *c. rationality as the guide to problem solving
    d. problem solving as a social process

2. In Kolb's model, problem solving proceeds
    *a. in wave-like expansions and contractions
    b. like a pendulum swings
    c. in a top-down fashion
    d. in a logical, linear fashion

3. When the problem solver is focusing on gathering information and problem definition, she or he assumes the role set of
    a. leader

    *b.   detective
    c.    inventor
    d.    coordinator

4. The dialectically related processes involved in the implementation analysis phase of problem solving are
    a.    valuing and priority setting
    b.    information gathering and problem solving
    c.    action and doing
  *d.   participation and planning

5. What are the four stages of Kolb's problem solving model?

<u>Answer</u>:
    situation analysis
    problem analysis
    solution analysis
    implementation analysis

6. Why is it best to look for "what" is the problem and not "who"?

<u>Answer</u>:
Problems are usually systemic, even though humans mistakenly tend to blame individuals. Even in the rare instance when an individual, rather than a systemic problem, appears to be the sole cause of a problem, there is nothing to be gained by identifying him or her as "the problem."

READER QUESTIONS:
## "Managing Creativity: A Japanese Model" by Min Basadur

7. According to Basadur, __(problem finding)__ may be the key to Japanese management success.

8. What are the three components of creative activity in an organization according to Basadur?

Answer:
a. continuous problem finding activity
b. problem solving activity
c. solution implementation activity

9. According to Basadur, what are the principal differences between the American and Japanese ways of managing creativity? (essay)

10. Japanese workers produce more suggestions than American workers because
    *a. they find it motivating
    b. they receive large bonuses for their ideas
    c. they must produce a monthly quota of suggestions
    d. Japanese workers are more creative

## "Of Boxes, Bubbles, and Effective Management" by Hurst

11. Under the soft bubble process of management, rewards are
    a. direct
    b. objective
    c. profit
    *d. fun

12. Which is an element of the hard box leadership model?
    a. roles
    *b. information systems
    c. groups
    d. networks

13. Soft bubble leadership relies upon
    a. sequence
    *b. wisdom
    c. rationality
    d. precise policies and rules

## Reader Articles

1. "Managing Creativity: Japanese Model" by Min Basadur
2. "Of Boxes, Bubbles, and Effective Management" by David K. Hurst

# Chapter 11
## INTERGROUP CONFLICT AND NEGOTIATION

**Materials Needed**: None.

**Objectives**  By the end of this chapter, students should be able to:

A. Describe behaviors that characterize group conflict.
B. Identify common sources of conflict.
C. Explain the five conflict handling modes.
D. Understand the functional and dysfunctional nature of conflict.
E. Differentiate between distributive and integrative bargaining.
F. Explain principled negotiation.

**Sample Design**

| | |
|---|---|
| 6:00 - 6:15 | Lecturette on Thomas-Kilman model |
| 6:15 - 6:45 | Groups prepare Nadir Case Report |
| 6:45 - 7:05 | Pairs negotiate criteria |
| 7:05 - 7:25 | Group discussion |
| 7:25 - 8:00 | Debriefing and principled negotiation |

**Setting the Stage -- Lecturette**

The purpose of this chapter is to provide students with an opportunity to practice negotiation skills and simulate a conflict situation. If you have more than two hours available, you can add another conflict simulation like the Red-Green game or other negotiating exercises. With shorter sessions, you can do one class on conflict and another on negotiation.

In the lecturette we present the Thomas-Kilman model, using the transparency T11-0. Warn students not to confuse the accommodation style in this model with the accommodator Learning Style. We give examples of each style, advantages and disadvantages, and the situations for which they are appropriate. To apply this model, we ask students to think back on a recent conflict situation and identify what style they used.

There is a good instrument, the Thomas-Kilman Conflict Mode Instrument, that measures these styles; Xiocom, Inc. of Tuxedo, New York has the copyright. The Strength Deployment instrument measures how people react both to "normal" conflict and when they are under the pressure of heavy conflict. If you obtain a self-assessment instrument, and we suggest you do, you can assign it as homework and go over their scores after explaining the theory.

If there is a major conflict in your environment (university, political, city), you can ask students to analyze the source of the conflict and identify what common characteristics are present.

We present the negotiation content after the exercise since the exercise is an example of distributive rather than integrative bargaining.

## Issues to Consider in Leading the Experiential Exercise

A. If you have more than 18 students, form more than one Nadir corporation. If you have an equal number of learning groups, you can make pairs of marketing and the manufacturing groups. When there are odd numbers of people in the groups, ask the extra people to be observers. In addition to tracking what occurs, have them write down interesting comments that they hear while they are observing.

B. The instructor or a student responsible for the class exercise can be Pat Cleary whose function is described in the memo in the Procedure for the Group Exercise. The marketing and manufacturing groups must come up with a list of five short criteria for choosing the next president of Nadir Corporation. Each individual in the group should make at least one copy of the list, since they will need to show it to their partner from the other team during Step Three.

The task during Step Three is to compare the two documents in the pairs (one person from manufacturing negotiates with one person from marketing) and allocate one hundred points between the two lists. **There can be no 50-50 allocation**, and they will have only twenty minutes to make the decision.

C. At the end of the twenty-minute Step Three period, you should record and tabulate the scores. This may be done privately, only announcing the totals for each team. However, the effects of the intergroup competition are often enhanced by asking each pair to state their allocation publicly and tabulating them in front of the class. If you opt to go public, you can make two columns and label one "Marketing" and the other "Manufacturing." Record the scores from each pair and then write the total at the bottom of each column.

D. The students then return to their marketing or manufacturing groups for a twenty-minute discussion of the group's functioning in Step 4. This is where much of the behavior described in the Follow-up section occurs. The losers will know they have lost by now and should be exhibiting some of the characteristics of losing groups. The winners should be fat and happy. The instructor should observe what goes on in the groups at this time.

E. The class then reconvenes and reads the Follow-up section, page 294-295. This is very important. The instructor then asks the **debriefing** questions in Step 5.

F. Sometimes students become frustrated because the exercise is designed so that one team must lose. This is one of the most potent lessons -- that organizations often needlessly "set people up" to be losers. Students may take their frustration out on the instructor or on group members who "gave up too many points." As it states in the Follow-up section, losers may blame a scapegoat or the rules. If students get angry, stay calm and don't become defensive. Point out that this is an example of structural conflict that often occurs in organizations -- our goal here is to learn how this feels, what type of behavior is provoked, and then to discuss how we can reframe this type of situation.

G. If students scapegoat individuals, ask the scapegoats for their opinion on what's happening and the effect on them. Draw a parallel to the pressures that negotiators experience in labor union disputes and diplomatic treaties.

H. This type of exercise brings out individual differences regarding competition and collaboration. It's important that students gain some awareness of their natural predisposition to conflict situations, so they can ensure that their approach is effective and not merely instinctive. Some people are competitive in a way that does not provoke a negative reaction, while others end up angering other class members. Help students focus in on the specific behaviors that provoke a positive or negative reaction to competitiveness ("What exactly did this group or person do that provoked such a strong reaction?")

I. One of the ways to prevent intergroup conflict is to have groups work together from the beginning before they become wedded to their position. It should come out in the debriefing that Cleary should have planned a joint brainstorming to produce a list that would be "ours" rather setting up a "we versus they" dynamic that only exacerbates the differences that already exist between two departments.

J. This is a good point to bring in Lawrence and Lorsch's concept of departmental differentiation. What differences exist between marketing and manufacturing departments that frequently serve as sources of conflict (time horizons, goals, formality, social vs. task orientation)? In addition, there are the usual problems of interdependence that cause problems (marketing making promises to clients that manufacturing cannot meet; manufacturing showing more concern for internal efficiencies than customer requests).

K.  Students are usually interested in how to resolve conflict once it begins. There are several suggestions in the Tips for Managers section that cover both preventing and resolving conflict.

L.  Before doing Step 6, we present principled negotiation. We give real life examples of each of the principles and point out that this model is heavily based upon things previously studied in the course such as communication and perception as well as conflict management techniques. Then the pairs evaluate their negotiation using the questions in Step 6. If there is time, the instructor can ask the reconvened class what they learned from doing this analysis.

**Transparency Masters**

11-0   Five Conflict-Handling Orientations

**Exam and Review Questions**

1.  When Sherif used equal status contact and superordinate goals as techniques for reducing intergroup tensions in his experiment
    - a.   both techniques proved successful
    - *b.  superordinate goals worked; equal status contact didn't work
    - c.   equal status contact worked; superordinate goals didn't work
    - d.   neither technique worked

2.  The conflict-handling orientation characterized by a desire to fully satisfy the concerns of both parties is
    - *a.  collaboration
    - b.   accommodation
    - c.   avoiding
    - d.   compromise

3.  A strategy that implies winning at the other's expense is called
    - a.   win-win
    - b.   lose-win
    - c.   appeasement
    - *d.  win-lose

4.  The phrase "winning the battle but losing the war" most often applies to which of the following conflict handling styles?
    - a.   collaboration
    - b.   accommodation
    - *c.  competition

d. compromise

5. Draw the Thomas-Kilman model of conflict handling styles.

6. What are the advantages and disadvantages of workplace reference groups?

Answer:
Advantages = they provide individuals with a sense of belonging and identity
Disadvantages = We-they attitudes between internal groups can foster competition and a lack of collaboration that hinders productivity and achievement of the overall goals of the organization.

7. Distributive bargaining is most closely related to
   a. collaboration
   b. accommodation
   *c. competition
   d. avoidance

8. Which of the sources of conflict identified in the workbook could contribute to problems between manufacturing and marketing departments?

Answer:
-Differences in goals, values, and education
-their interdependency and the usual problems that occur at the joints of organizations

9. Which is not a common characteristic of conflict?
   a. polarization
   *b. increased communication
   c. escalation
   d. overvaluing one's own group

10. Name the four steps in principled negotiation.

Answer:
Separate the people from the problem
Focus on interests, not positions
Invent options for mutual gain
Insist on objective criteria

READER QUESTIONS:
**"Managing Group Conflict" by Brown**
11. According to Brown, what level of conflict is most desirable
    a. minimal
    b. high degree
    *c. moderate amount
    D. no conflict whatsoever

12. Brown states that conflict between groups promotes
    *a. increased emphasis on differences
    b. decreased group loyalty
    c. decreased stereotyping
    d. decreased polarization

13. Brown calls the pattern between groups that is generated by positive stereotypes, trust and cooperative action
    *a. a benevolent cycle
    b. a positive prophecy
    c. a vicious cycle
    d. a generative cycle

14. Which is not identified by Brown as a category for diagnosing group relations.
    a. attitudes
    b. behavior
    c. structure
    *d. performance

**"Ingroup and Intergroup Relations" by Sherif and Sherif**

15. According to Sherif and Sherif, which is characteristic of two established groups that participate in competitive activities that only one can win?
    a. conflict between groups serves to decrease in-group hostility
    b. interaction between the groups (i.e., conflict) will result in no change in the in-group's organization and practices
    c. the groups will become more and more similar
    *d. over time, friendly competition will turn to intergroup hostility

16. Research by Sherif and Sherif suggests that one means of reducing intergroup hostility is to
    a. encourage competition between the groups
    *b. develop a superordinate goal shared by the groups
    c. provide a facilitator who observes the groups
    d. focus their attention on different issues

**"Negotiating with 'Romans' -- Part 2" by Stephen E. Weiss**

17. Relate the Thomas-Kilman Conflict Handling Model to the model of Culturally Responsive Negotiation Strategies found in Weiss' article. (essay)

18. Name three aspects of the negotiator's profile presented in Weiss' article.

Answer: general model, role of the individual, interaction dispositions, interaction processes, and outcome

**Reader Articles**
1. "Managing Conflict Among Groups" by L. Dave Brown
2. "Ingroup and Intergroup Relations" by Musafer Sherif and Carolyn W. Sherif
3. "Negotiating with 'Romans' -- Part 2" by Stephen E. Weiss

## Chapter 12
## MANAGING DIVERSITY

**Materials Needed**: Two rooms large enough for half the class to meet privately.

**Objectives:** By the end of this chapter, students should be able to:

A. Explain the advantages and disadvantages of culture.
B. Define ethnocentrism and stereotyping.
C. Describe four dimensions of cultural differences.
D. List the positive aspects of managing diversity well.
E. Explain what happens to tokens in organizations.
F. Understand how to manage diversity in organizations.

**Sample Design**

| | |
|---|---|
| 6:00 - 6:15 | Lecturette on managing diversity |
| 6:15 - 7:00 | Groups plan strategy |
| 7:00 - 7:30 | The Embassy Reception |
| 7:30 - 8:00 | Debriefing and summary |

**Setting the Stage -- Lecturette**

This chapter focuses upon both domestic and international diversity. With shorter class sessions, the instructor may wish to do domestic diversity one day and international diversity in the next session. Kanter's "Tale of O" video, based upon the findings from *Men and Women of the Corporation* (Goodmeasure Co.), and the diversity videos from Griggs Intl. can be effective in this session. Some instructors use the pre-meeting preparation as the basis for an Individual Differentness Exercise that appeared in a previous edition of the workbook. The instructions for that are also included here in the manual.

We begin the lecture by reiterating the need for managing diversity both domestically and internationally. We briefly present the material in the Topic Introduction -- the pros and cons of culture, ethnocentrism and stereotyping, individualism versus collectivism, and Hofstede's four dimensions. We mention that Hofstede's theory has its critics and, while we don't necessarily agree with all the characteristics in his dimensions, the four dimensions do help us understand cultural differences. At this point, we show students the transparency (T12-0), "Geert Hofstede's Four Value Dimensions of National Culture."

C. As a way to segue into the exercise and profit from the resources in the classroom, we ask who has had (or is having) a cross-cultural experience. Next we ask these students what cultural differences they noted and why these differences exist. This helps students understand how cultures do things differently so they are more prepared to come up with ideas for the exercise.

## Issues to Consider in Leading the Experiential Exercise

A.  This exercise is usually very entertaining and a wonderful opportunity for students to be creative. However, there is a danger that some students may clown around too much. It's good to have fun with the exercise as long as students are learning from it. Instructors can avoid problems here by taking a business-like approach, conveying that students should take the exercise seriously, and ensuring in the beginning of the strategy section that groups are working well.

B.  The purpose of this simulation is to have students create a culture from scratch by applying Hofstede's value dimensions. Make sure that students understand the task; some will be confused or even annoyed when told to create their own culture. State the instructions in your own words and remind them of all the different things they notice in another culture and encourage them to be creative. It is normal for groups to struggle with this task in the beginning moments.

C.  Emphasize that groups should not read each other's instructions. Encourage students to try to be loyal to the description of their culture to gain maximum learning.

D.  During the **debriefing**, we often find that the words used to describe the other group (question #a) are negative. If this occurs, we ask students why. They usually respond that we usually perceive differences in other cultures in a negative rather than a positive fashion.

In response to question #b, look for similarities and differences concerning interacting with the other culture. There are many common feelings (uncertainty, awkward, suspicious, scared, etc.) that are good to point out, especially if there are international students in your class who are not completely integrated.

The questions on norms and values may highlight that other cultures make perfect sense to their members, but outsiders make attributions that are often incorrect.

E.  Instructors can take advantage of this chapter to help the class manage its own diversity better. Be careful not to put minority students on the hot seat without their permission. You can do this by directing questions to everyone, "What do you think it's like to be a minority or international student on this campus?" "What could we do to make minorities and international students feel more comfortable in this class or on campus?"

<u>Instructions for the Individual Differentness Exercise</u>

The purpose of this exercise is to explore group members' experiences of being different, to appreciate and learn from these experiences, and to use this learning to generate practical principles for the constructive management of differences among people -- principles that would have helped you in the situation you described in the pre-work.

Step 1. Find the person in the group who is most similar to you on the "intensity of differentness" scale (20 minutes). Members of the total group should circulate to find the person with a similar score. Start with similar total scores and then try to find someone you agree with on each question. If there is an odd number of people, form one trio of individuals who are similar. Try not to pair up too quickly. Take your time to find the person most like you.

Step 2. Pair off with this person and share your experience of "differentness" with them (20 minutes). Listen carefully to your partner's description, asking questions of clarification only. In the next step you will need to be able to describe your partner's experience to someone else.

Step 3. Each pair should now find the pair of persons in the room who were most different from them on the intensity of differentness scale (10 minutes).

Step 4. In the resulting <u>quartets</u>, each individual's experience of difference should be reported by his or her partner (30 minutes).
-- Discuss and ask questions about these experiences so that all four individual experiences are understood by everyone.
-- Prepare a report for the total group listing ways in which the situations described in your group could have been managed more effectively -- things the individual who felt different could have done and things that other people in the situation could have done.

Step 5. Reports and discussion in the total group (40 minutes). Each quartet should report its findings to the larger group. Discuss the following questions that relate the conclusions reached in the quartets to your here-and-now experiences in the exercise.

a. During today's exercise, did I at any time feel different from others in the group?
b. In what ways?
c. Did others in the group experience my differences? How did they show it? Do they share this perception now?
D. In what ways did I feel similar to others in the group?
E. Are these differences and similarities the same as or different from the one(s) I listed in my preparation?
F. How did the group(s) I was part of today manage difference?
G. How did we use our differences to enrich our work? Or hinder it?
H. How did we suppress our differences?

**Leading the Exercise**

A. The aim in creating this exercise is to legitimize discussion of racial and sexual differences that often exist in groups. By beginning with a focus on each individual's experience of being treated as different, some empathy for others' feelings is stimulated.

B. Encourage members to explore the group thoroughly to find the person whose score is most like theirs. There is a tendency to quickly pair up with the first person individuals talk to, which should be avoided. This is a chance for students to see the range of experiences in their class.

C. Students are in a sensitive place when they return for the class discussion and somewhat hesitant to discuss any further their experiences, which were unpleasant for many of them. At this point, one instructor talks about a situation that all or most members of the class share, for example, living in a particular region of the country and being made to feel different because of that. This helps students rejoin the class.

## Transparency Masters

12-0 Geert Hofstede's Four Value Dimensions of National Culture

## Exam and Review Questions

1. Those parts of you or your actions that do not fit into your organization's image of the "ideal person" are called
   a. perceived competence
   *b. perceived eccentricity
   c. perceived performance
   d. perceived image

2. Kurt Lewin believed that behavior is a function of
   a. actions and results

b. heredity and age
c. freezing, moving, unfreezing
*d. personality and environment

3. The tendency to think that one's own group or race is superior to another group or race is known as
   a. cultural bias
   b. attribution error
   c. superiority complex
   *d. ethnocentrism

4. Stereotypic perception of individual differences is called
   a. ascription
   b. projection
   *c. prejudice
   d. tokenism

5. Which does Kanter identify as a typical experience of tokens in large organizations?
   a. they are virtually ignored
   *b. their behavior is closely scrutinized
   c. performance pressures are low
   d. as long as there are only a few of them, they are embraced and welcomed into the dominant group

6. What are the three perceptual tendencies that affect tokens and their results?

Answer:

| TENDENCIES | RESULTS |
|---|---|
| a. high visibility | performance pressures |
| b. contrast effects | heightened boundaries of dominant group (isolation of token) |
| c. assimilation by use of stereotypes | role encapsulation |

7. Kanter's suggestion for decreasing the stress experienced by tokens is to
   a. hire another minority member to accompany the token
   b. restrict tokens to jobs they have traditionally held and where they'll be comfortable
   *c. increase the number of minorities so they're seen as individuals, rather than tokens
   d. demand less of minorities

READER QUESTIONS:
**"The Multicultural Organization" by Taylor Cox, Jr.**

8. Your boss has asked you to develop recommendations for improved management of diversity within your organization. (a) Describe the characteristics of

organizations that manage diversity well, (b) evaluate your own organization using these standards, and (c) determine what improvements and steps should be taken. (essay)

9. What does Cox identify as the potential costs of increased cultural differences within a workforce?

Answer: higher turnover, interpersonal conflict, communication breakdowns

10. What are the potential benefits of a diverse workforce, according to Cox?

Answer: better decision making, greater creativity and innovation, and more successful marketing to different types of customers

11. If a woman complains that she is left out of the decision making and bonding that goes on during golf outings because she must stay at home with her children on weekends, this is a lack of
    a. acculturation
    b. structural integration
    *c. informal integration
    d. organizational identification

12. __(Acculturation)__ refers to modes by which two groups adapt to each other and resolve cultural differences.

13. An organization characterized by assimilation, prejudice, a minimal degree of structural integration and virtually no informal integration, and a large majority-minority gap is, according to Cox,
    a. multicultural
    b. plural
    *c. monolithic

**"Viva la Difference: Gender and Management in the Workplace" by Gary Powell**

14. What are Powell's two key recommendations for the way organizations should treat women?

Answer: 1. Be gender-blind in how they fill open managerial positions, except when trying to offset effects of past discrimination. 2. Try to minimize differences in job experiences of equally qualified male and female managers so artificial gender differences do not arise.

15. Powell concludes that
    a. males are superior managers compared to women
    b. females are superior managers compared to men
    c. men are more participative than women

81

  *d.  there is little difference between male and female managers

**"Motivation, Leadership, and Organization: Do American Theories Apply Abroad?" by Geert Hofstede**

16. Uncertainty avoidance refers to a country's
  a.  social framework
 *b.  need for rules and regulations
  c.  centralization
  d.  power distribution

17. Hofstede characterizes the U.S. as a culture that is
 *a.  below average on power distance
  b.  average on individualism
  c.  above average on uncertainty avoidance
  d.  below average on masculinity

18. Identify and define each of Hofstede's value dimensions and provide cultural examples of each dimension. (essay)

## Reader Articles

1. "The Multicultural Organization" by Taylor Cox, Jr.
2. "Viva la Difference: Gender and Management in the Workplace" by Gary Powell
3. "Motivation, Leadership, and Organization: Do American Theories Apply Abroad?" by Geert Hofstede

# Chapter 13
## LEADERSHIP

**Materials Needed**: Blindfolds for everyone but the observers. (You can cut up old sheets if you have no budget for materials.) A length of rope or clothesline for each group of no more than 18 people. For the length of the rope, figure a yard for each person and then add at least 4 yards more. It does not hurt if the rope is much longer than that if permitted by the space you are using; the exercise will be compromised, however, if the rope is too short. **Please note that the facilitator instructions for the exercise are in this manual, not the workbook.**

**Objectives:** By the end of this chapter, students should be able to:

A. Define leadership.
B. Describe what followers expect of leaders.
C. Differentiate between leadership and management.
D. Identify the traits related to leader success.
E. Define initiating structure and consideration behavior.
F. Explain what we mean by a contingency theory of leadership.
G. Describe the behavior of effective transformational leaders.
H. Describe how charismatic leaders function.

**Sample Design**

```
6:00 - 6:30     Lecturette on leadership
6:30 - 7:00     Group exercise
7:00 - 7:10     Individual reflection
7:10 - 7:30     Group discussion
7:30 - 8:00     Debriefing
```

**Setting the Stage -- Lecturette**

This is the first chapter in the third part of the book. The focus in this part of the course is upon leadership in relation to organizational culture, decision making, power and influence, empowerment and coaching, and performance appraisal.

In the opening lecturette, we briefly explain the evolution of leadership theory. There are transparencies that show leadership continuums (T13-0 and 13-1) and the "Path Goal Theory" (T13-2). We try to make sure that students have a thorough understanding of the contingency aspect of leadership, especially since the exercise provides an opportunity to see what type of leadership emerges in a unique situation.

## Issues to Consider in Leading the Experiential Exercise

A.  This is a very effective exercise.  However, the larger the groups, the more difficult and frustrating the exercise becomes.  If your class is large, divide it into smaller groups of no more than 18 people and make at least three people per group into observers.  The ideal group size is 8-12.  This is an exercise in which students may learn more by <u>not</u> being in their normal learning groups with established leadership patterns.  It is not difficult to run several groups at a time if you have a large area so that you can keep your eye on all of them at once.  Another way to work with a very large class is to assign facilitators for each group and give them responsibility for managing the exercise, a bag with blindfolds and rope, and the **Facilitator Instructions for the Perfect Square** found at the end of this section.  Tell them when they need to return to the classroom.  Make sure they read and assimilate the instructions.  You may want to give them a copy before the class with the understanding that they will not tell other students what will happen in the exercise.

B.  The instructor should ask if anyone has done the Perfect Square exercise in the past and would therefore like to be an observer.  (Even if a person has done the exercise before, that is no guarantee that the rest of the group will listen to his or her instructions.)

C.  Keep your eye on the person who has the excess rope. What did that person do about it?  How long did it take for the group to become aware of this?  This is an analogy for people in organizations who have information that the leaders do not.

D.  Some groups will come up with the idea of having a member go inside the square and walk around it to measure off the sides.  That is permissible; in fact, some instructors suggest this to the groups near the end of their time period.  If you don't suggest it and one group does it on their own, this can be a lesson in taking initiative and pushing against perceived constraints.

E.  In the **debriefing**, do not let the group focus too much on strategies for making the square.  There are a variety of ways to form the square successfully; there is no one best strategy.  The factor that determines whether a particular strategy works is how effectively the group functions.  For the sake of their learning, keep the focus on the process issues ("We could continue talking about strategies for making perfect squares, but we can probably learn more useful lessons from how you worked together as a group.")

F. The major issues that usually surface in debriefing this exercise are leadership, communication, and decision making. Many students have trouble hearing or being heard in this exercise and therefore become angry or frustrated. It is not uncommon to see students whose body language indicates that they have "given up" and are simply waiting for the exercise to end. Students often remark that they need basic communication norms -- listening to everyone, active listening, and two-way communication.

G. Because the students are blindfolded, an autocratic leader often emerges (he or she who talks the loudest). If the group is not successful, they may blame the leader. This points up the dangers of autocratic leadership -- heaven help you if you're wrong. If this occurs, support the leader by acknowledging there's a price to be paid for taking on leadership and help the leader see the effect of his or her leadership style.

H. You may want to write on the board the answers to questions 4 and 5 (things that helped and hindered).

I. Sometimes leaders push the group to follow a strategy without gaining their approval or commitment. In the debriefing, students often mention that they should have followed the problem-solving cycle -- asked for solutions from everyone, chosen the best solution, and then moved ahead. Most groups who have not worked together have no vehicle for making decisions.

J. One of the best leadership analogies that usually comes out in this exercise is the importance of communicating the leader's vision. Because people are blindfolded, someone has to transmit a vision (the strategy for making the square) to all the members. If a leader just gives instructions without communicating the overall plan and its logic, group members unwittingly make mistakes during the exercise (e.g., letting go of the halfway point of the rope that a leader has painstakingly measured).

K. At some point, students will probably talk about the effect of being blindfolded. Question 7 often raises this issue. In response to question 8, students define good followers as good listeners, being disciplined and not taking up air time for frivolous reasons, asking for clarification when they are not sure about what's been communicated, voicing reservations, and having a positive attitude.

L. We bring in Kouzes and Posner's five practices and ask students to identify examples of these practices during the exercise. After a brief summary of the findings on charismatic leaders, we mention the concept of servants as leaders.

# FACILITATOR INSTRUCTIONS FOR THE PERFECT SQUARE

**General Procedure** (read to yourself) The group should form a moderately tight circle away from a wall of sidewalk that would make it too easy for them to determine their location. Pass out the blindfolds. Ask for a predetermined number of volunteers to be observers. When the others are blindfolded and cannot see, give them the following instructions and pass out the rope. Don't let them see the rope ahead of time because they should not know its length. When you pass out the rope, make sure there is a lot of rope left over at one end that you will leave behind the last group member to receive the rope. This should be a quiet group member so we can see whether the group listens to people who aren't leaders. Don't tell the group that there is leftover rope. Note what time they start and when 15 minutes have passed, tell them they have 5 minutes left. Call time and have them answer the questions in Step 5 individually. Then discuss these as a group during the next 20 minutes and choose a represen-tative to report back to the class as a whole.

**READ THE PARTICIPANTS THESE INSTRUCTIONS:**
　　Please form a circle. Who would like to observe this exercise? Everyone else should put on a blindfold so you cannot see. I'll give you the rest of the instructions once everyone is blindfolded.
　　Your task is to form a perfect square utilizing all the rope that I am passing out. Here are the rules:
1. Use all the rope so that your square is taut, with no slack.
2. You must keep both your hands on the rope at all times.
3. You have 20 minutes to form a perfect square.

I can repeat these rules if you like, but after that I cannot answer any questions. Shall I repeat the rules?

**OBSERVER AND FACILITATOR INSTRUCTIONS:**
Please don't talk, laugh or distract the group. You should only intervene if it looks as if someone is about to back into a tree or wall. Both the facilitator and the observer(s) should follow the Observer Instructions in the workbook.

**FURTHER INSTRUCTIONS FOR THE FACILITATOR:**
- Give a 5 minute warning after 15 minutes have passed
- When 20 minutes have passed, tell them to take off their blindfolds
- Immediately ask the group members to answer by themselves the questions found in Step 5, Individual Reflection.
- Lead the group discussion in Step 6.
- Return the group to the classroom at the prearranged time.

**Transparency Masters**

13-0          Continuum of Leadership Behavior
13-1          The Path Goal Theory

**Exam and Review Questions**

1. Which of the following is <u>not</u> part of the definition of leadership?
   a. establish direction for a group
   b. motivate followers to achieve goals
   c. establish goals for other people
   d. gain the commitment of their followers

2. What's the difference between managers and leaders?

Answer:
Leaders tend to produce change while managers tend to produce order, predictability, and the key results expected by stakeholders.

3. Which of the following leader traits are inherited?
   *a. high energy and intelligence
   b. honesty and integrity
   c. self-confidence and creativity
   d. flexibility and drive

4. What is the primary difference between male and female leadership styles?

Answer:
Women tend to prefer a more participative decision making style.

5. Leader behavior that organizes and defines what group members should be doing to maximize output is called
   a. consideration
   b. participative
   c. supportive
   *d. initiating structure

6. Name three things followers expect of leaders.

Answer:
integrity, competence, forward-looking, and inspiring

7. Why is House's Path Goal Theory called a contingency theory? Provide an example by applying this theory to an organizational situation.

Answer:
The leader analyzes both employee and environmental contingency factors and then decides which of the four

leadership styles (supportive, directive, achievement-oriented, participative) is most appropriate. Example =

8. Which of the following characteristics describe the relationships of charismatic leaders with their followers?
   a. empowerment, respect, compromise
   *b. loyalty, sacrifice, enthusiasm
   c. commitment, tit-for-tat, respect
   d. devoted, non critical, respect

Reader Questions.
**"The 4 Competencies of Leadership" by Warren Bennis**

9. Bennis defines leaders as
   a. people who do things right
   *b. people who do the right thing
   c. people who do things differently
   d. people who make small improvements at work

10. Which is not one of Bennis' competencies of leadership?
    *a. management of people
    b. management of self
    c. management of meaning
    d. management of attention

11. Analyze your boss' leadership using Bennis' four competencies. Define each competency and provide examples to substantiate your evaluation.

**"Superleadership: Beyond the Myth of Heroic Leadership" by Charles C. Manz and Henry P. Sims, Jr.**

12. Define and describe the four types of leaders mentioned by Manz and Sims. What are the pros and cons of each type of leader? (essay)

13. __(Self-leadership)__ is the influence we exert on ourselves to achieve the self-motivation and self-direction we need to perform.

14. Which of the following is not one of Manz and Sims' Seven-Step Process of SuperLeadership?
    a. encourage self-set goals
    b. create positive thought patterns
    *c. develop self-leadership through transactions
    d. promote self-leadership through team work

**"Firms With a Superior Leadership Capacity: Practices That Create Better-Than-Average Management Teams" by John P. Kotter**

15. One practice that seems to distinguish Kotter's "Best

Practices" firms from today's business norms is that they
- a. target an unlimited number of colleges and universities as sources of future leadership
- b. evaluate their recruiting effort every five years
- *c. hire people with leadership potential
- d. give employees sole responsibility for their own development

16. Data from Kotter's "best Practices" study indicate
- a. sophisticated recruitment is the key to success
- *b. no single practice, but rather a set of practices, results in success
- c. the best predictor of leadership capability is a person's need for personal power
- d. the organizational culture determines the type of leadership to be found in an organization

## Reader Articles

1. "The 4 Competencies of Leadership" by Warren Bennis
2. "Superleadership: Beyond the Myth of Heroic Leadership" by Charles C. Manz and Henry P. Sims, Jr.
3. "Firms With a Superior Leadership Capacity: Practices That Create Better-Than-Average Management Teams" by John P. Kotter

# Chapter 14
## LEADERSHIP AND ORGANIZATIONAL CULTURE

**Materials Needed**: You may want to bring a non-permanent marker for each learning group and make a transparency of the G.B.A. Co. Case Summary on page 357. You can also use flip chart paper for the group summaries if you want the results to be posted for comparison purposes.

**Objectives:** By the end of this chapter, students should be able to:

A. Define organizational culture and explain its function.
B. Explain how it evolves and is maintained.
C. Describe the characteristics of a strong culture.
D. Explain the relationship between strong cultures and high performance.
E. Identify the four stages in the organizational life cycle.

## Sample Design

| | |
|---|---|
| 6:00 - 6:15 | Lecturette on organizational culture |
| 6:15 - 6:45 | G.B.A. Construction Case |
| 6:45 - 7:05 | Group Reports |
| 7:05 - 7:25 | Case Part II and debriefing |
| 7:30 - 8:00 | Assessing the class culture (students come with Step 1 prepared ahead of time) |

## Setting the Stage -- Lecturette

Assign students to write up the pre-meeting preparation if you have doubts that all students will come to class having prepared the case. Valuable class time will be lost if they have not read Part I. **Warn students ahead of time not to read Part II of the case.**

Some instructors do only the case in this session and combine the class culture assessment with the following chapter so there is more time to debrief the case. If you are going by the sample design, students should prepare their statements for Step 1 to decrease the time needed in class.

The purpose of this chapter is to help students discover the relationship between leadership and organizational culture. We highlight the fact that organizational culture is another tool that managers can use to influence motivation and performance.

Instructors sometimes assign Pascale's Chapter One article or Pitre and Sims' Chapter 8 article in the Reader with this chapter.

In the lecturette, we briefly question students about key points in the Topic Introduction: definition of organizational culture, challenges of external adaptation and internal integration, definition and characteristics of strong cultures. We ask students to name the most popular employer in town and figure out what makes them so popular. They usually identify a company with a strong culture. Then we ask them to analyze that organizational culture and make the point that strong cultures attract employees. We ask students what they see as the pros and cons of strong cultures. We point out the link between high performance and strong cultures that focus on key constituencies (customers, stockholders, and employees) and have good leadership at all levels. We ask MBAs for (and give undergraduates) examples of organizational culture and "fit" issues in local companies.

Sometimes students ask us to distinguish between climate and culture. Many large organizations periodically undertake climate surveys to "take the temperature" of their organizations. Climate measures the extent to which individuals' expectations about what it should be like in an organization are being met. Culture, on the other hand, is a pattern of beliefs and expectations. Culture is more concerned with the nature of the expectations themselves than with measuring them.

We present the growth stages after the group exercise.

## Issues to Consider in Leading the Experiential Exercise

A. If you are using transparencies or flip charts, pass those out in the beginning of the exercise.

B. The purpose of the case is to determine the person with the optimal managerial style and motive profile to take the company through a coming period of transition in which there will be more of a premium on rational management and less on entrepreneurial activity.

C. As with most case discussions, there will be much disagreement about who the appointee should be and what should be done to provide continuity. This may even be a little exaggerated by the procedure, which asks the students to do the original analysis first as individuals and then as a small group before sharing their recommendations. As a result, positions sometimes harden.

D. You may want to remind students to use their group skills to come to a consensus. Usually by this time in the course, the groups do not experience too much difficulty making a decision. If there is a group that cannot compromise and their time is running out, ask them what process skills they could use to arrive at a decision. Usually all the instructor has to do is remind them of the time deadline and their upcoming presentation.

E. In Step 3.a., ask the group representatives to give their report from the front of the room when it's their turn. You may want to announce that it is not necessary to repeat points (characteristics of each manager) that other groups have already made. This prevents boredom from hearing the same thing numerous times and encourages students to listen to other groups, think on their feet, and consider their audience. We clap for presenters.

F. Have the students read Part II to themselves and do the debriefing questions that follow. In the **debriefing**, you should avoid getting caught up in a right-wrong decision. This case underscores the complexity of succession decisions and the difficulty of predicting human behavior.

In regard to question #1, the strongest additional clue was probably Manager II's low need for power. Another example of this was his remark to G.B.A. Jr. that he didn't know if he wanted to be the head of a big company.

When answering question #2, students often mention that manager I was probably too young in 1973 and that the other managers might have quit en masse if he had been chosen over them. In the interim, he could have learned some valuable lessons by watching Manager II's experience taking over from G.B.A. Jr.

Students are often concerned with Manager I's carelessness with details, returning phone calls, arriving on time to meetings. Someone else usually points out that as long as he is careful about clients (which he is) and hires a good assistant to take care of details, this is not a major problem for a CEO. He can be eccentric in this regard if he is perceived as highly competent in other areas.

Undergraduates may not perceive the importance of the structural changes because of their lack of experience. Students who have no exposure to family business and the tension that surrounds succession issues may need the instructor to highlight this. We ask who has worked in family businesses and have them describe some of the key problems that relate to this case. The structural changes described here helped decentralize decision-making and provided more security to the top managers.

Another aspect of this case (question #4) is what happens to people who take over from strong leaders. Students sometimes suggest that no one could have survived if G.B.A. Jr. meddled and refused to fully turn over the reins to his successor. Perhaps the first successor is often a type of sacrificial lamb unless everyone involved quickly learns to deal with the change.

G. At this point, some instructors ask students what stage of growth the company is in (high-growth and needing to move towards maturity). They also show them the transparency T14-0, "The Five Phases of Growth," and ask students to determine which stage best describes the G.B.A. Company. Most students opt for a *crisis of control*. Since the company is growing and expanding and has had a benevolent autocrat in G.B.A. Jr., they needed to decentralize. This is further justification for choosing Manager II.

H. One of the most significant lessons of the case, which is stated in the Postscript, is the importance of fit with regards to leadership and organizational culture. Sometimes students ask if the failure of Manager II means that an organization is doomed to always having the same type of leader. The lesson of Greiner's "Evolution and Revolution" article is that organizations do need different types of leaders to pilot companies through different stages of growth. The answer to the students' question then is that organizations can and should hire different types of leaders. However, the success of doing so will depend upon several factors: an understanding of the organizational culture and its strength and resistance to change, the new leader's capacity to modify the culture and make the necessary organizational changes, and, if necessary, the leader's ability to adapt his or her own leadership style so there is a closer fit with the culture. This leads into the Follow-up material, Schein's mechanisms for creating or modifying culture.

I. The last portion of the class (or a second session in the case of shorter class sessions) allows the instructor to check on how students feel about both the classroom and their learning group. This is an excellent time to trot out the transparency (T1-1) of Sherwood and Glidewell's model of planned renegotiation from Chapter 1. If the data seem to indicate dissatisfaction with the way the class is going, it is useful to renegotiate the original understanding in light of what has happened since then. There should be no blaming, just an acknowledgment of changing needs and the necessity of taking corrective action.

If you have used a mid-course evaluation form like the one in Appendix E before this session, this is a good time to make some of that feedback known to students. In addition to suggestions for the instructor, there is often feedback for students, elicited by the question, "Is anything hindering your learning?".

NOTE: If you are using Chapter 15 next, it helps to take a few minutes at the end of this class and explain what they must do in the premeeting preparation for Chapter 15.

**Transparency Masters**

14-0 The Five Phases of Growth

**Exam and Review Questions**

1. What is the definition of organizational culture?

Answer: The pattern of shared values and beliefs which produce certain norms of behavior.

2. Which of these factors has the least influence on determining an organizational culture?
   *a. attitudes about one's boss
   b. the values of the founder
   c. the external environment
   d. solutions to problems over time

3. Which is not a characteristic of a strong culture?
   a. behavior consistent with dominant values is rewarded
   b. more time and effort are devoted to socialization
   *c. dominant values tend to be ambiguous
   d. employees who do not fit the culture are sometimes fired

4. What is the difference between weak and strong cultures?

Answer: Strong cultures have more values and beliefs that are more widely shared and more ordered.

5. There should be a "fit" between organizational culture and
   a. people, ecology, groups, and strategy
   b. people, groups, systems, and strategy
   *c. people, organizational task, environment, and strategy
   d. people, organizational task, groups, and strategy

6. The disadvantages of strong cultures are
   *a. pressure for conformity and resistance to change
   b. sense of identity
   c. lack of control
   d. people are more likely to be fired than in a weak culture

7. Which of the following is not a stage of organizational growth
   a. inception
   b. high-growth
   *c. assimilation
   d. maturity

8. Which of the following is not one of the ways leaders can change organizational cultures?
   a. what leaders pay attention to, measure, and control
   *b. edicts about changes
   c. observed criteria by which leaders allocate scarce resources
   d. criteria for allocating rewards and status

READER QUESTIONS:
**"Coming to a New Awareness of Culture" by Edgar H. Schein**

9. Schein's definition of culture highlights that culture
   a. tends to cover one major aspect of human functioning
   b. is ultimately embodied as an unrelated set of values with no set pattern
   *c. is learned around the major issues of external adaptation and internal integration
   d. is unchanging

10. Schein states that attempts at culture management strategies must begin by considering
    *a. the organizational life cycle
    b. sources of stability
    c. sub-cultures
    d. employee motivation

11. Which level of culture is the easiest to decipher, according to Schein?
    a. values
    b. basic assumptions
    c. theories in action
    *d. artifacts & creations

**"Evolution and Revolution" by Larry E. Greiner**

12. Which of the following statements concerning organizational growth is true?
    a. most growing organizations expand for two years and then retreat for one year
    *b. evolutionary periods tend to be relatively short in fast-growing organizations
    c. revolutions are easier to resolve when the market environment is poor
    d. periods of evolution have little effect on periods of revolution

13. The coordination phase of organizational growth is caused by demand for
    a. a strong business manager
    b. greater autonomy on the part of lower-level managers
    c. decreased red tape
    *d. control over the total company

14. Greiner writes that organizational solutions cause problems for the future. _x_ True ___ False  Why?

Answer: The solution to a growth problem is often carried to extremes or becomes unwieldy as the organization grows. Therefore, the solution becomes a problem as the organization becomes larger. Each of Greiner's revolutions has its seeds in the solution to the previous phase.

**Reader Articles**
1. "Coming to a New Awareness of Organizational Culture" by Edgar Schein
2. "Evolution and Revolution as Organizations Grow" by Larry Greiner


NOTE: You may wish to use Schein's article, "The Role of the Founder in Creating Organizational Culture," *Organizational Dynamics*, Summer 1983, p. 13-28.

# Chapter 15
# LEADERSHIP AND DECISION MAKING

**Materials Needed**: None.

**Objectives:** By the end of this chapter, students should be able to:

A. Explain why decision making is a social process.
B. Identify your personal approach to organizational decision making.
C. Describe and apply the Vroom-Yetton model of decision making.
D. List the five leadership styles included in the Vroom-Yetton model.

## Sample Design

6:00 - 6:30     Lecturette on decision making
6:30 - 7:15     Teams reach consensus
7:15 - 8:00     Debriefing and Follow-up

## Setting the Stage -- Lecturette

This is another chapter where it is essential that students come to class with the cases prepared.

We've studied Vroom and Jago's latest version of the model in *The New Leadership* and have included slight modifications in the model. However, we decided it was not feasible to teach the latest version without the computer software they now use. Vroom is in the process of simplifying some of the language in the model, but he had not finished by the time we went to press. We have tried to make the model more user-friendly than in previous editions.

Previous work on the issue of leadership and decision making consistently identifies three factors that need to be taken into account in determining appropriate decision making styles (e.g., Tannebaum and Schmidt leadership continuum):
 1. Leaders' personal preferences and predispositions
 2. Subordinates' personal preferences and predispositions
 3. The nature of the situation or decision

Earlier units in this text have as their primary focus the first two of these factors -- the motives, needs, and interpersonal styles of individuals. Vroom's work (with others) allows for examination of how decisions ought to be made from a rational analysis of the nature of the situation or decision. Vroom's theory seems complex to some students, so make sure they have a good understanding of the theory before you begin the exercise.

In the lecturette we state that, as we saw in the Perfect Square exercise, the leader does not have to come up with the solution or decision. He or she is responsible, however, for determining how the decision should be made. When should managers make decisions on their own and when should they involve others? To determine this, managers have to know who has the necessary information and what are the attitudes and likely reactions of people affected by the decision. We introduce the idea of compliance and commitment here (which comes up again in the power and influence chapter) in relation to the implementation of decisions. Thus, decision making is a social process rather than a logical choice. The difference between Vroom's model and decision trees that students may come across in other business courses is that it includes contingencies that reflect our knowledge of human behavior.

We acknowledge a few intellectual debts that help us understand Vroom's model:
(1) Follett's contribution that the natural reaction of people being bossed is to become less and less proactive. This is a built-in danger to an autocratic style. Her suggestion that we look at the "situation as the boss" helps set students up for a contingency approach to decision making.
(2) Barnard's "zone of indifference" helps us zero in on the idea of the acceptance of the decision made by a boss. At any point in time, there's usually at least one juicy example on a university campus in which the administration has made a decision that was outside the students' zone of indifference. It's also easy to come up with examples of administrators asking faculty to participate in decisions that fall within their zone of indifference, provoking another round of complaints about time-wasting committee meetings. The lesson here is that managers have to know their employees or stakeholders well enough to know what falls within and without their zone of indifference.
(3) Schmidt and Tannenbaum's "Continuum of Leadership Behavior" (transparency 13-1) to give students a visual image of the leadership continuum. We note that we are building upon the contingency theory groundwork laid in the preceding chapter on leadership.

We put Vroom's contingency on the board and explain the letters and numbers (II = farther along on the continuum). Note that delegation has been added to GII on Group Problems. So far, Vroom has opted to do this rather than add a DI to the Group Problem styles. This addition is in keeping with the emphasis upon empowerment.

We explain the key concepts: the difference between group and individual problems, the three criteria of decision effectiveness, and the difference between structured and unstructured problems. Some students have difficulty with "the quality or rationality" of the decision so you may have to explain this in greater depth.

We try to convey the logic of the model, which is captured in Table 15-2. Then we put up the transparency, "Decision Process Flow Chart," read aloud the example on page 382, and have students trace it through the tree. Note that the decision styles within a set are not simply in order along the autocratic-delegation continuum; they are arranged from the least to the most time-consuming from the manager's point of view. Therefore, delegation appears to the left of the consultative or group styles.

## Issues to Consider in Leading the Experiential Exercise

A. Make it clear when reading the Procedure for Group Meeting that learning groups should trace through the tree for each case, just as we just did for the example. If the group traces the cases in different workbooks and labels them, it is much easier for the group to know where their analyses differed from Vroom's.

B. We tell groups to quickly record their answers on the Case Analysis Record Form so they have enough time to trace through the decision tree with every case.

C. It saves time if the instructor makes a chart on the blackboard, similar to the Case Analysis Record Form, where groups can write the style they chose for each case.

D. As the groups are working, we circulate and answer occasional questions about the definition of quality requirements, structured problems, and individual versus group problems.

E. Sometimes groups have trouble figuring out how they came up with such a different set of answers from Vroom's. If you suggest that they follow their trail for a particular case as you read the answers, you can avoid this problem.

F. Before reviewing Vroom's choices in the **debriefing** section, we remind students that the major opportunity for learning is to see how and where they differ from Vroom's analysis. Sometimes they depart from Vroom's trail because they are not clear on a definition; other times it's due to their own predispositions and experiences. When they've missed the definition, we point that out. However, there are instances when people can make a good case for disagreeing with Vroom. Therefore, we don't set ourselves up as the defenders of his choices or state that his are the only right answers; we merely explain why we think he made that decision. ("You have a good point there, but it looks like Vroom interpreted it like this...and that's why you came out differently on the tree.") Make sure you can explain to them why he made each decision.

G. The focus in the debriefing should be upon factors that led people to interpret the situation as they did and how personal preferences may have intervened. For example, students often disagree with the GII decision on Case Three. If you ask them why, they say things like, "What if nobody wants to go and they start fighting about it?," or "The employees should accept the assignment whether or not they want to go." If you follow up with the question, "What assumption underlies your opinion?", they begin to understand their personal predispositions. Incidentally, Osland's research on expatriate managers found that people who had a strong desire to go abroad were more effective and more satisfied overseas (in press, Jossey-Bass, 1995). Therefore, acceptance of this particular decision is very important.

H. At times students will have difficulty distinguishing between individual and group problems and raise the question of precedents. Managers do need to understand that every decision made sets a precedent, even when it only impinges upon one individual. But merely setting a precedent for handling individuals with problems does not mean Case Two is a group decision.

I. With the last case, the discussion often centers on how much participation to allow. Students may mention the zone of indifference here. We ask why a manager would ever use a style that is more time-consuming. Among other answers, we highlight the idea of developing employees and teaching them to make good decisions (which lays some groundwork for Chapter 17, Empowerment and Coaching). We mention that it's unrealistic to expect employees who have never made any decisions to be proficient when they are first promoted to a supervisory or managerial job.

J. The last debriefing question is a good lead-in to the underlying assumptions of the model that are noted in the Follow-up section:
1. Managers are equally skilled in using the different styles.
2. Groups are equally skilled in their adaptation to these styles.
3. Organizational history and culture have no impact on a single decision.

Therefore, we have to understand decision making within the broader context which a normative model like this cannot do.

K.  We summarize the findings regarding the effectiveness of the model -- managers who follow the model have more productive operations and satisfied subordinates.  The statistics on these studies have changed slightly from those in the last edition.

L.  Students often ask, "Do managers actually use this model?"  In our experience, many good managers who have not studied the model use some or most of it intuitively -- often because they have been burned in the past by handling decisions poorly.  Former students have written to say they still refer to the model when they are faced with an especially tough decision.  This question is a good lead-in to the considerations listed in the Follow-up.

M.  We cover the remaining key points in the Follow-up: the new Vroom model, pros and cons of group decisions, and cultural differences regarding decision making.  There's a lot of practical information in the Tips for Managers that we include at this time.

N.  For a shorter class session, you can present the theory and begin analyzing the cases in the first class.  In the second session, you can complete the cases and do the debriefing.

**Transparency Masters**

15-0 Decision Process Flow Chart

**Exam and Review Questions**

1. Why is Vroom's theory a contingency model of leadership?

<u>Answer</u>:  The leadership style chosen depends upon factors relating to the situation.

2. When making effective decisions, managers tend to under-emphasize the importance of
   a.  quality
   *b. acceptance and commitment
   c.  resources
   d.  efficiency

3. The "zone of indifference" refers to the area within which employees
   a.  will carry out directives with resistance
   b.  will be committed to decisions
   *c. will accept directives without questioning their boss' right to decide
   d.  do not care about organizational performance

4. According to Vroom, under what circumstances would an autocratic decision be justified?

Answer: When the leader has all the necessary information, the problem is structured, subordinates are likely to accept an autocratic decision

5. List and explain the three criteria for decision effectiveness.

Answer:
a. quality or rationality of the decision = extent to which decisions influence employee performance
b. acceptance of the decision = degree of employee commitment to executing the decision effectively
c. amount of time available to make decision = efficiency

6. Which of the following is <u>not</u> a criteria for decision effectiveness
   a. acceptance of the decision
   b. amount of time available
*c. opportunity to develop subordinate decision making capacity
   d. quality or rationality

7. (Unstructured problems) are novel, with no procedures to handle them because they are infrequent and/or complex.

8. You are the president of a student organization. You won a very close election last fall and, quite frankly, not all the members seem pleased to have you as president. You've just received a letter from the president of your alumni group asking whether your group is willing to put on a show for them when they have their national meeting in town at the end of the semester. It's hard to refuse them because they donate funds to groups like yours, based upon how active and productive each campus organization is. So if you agree to do the show, it must be well done. The show would require a lot of extra work right around exam time, which might annoy some members.

a. Using Vroom's theory of decision making, which leadership style would be most appropriate for making this particular decision?

Answer: participative -- GII

B. Why did you choose this particular style? How did you apply Vroom's decision tree?

Answer:

a. there's a quality requirement -- otherwise the organization would lose face and perhaps funds
b. the leader doesn't have the information about whether the members can do it
c. leader's decision would not be accepted due to lack of confidence and exam conflicts

9. A structured problem requires more interaction and participation. ____ True __x__ False    Why?

Answer: because structured problems can be resolved with an autocratic or consultative style since it is easier to gain the information needed for resolving routine problems with known procedures. Unstructured problems require more interaction and participation because the necessary information is found in various people. More brains are needed to resolve these novel problems.

10. In Sweden, rationality is highly valued.
     ____ True __x__ False    Why?

Answer: Swedes are more comfortable with intuitive decision making. It's Americans who revere rationality.

READER QUESTIONS:
**"Leadership Revisited" by Victor H. Vroom**

11. Managers tend to use non-participatory decision processes when
    *a. they possess all the necessary information
    b. the problem they face is unstructured
    c. their subordinates' acceptance of the decision is critical
    d. subordinates' personal goals are incongruent with the goals of the organization as manifested in the problem

**"Speed and Strategic Choice: How Managers Accelerate Decision Making" by Kathleen M. Eisenhardt**

12. Which of the following is not a characteristic of speed in strategic decision making, according to Eisenhardt?
    *a. develop a single alternative
    b. track real time information
    c. seek advice of experienced counselors
    d. integrate the decision with other decisions and tactics

13. What does Eisenhardt mean by the term "consensus with qualification?"

Answer: Executives talk over an issue and attempt to gain consensus. If consensus occurs, the choice is made. However, if consensus is not forthcoming, the key manager and most relevant functional head make the choice, guided by the input from the rest of the group.

14. Speed in strategic decision making is a competitive advantage.  _x__ True   ____ False   Why?

Answer:  Speed in strategic decision making is linked to high performance; companies who are fast can take advantage of opportunities.  A company can have a good strategy but if they take to long to decide upon it, it could be obsolete.  The business environment is too turbulent for slow decision making.

**Reader Articles**

1. "Leadership Revisited" by Victor H. Vroom
2. "Speed and Strategic Choice:  How Managers Accelerate Decision Making" by Kathleen M. Eisenhardt

## Chapter 16
## POWER AND INFLUENCE

**Materials Needed**: None.

**Objectives:** By the end of this chapter, students should be able to:

A. Identify the three possible outcomes of an influence attempt.
B. Describe the various sources of power.
C. Identify the influence tactics people use at work.
D. Describe and recognize the four influence styles.
E. Identify four behaviors that foster win-win outcomes.
F. Identify ways that managers maintain their influence.

## Sample Design

| | |
|---|---|
| 6:00 - 6:15 | Lecturette on power and influence |
| 6:15 - 6:40 | Share self-diagnosis pre-work Prepare for role plays |
| 6:40 - 7:40 | Role plays |
| 7:40 - 8:00 | Debriefing |

## Setting the Stage -- Lecturette

We begin the lecturette with a demonstration of power (ordering them to do something and then asking why they did so -- if you're lucky they'll say you have expert power rather than just position power) which leads into identifying powerful people and the source of their power. We ask students why it's a good thing to have power in organizations.

After defining power and influence, we present the three potential outcomes of influence attempts (commitment, compliance, or resistance) and link this back to the need for acceptance in Vroom's decision making model. We ask students how they see people exerting influence at work and then review the "Definition of Influence Tactics" transparency, T16-0. After noting that people usually exert power in organizations by either pushing or pulling, we explain more carefully each of the four influence styles, using the "Influence Styles" transparency (T16-1) and examples (analyzing the style of well-known politicians is something the American students can easily relate to). We ask students what happens when someone uses a "push" style of influence; the result is often pushing back, resistance, compliance when the person really wanted commitment, and "winning the battle but losing the war." This brings up the importance of understanding our particular level of competitiveness; people who are both excessively competitive and non-competitive have difficulty exerting influence. We relate this back to the competitive and accommodative conflict handling styles.

We mention once again that we need to take a contingency approach with these styles and ask students under what circumstances they would use each style. We present the win-win behaviors and emphasize that students can use these behaviors no matter which influence style they have chosen to use. Not harming the relationship is important in influence attempts, just as it was in negotiation.

## Issues to Consider in Leading the Experiential Exercise

A. The purpose of the exercise is to give students practice in both spotting and using influence styles and seeing the results of their influence attempts.

B. Forming four-person groups often means that students must join up with people from different learning groups. This does not cause any problems at this point in the course.

C. If you have a class that seems to benefit by seeing examples, you may want to ask for two volunteers to act out one of the role plays in front of the entire class and then critique it together. This takes more class time, but clarifies the task and models good critiqueing behavior. Before doing a role play like this, we mention that we are not expecting perfection from the person in the influencing role -- they are simply providing a live example from which we can learn. When it is over, we ask that person to evaluate his or her performance first, before asking the class members to voice their opinions.

D. Make sure students do the planning questions before the role plays to emphasize that this should be a conscious, well thought out process.

E. If students do not like any of the cases, they can use an example from their own life -- someone they want to influence. The only problem with this is they sometimes get so involved in explaining the details to the person playing opposite them, that they have little time left for the role play.

F. In the general **debriefing** after the role plays when you ask what they learned from doing the role plays, students often mention how difficult it was to deviate from their natural style. We suggest they try to spot influence styles (both their own and others) in the next week since recognition is the first step towards expanding their behavioral repertoire.

We point out how managers establish influence, which is located in the Follow-up section. We mention cultural and gender differences and ask if they observed any differences of this type in the role play exercise. Finally, we end with Drucker's advice on managing the boss. It is natural in this type of course for students to focus on what their boss and organization does wrong. Drucker's advice adds another perspective on the employee-boss relationship and emphasizes the employee's responsibility for working well with the boss.

**Transparency Masters**

16-0 Definition of Influence Tactics
16-1 Influence Styles

**Exam and Review Questions**

1. Drucker states that the subordinate's duty is to
   a. protect the boss from unpleasant information
   *b. make the boss as effective and achieving as possible
   c. be responsible for his or her own performance
   d. wait for the boss to declare what he wants from the subordinate

2. Which of the following is not part of Drucker's advice on managing the boss?
   a. Never expose the boss to surprises
   *b. Never overrate the boss
   c. Accept the boss as a fallible human being
   d. Create a relationship of trust

3. Individuals who are high in socialized power
   a. are unconcerned about group goals
   *b. use a win-win approach
   c. use a win-lose approach
   d. desire personal dominance

4. The two "pull" influence styles are
   a. common vision and assertive persuasion
   *b. participation and trust and common vision
   c. reward and punishment and participation and trust
   d. reward and punishment and assertive persuasion

5. Which influence style is least likely to result in commitment?
   *a. reward and punishment
   b. common vision
   c. assertive persuasion
   d. participation and trust

6. Active listening is associated with which influence style?
   a. reward and punishment
   b. common vision
   c. assertive persuasion
   *d. participation and trust

7. Which of the following is not a characteristic of people who obtain and exercise a great deal of power
   *a. extremely ambitious and political
   b. energy and endurance
   c. personal toughness
   d. flexibility

8. What's the difference between power and influence?

Answer: Power is defined as the capacity to influence the behavior of others. Influence is the process by which people successfully persuade others to follow their advice, suggestions, or orders.

9. What's the difference between compliance and commitment?

Answer: Commitment implies internal agreement while compliance is merely going along with a request or demand without believing in it.

10. Which of these influence tactics is least preferred by managers?
    a. consultation
    *b. pressure tactics
    c. inspirational appeals
    d. rational persuasion

11. Which is not a win-win behavior
    a. attending
    b. asking
    c. empathizing
    *d. being assertive

READER QUESTIONS:
**"The Leadership Challenge -- A Call for the Transformational Leader" by Noel M. Tichy and David O. Ulrich**

12. According to Tichy and Ulrich, what would President (incumbent) have to do to be perceived as a transformational leader by the American people?

Answer: Make fundamental changes in basic political and cultural systems. Create something new out of something old. Create a vision. Mobilize commitment. Institutionalize change.

13. The transformational leader
    a. maintains the organization's old structure while making other changes
    *b. revamps the political and cultural systems
    c. makes minor adjustments in the organization's mission, structure, and human resources
    d. relies on quick-fix solutions

**"Who Gets Power -- and How They Hold Onto It: A Strategic Contingency Model of Power" by Gerald R. Salancik and Jeffrey Pfeffer**

14. Which set of conditions is presented by Salancik and Pfeffer as likely to affect the use of power?
    a. scarcity, contingency, uncertainty
    b. contingency, uncertainty, criticality
    *c. scarcity, criticality, uncertainty
    d. scarcity, criticality, contingency

15. Salancik and Pfeffer view traditional "political" power as
    a. a dirty business
    *b. a mechanism for reality testing in organizations
    c. synonymous with institutional power
    d. obscuring the demands of the environment

16. Once upon a time there was an organization that was facing a major new regulatory threat from the government. The situation required constant monitoring and contact with government officials. The lawyer who served as the liaison with the regulatory body became the most powerful person in the organization.
    a. What is the name of this type of power?
    b. What made the lawyer powerful?

Answer:
a. strategic contingency
b. The lawyer dealt with the critical problem and major uncertainty in the organization's environment.

**"Influence Without Authority: The Use of Alliances, Reciprocity and Exchange to Accomplish Work" by Allan R. Cohen and David L. Bradford**

17. Define the law of reciprocity and provide an example.

Answer: the almost universal belief that people should be paid back for what they do. Example =

18. Name three things influencers should do to make the exchange process effective.

Answer: a) think about the person to be influenced as a potential ally, not an adversary; b) know the world of the potential ally, including the pressures as well as the person's needs and goals; c) be aware of key goals and available resources that may be valued by the potential ally; d) understand the exchange transaction itself so that win-win outcomes are achieved.

19. Think of a person at work that you need to influence. Apply the lessons from Cohen and Bradford's article to your situation. Analyze the situation and devise an action plan for yourself. (essay)

## Reader Articles

1. "The Leadership Challenge -- A Call for the Transformational Leader" by Noel M. Tichy and David O. Ulrich
2. "Who Gets Power -- and How They Hold Onto It: A Strategic Contingency Model of Power" by Gerald R. Salancik and Jeffrey Pfeffer
3. "Influence Without Authority: The Use of Alliances, Reciprocity and Exchange to Accomplish Work" by Allan R. Cohen and David L. Bradford

# Chapter 17
## EMPOWERMENT AND COACHING

**Materials Needed**: None.

**Objectives:** By the end of this chapter, students should be able to:

A. Describe the characteristics of high-performance organizations.
B. Define empowerment.
C. Explain the four aspects of empowerment.
D. Describe how managers can empower employees.
E. Identify four different types of coaching.
F. Distinguish between effective and ineffective feedback.

## Sample Design

| | |
|---|---|
| 6:00 - 6:15 | Lecturette on empowerment and coaching |
| 6:15 - 6:35 | Enterprise prepares for production Facilitators plan and observe |
| 6:35 - 6:45 | Production Period I and buying |
| 6:45 - 7:10 | Facilitators help Enterprise teams |
| 7:10 - 7:20 | Production Period II and buying |
| 7:20 - 7:35 | Group Analysis of facilitation process |
| 7:35 - 8:00 | Group reports and debriefing |

## Setting the Stage -- Lecturette

In the lecturette, we explain the difference between the command-and-control mentality and the involvement-oriented approach. We define empowerment, the four components, and what empowering managers actually do and don't do. Then we present the four types of coaching and go over the steps in the coaching process.

Some instructors use Walton's article in the *Reader*, "From Control to Commitment in the Workplace," in conjunction with this chapter.

## Issues to Consider in Leading the Experiential Exercise

A. This exercise was previously located in the chapter on Managing Change and has been modified to focus upon the empowerment and coaching process. This is a paper folding exercise that fabricates the Space Ship Enterprise, an aerodynamically unsound aircraft with nice lines. The lines on the materials may be off-center. We have tried repeatedly to remedy this problem, but apparently the thickness of the workbook makes it impossible to print the lines correctly. Once students understand they should guide themselves by the corner fold rather than the lines, this doesn't present a problem. You need to do the same when you are buying the planes.

B. We usually have pairs of learning groups work together -- one becomes the Enterprise Team and the other the Facilitator team. If you have an uneven number of learning groups, you can have the class count off to form the appropriate number of groups. The ideal production group size is approximately 5-6 people. Facilitator teams can have fewer members (3-4) if you are not working with set learning groups.

C. The instructions to this game sound complex, so you may want to put the schedule on the board so they can refer to it during the exercise. We usually bring an assembled space craft to class to serve as a prototype. If you do that, make sure you have observed the quality requirements found at the end of the instructions. Students always manage to figure out the assembly instructions, so there is no need to do more than read them the procedure instructions.

D. We usually serve as the game coordinator and also evaluate and buy the spacecraft. If you do the same, you will need to be familiar with the time schedule and stick to it pretty rigidly so there is enough debriefing time. You also have to master the quality control points for the spacecraft. When you are buying the spacecraft, students will usually try to influence your decisions. Be strict on quality control and consistent in your judgments so you don't become a target of frustration in the exercise. Have students throw away the practice spacecraft before the first production round begins. We throw rejects directly into the wastebasket to avoid confusion.

E. Put a chart like the Enterprise Team Accounting Form on the blackboard so teams can compare their scores. Ask the students to figure out and post their own statistics.

F. It is very common to see intergroup dynamics and even conflict in this exercise. Many pairs of teams will have amicable, positive relationships, but Facilitator teams sometimes act in an autocratic, arrogant fashion that provokes strikes, slowdowns, or barely concealed impatience on the part of the Enterprise teams. Occasionally, the Enterprise teams want nothing to do with the Facilitator teams. Other than calling out warnings about time deadlines, we don't intervene.

G. Try to observe carefully how the Facilitator teams approach the Enterprise teams to offer help. The Facilitator teams often focus more upon task issues -- technical improvements and finances -- rather than the process issue of how the two groups will work together.

H. Have individuals on the separate teams fill out the Analysis of the Facilitation Process in Step 6 and average their Enterprise or Facilitator team score. Put these scores on the board so students can compare the scores for each pair of teams. Invariably there will be one pair in which the Facilitator team evaluated themselves more highly than their Enterprise team. Sometimes this results in disbelief, hurt feelings, or a sense of betrayal, i.e., a reflection of the difficulty of helping relationships. During the **debriefing**, we acknowledge these negative feelings and push the class to figure out why they occurred. That is the purpose of the helped and hindered question. It allows the class to approach it more generally and takes the heat off groups that were unsuccessful. However, sometimes it becomes obvious that a team or individual is very frustrated with what occurred and wants to focus specifically on their group experience. To use this as a learning opportunity, we first ask them to briefly list what their feelings are (so they can move beyond them) and move to analysis ("Let's figure this out; what behaviors on the part of each team contributed to this result and why are the scores so different?). If possible, we diagram their behaviors on the board as you would an escalating conflict situation -- team A did this, Team B responded with this, so team A did that, and so forth. Help them see what both teams contributed to the situation.

I. Frustrated Facilitator teams sometimes ask, "What can you do if the other team doesn't want you there at all?" We answer that this is not uncommon in real-life situations and you can at least acknowledge that they don't want you and try to negotiate a psychological contract that you can both live with ("We know you'd rather not work with us, but our boss wants us to. Frankly, this isn't easy for us either, but how can we make the best of it?")

J. The way the Facilitator teams begin their relationship with the Enterprise teams receives a lot of attention in the debriefing section. Because the latter groups have just seen the results of their efforts and how much money they won or lost (most groups lose money in the first round), their first reaction is to discuss how they can make improvements. Facilitator groups often unwittingly interrupt this process and disempower the Enterprise team. This is what makes this exercise such a good way to learn about empowerment and coaching. Students usually learn that they should first gauge what's happening in the Enterprise team and ask what they have come up with before telling Enterprise what they should do. Students often find that the teams have misconceptions about each other. Another issue that surfaces here is Theory Y and the learning curve of the Enterprise team. For example, does the Facilitator team assume that Enterprise people will improve from one production round to another or do they immediately opt to replace less productive members with their own people?

K.  This is a jam-packed class session.  If you have shorter class sessions, you can run the simulation one day and assign the Analysis of the Facilitation Process as homework for the next session.  It's not ideal to separate the debriefing from the exercise, but if you have students write down their reactions they will not be lost.  We present the characteristics of effective and ineffective feedback (T17-0) in the beginning of the Performance Appraisal class, which follows.

**Transparency Masters**
17-0  Effective and Ineffective Feedback

**Exam and Review Questions**

1.  What are the four characteristics of today's high performance companies?

Answer:  cost competitiveness, high-quality products and services, innovation, and speed

2.  In which management approach do managers make decisions, give orders, and make sure they are obeyed?
    a.  involvement-oriented
    b.  empowerment
    *c.  command and control
    d.  coaching

3.  (Empowerment) is defined as granting employees the autonomy to assume more responsibility within an organization and strengthening their sense of effectiveness.

4.  Which of the following is not an aspect of empowerment?
    *a.  coaching
    b.  meaning
    c.  competence
    d.  impact

5.  Which of the following is not a part of the definition of coaching?
    a.  follows a predictable process
    b.  leads to superior performance
    c.  leads to commitment to sustained improvement
    *d.  positive regard

6.  Fill in the blanks concerning effective and ineffective feedback.
    EFFECTIVE                rather than         INEFFECTIVE
    descriptive                                  _____
    _____                                  general

solicited                                    _____
immediate                                    _____

7.  What are the four types of coaching?

Answer: tutoring, counseling, mentoring, and confronting

8.  Which type of coaching would you use with an employee who does not have the necessary job skills?  (tutoring)

9.  Which type of coaching would you use with an employee when the purpose is to improve employee performance?  (confronting)

10. Mary Parker Follett's notion of "taking the situation as the boss" suggests
    a.  hierarchical position determines who gives orders
    b.  autocratic decision making
    c.  anarchy
    *d. depersonalizing authority and the giving of orders

READER QUESTIONS:
**"The Empowerment of Service Workers: What, Why, How and When" by David E. Bowen and Edward E. Lawler III**

11. According to Bowen and Lawler, what is it that empowered companies share with front-line employees in the service sector?

Answer: a) information about the organization's performance, b) rewards based upon the organization's performance, c) knowledge that enables employees to understand and contribute to organizational performance, and d) power to make decisions that influence organizational direction and performance.

12. Which of the following is not a benefit of empowering service workers?
    a.  employees feel better about jobs and selves
    b.  employees are a source of service ideas
    c.  employees interact with customers with more warmth and enthusiasm
    *d. reduced training costs

**Management Dialogues: Turning on the Marginal Performer" by John R. Schermerhorn, Jr. and William L. Gardner**

13. What are the three factors that comprise the individual performance equation, according to Schermerhorn and Gardner?

Answer: ability x support x effort

14. Identify a marginal performer in your organization. Apply the lessons from "Turning on the Marginal Performer" to this person. Analyze the situation and devise an action plan for improving his or her performance. (essay)

15. __(Learned helplessness)__ refers to the tendency for people who are exposed to repeated punishment or failure to believe they do not possess the skills needed to succeed at their job.

16. When people feel competent in their work they can be expected to work harder at it. __x_ True ___ False Why?

Answer: The effectance motive comes into play. This is a natural motivation that occurs from feelings of self-efficacy.

**Reader Articles**

1. "The Empowerment of Service Workers: What, Why, How and When" by David E. Bowen and Edward E. Lawler III.
2. "Management Dialogues: Turning on the Marginal Performer" by John R. Schermerhorn, Jr. and William L. Gardner

# Chapter 18
## PERFORMANCE APPRAISAL

**Materials Needed**: None.

**Objectives:** By the end of this chapter, students should be able to:

A. Explain the importance of performance feedback.
B. Describe the process of performance appraisal.
C. Identify the components of effective appraisals.
D. Demonstrate the skills required for a good appraisal.
E. Explain the opposition to appraisal systems.

## Sample Design

| | |
|---|---|
| 6:00 - 6:20 | Lecturette on performance appraisal |
| 6:20 - 6:40 | Role play demonstration |
| 6:40 - 7:40 | Performance Appraisal Role Plays |
| 7:40 - 8:00 | Debriefing |

## Setting the Stage -- Lecturette

We begin the lecturette by asking how many students receive performance appraisals at work. Next we ask students to identify the characteristics of effective and ineffective appraisals. The class creates a list on the board that is based partly on Lawler et al's article in the *Reader* and their own experiences.

We cover the purpose and importance of appraisals, what they symbolize to employees, and emphasize that it's a process, not an event. We ask students about the link between perception and appraisal to cover the dangers of bias. If we haven't already done so, we go over the characteristics of effective and ineffective feedback (T17-0). We also remind students about I-statements in Chapter 7 and Gibb's defensive and nondefensive climates (T7-2) since defensiveness is one of the major difficulties in the appraisal interview. Finally, we go over very carefully the steps in the **Performance Appraisal Interview Guidelines,** which are found after Step 7 in the Procedure for Group Meeting, page 483-4.

## Issues to Consider in Leading the Experiential Exercise

A. The purpose of this exercise is to give students an opportunity to practice performance appraisal skills and consider their own performance in the course. For this reason, some instructors use this chapter near the middle of the course because that gives students time to modify their performance.

B. It is very helpful to model for the students an appraisal interview before they evaluate one another. One of the authors asks students if they would like to see a demonstration, but if so, she needs a volunteer to be evaluated. The instructor notes that she will probably not do a flawless interview with everyone watching but the point is to learn from the attempt. The other students are asked to analyze the role play using the Observer Worksheet. A student volunteers and the role play becomes a real evaluation and coaching session. This can be very helpful, for example, when the volunteer brings up a problem like speaking up in class that other students may share. When the interview is done, we go over the Observer Worksheet questions. If the instructor is open and non-defensive about shortcomings, this creates a good learning climate for the class. Obviously, if instructors make glaring errors and come nowhere close to the guidelines, they will lose credibility.

C. Occasionally students will complain that they do not know how another student is performing in class. It's true they may be unaware of grades, but members of one's learning group will know whether students come to class prepared and if they devote energy to the class exercises. By this time in the course, they have also had an opportunity to observe the student in a variety of situations. This is why it is important that students evaluate members of their own learning group.

D. If your learning groups have more than six members, time considerations may determine whether you use trios or some other formation. Try to have groups of the same number since smaller groups will finish earlier than larger groups. You may wish to diagram on the board how the exercise will work so that everyone in the groups has a chance to both evaluate and be evaluated (Person A evaluates Person B; Person B evaluates Person C; and Person C evaluates Person A).

E. In the <u>debriefing</u>, students usually mention that they found the exercise very helpful and that it is difficult to give negative feedback to a peer. Many students report that it is difficult not to give gratuitous advice when they are playing the manager.

F. We cover the TQ opposition to performance appraisal, summarized in the Follow-up, at the end of the class.

G. Carolyn Jensen, an MBA student of Dr. Jay Liebowitz at Duquesne University, designed the excellent role play exercise found in Appendix L. This exercise can be used in place of the workbook exercise.

**Transparency Masters**

18-0 General Beliefs About Performance Appraisal

**Exam and Review Questions**

1. Performance appraisal should be viewed as
    *a. an on-going process
    b. a chance to rank and compare employees
    c. a once-a-year event
    d. a chance to weed out troublemakers

2. Which is not an objective of the "ideal" performance appraisal system?
    a. provide feedback to employees
    b. provide management with data to make salary decisions
    *c. clear up personality differences
    d. motivate employees to be more effective workers

3. When doing performance appraisals, people tend to rate those who are similar to them
    a. lower than those who are different from them
    b. about the same as those who are different from them
    c. less often than those who are different from them
    *d. higher than those who are different from them

4. One way organizations can stimulate attention from managers to the performance appraisal process is to
    *a. evaluate managers on how well they develop their subordinates
    b. reward managers on the length of their appraisals
    c. evaluate managers on the number of subordinates who receive high appraisals
    d. reward managers with the least staff turnover

5. Performance appraisal requires that managers take on the role of
    a. persuader
    *b. helper/consultant
    c. policeman
    d. therapist

6. Which is the correct order of the beginning of the performance appraisal interview?
    a. employee self-appraisal, explanation of format, supervisor appraisal
    b. explanation of format, supervisor appraisal, employee self-appraisal
    c. supervisor appraisal, employee self-appraisal, explanation of format
    *d. explanation of format, employee self-appraisal, supervisor appraisal

7. What do TQ proponents suggest instead of performance appraisals?

Answer: continuous feedback and coaching

READER QUESTIONS:
**"Performance Appraisal Revisited" by Edward Lawler III, Allan M. Morhman, Jr., and Susan M. Resnick**

8. Lawler et al's study on performance appraisal indicates that appraisers (those appraising subordinates), more than subordinates, believe
   *a. that the purpose of performance appraisal should be to allow subordinates input on the definition of work
   b. that the purpose of performance appraisal is to explain and communicate pay decisions and to mutually plan future goals
   c. that subordinates should have several appraisal interviews during the year
   d. that performance appraisal should be eliminated

9. One finding in Lawler et al's study on performance appraisal is
   a. general climate of the organization has little impact on how well the performance appraisal process goes
   *b. content of the performance appraisal form has little if any effect on the actual appraisal event
   c. those who view their jobs as enriched are less likely to perceive performance appraisal as beneficial
   d. pay actions and consequences should be separate from the appraisal discussion

**"On the Folly of Rewarding 'A' While Hoping for 'b'" by Steven Kerr**

10. Kerr argues that often behaviors which are rewarded are those
    a. that most resemble the behavior of the evaluator
    b. that the rewarder desires
    c. that demonstrate emotional behavior
    *d. that the rewarder is trying to discourage

11. Define goal displacement and provide an example that did not appear in the article.

Answer: Goal displacement occurs when the means become the ends, displacing the original goal. Example =

12. Explain Kerr's principal argument and provide an

example that did not appear in the article, which proves his thesis. Analyze your own organization -- are there instances of rewarding 'A' while hoping for 'B' and if so, what are they? (Essay)

## Reader Articles

1. "Performance Appraisal Revisited" by Edward Lawler III, Allan M. Morhman, Jr., and Susan M. Resnick
2. "On the Folly of Rewarding 'A' While Hoping for 'B'" by Steven Kerr

# Chapter 19
## ORGANIZATIONAL ANALYSIS: THE ORGANIZATION AS AN OPEN SYSTEM

**Materials Needed**: None.

**Objectives:** By the end of this chapter, students should be able to:

A. Explore the implications of the open systems view of organizations.
B. Identify and analyze their own personal theory of organizational functioning.
C. Explore relationships between theories of organization and managerial action.
D. Explain the 7-S model.

## Sample Design

| | |
|---|---|
| 6:00 - 6:15 | Lecturette |
| 6:15 - 6:45 | Compare and refine individual models |
| 6:45 - 7:45 | Evaluation of organizational health and effectiveness |
| 7:45 - 8:00 | Debriefing and summary |

## Setting the Stage -- Lecturette

If the instructor is following the chapter sequence found in the book, this is the first chapter of the last part of the book. The last four chapters focus upon organizational effectiveness. Instructors can tie this chapter to the groundwork laid in Chapter Two concerning theories of management and the fact that our theories determine what we see. This chapter allows students to gain more specific knowledge on their own theory of organizational functioning.

Some instructors use this chapter in the beginning of the course as a kind of base-line measure of how students think of organizations. When used near the end of the course, it serves to integrate what students have learned throughout the course.

In the lecturette we review open systems theory and focus on examples of the relationship between theories of organization and managerial action (e.g., the Atari example). We also summarize the 7-S model before the exercise.

## Issues to Consider in Leading the Experiential Exercise

A. It is important to have the students take at least an hour and a half prior to the class meeting to choose key variables in their thinking about organization, sort them, and arrange them under unifying concepts that make sense to the individual. Since the class meeting will begin with a review and sharing of the outcome, it is absolutely essential that this be completed ahead of time.

B. Students with abstract learning styles especially appreciate this exercise because they are required to think and sort out their thoughts on organizational functioning.

C. The procedures for this unit are complex and may take several readings before the class understands them well enough to proceed. **Instructors should carefully explain the pre-meeting preparation instructions in the previous class session.**

D. There may be resistance to the exercise as "busy work" with no clear objective. This would most likely come from students who resist theoretical formulations. One response is that all of our approaches to organizations represent a theory, however implicit and unarticulated. The purpose of this unit is to articulate some of the most meaningful aspects of our own personal theories, make them explicit, and understand a little more fully what assumptions are behind our concerns and behaviors in organizations. This exercise can be related to the need to question assumptions in organizational learning (see Senge's article in the *Reader*).

E. After the debriefing, we show students the transparency, entitled "The Open System View of Organizations." This diagram should help students pull together the different things we have studied in the course. We also discuss the significance of boundaryless organizations.

**Transparency Masters**

19-0 Components of an Open System
19-1 The Open System View of Organizations

**Exam and Review Questions**

1. A central characteristic of the open systems view of organizations is
   a. impermeable organizational boundaries
   b. positive entropy
   *c. environmental influence
   d. independence of structural components

2. When applying concepts of open systems theory, the knowledge that students gain from colleges and universities would be identified as

a. input
*b. output
   c. feedback
   d. creative transformation

3. In the 7-S framework for organizational analysis, staff is
   a. distinctive capabilities of key personnel
   b. line staff
   c. administrative personnel
*d. demographic description of personnel categories

4. Which is not a hard S within the 7-S framework?
   a. strategy
*b. skills
   c. systems
   d. structure

5. Our personal theories are often designed to create a self-fulfilling prophecy. __x__ True ____ False   Why?

Answer: Many of our theories are self-sealing and untestable. They determine what we see, so we see things that confirm our beliefs.

6. __(Boundaryless organizations)__ work at eliminating or diminishing the boundaries between both internal and external entities to increase their effectiveness.

7. Which of the following is not a characteristic of healthy, effective organizations?
*a. function following form
   b. relatively undistorted communication
   c. feedback mechanisms that enable learning from experience
   d. acknowledgment of interdependence among subparts and the larger environment

READER QUESTIONS:
**"A Congruence Model for Diagnosing Organizational Behavior" by David A. Nadler and Michael Tushman**

8. The first step in Nadler and Tushman's model for organizational diagnosis is
   a. identify critical system problems
*b. identify the system
   c. bring in a consultant
   d. brainstorm possible implementation strategies

9. The notion that the same end point can be reached by a variety of different processes is known as
*a. equifinality
   b. energy importation
   c. equilibrium seeking

    d.    throughput

**"Structure is not Organization" by Robert H. Waterman, Thomas J. Peters, and Julien R. Phillips**

10. Actions planned in response to or in anticipation of environmental changes are called
    a. system
    b. superordinate goals
    c. structure
    *d. strategy

11. Analyze your own organization using the 7-S model. Where do you find "fits" or lack of fit between the various components? (essay)

12. According to Waterman et al, the variable in the 7-S model with the potential of dominating all others is
    *a. systems
    b. staff
    c. style
    d. structure

**Reader Articles**
1. "A Congruence Model for Diagnosing Organizational Behavior" by David A. Nadler and Michael Tushman
2. "Structure is not Organization" by Robert H. Waterman, Thomas J. Peters, and Julien R. Phillips

# Chapter 20
## ORGANIZATION DESIGN

**Materials Needed**: None.

**Objectives:** By the end of this chapter, students should be able to:

A. Distinguish between mechanistic and organic structures.
B. Distinguish between formal and informal organizational structure.
C. Describe the three pure types of organizational structures and their advantages and disadvantages.
D. Describe horizontal and network organizations
E. Explain the differentiation-integration issue in organization design.

## Sample Design

| | |
|---|---|
| 6:00 - 6:45 | Lecturette on organization design theory |
| 6:45 - 7:00 | Preparation: Family Hotel Role Play |
| 7:00 - 7:30 | Family Hotel Role Play |
| 7:30 - 8:00 | Debriefing |

## Setting the Stage -- Lecturette

This is a complex unit for some students since it asks them to be both analytical and creative. The shift in focus from micro issues to macro issues may require some adjustment. This is the rationale for spending more time than usual on the theoretical aspect of the class and allowing students time to prepare for their roles. Let students know ahead of time that they should become thoroughly familiar with the case and complete the premeeting assignment that calls for them to redesign the hotel. Impress upon them that what's important here is not a right or wrong answer but an awareness of the considerations that should be kept in mind when evaluating the situation.

In the lecturette, we ask students what type of structure is found in their own organizations and refer back to them for more information when we discuss the different types of structure. We review the three pure models of organization structures using the transparencies (T20-0, T20-1, T20-2) and discuss their advantages and problems. We present horizontal and network organizations and focus on the new skills such structures demand. We show students the 7-S model once again to remind them of the necessity of aligning all aspects of the organization.

We discuss the design principles and ask for applications to the students' own organizations. We cover both formal and informal integrative mechanisms and mapping organizational structures.

## Issues to Consider in Leading the Experiential Exercise

A. This is a real case about a hotel that outgrew its structure and experienced many of the classic design problems. You may want to develop your own design for the Family Hotel when preparing for this class.

B. There are several ways to run this exercise. (1) You can do the case as a role play that is observed by the rest of the class who may or may not choose to occupy the empty chair. (2) You can run simultaneous role plays with groups of nine students. (3) You can scrap the role play and assign the task of redesigning the Family hotel to the learning groups. In the last instance, a representative of each group presents its design on newsprint to the entire class and the pros and cons of the designs are discussed at that time.

C. At present, the hotel is formally differentiated by a functional design. Formal integration occurs via rules that apply to all hotels. Communications and decision making are closed and one-way. The theory of motivation that can be assumed to be operating here is that individuals are motivated by security (money). Planning (owners) and doing (workers) are separate.

The Schmidt family contributes to many of the problems by reinforcing certain aspects of the informal integration system. It's an informal norm, for instance, that when older workers want a managerial decision countermanded, they simply contact Schmidt family members directly. This breeds an informal hierarchy in which older workers are perceived to be more influential than managers. Informal status differentiation appears in several examples: individuals who are personal friends of the Schmidts and those who are not; department heads who get bonuses while other salaried and hourly workers do not; the Food and Beverage director who is second in prestige only to the GM; and sales people who are the only workers who go home at 5:00.

The informal goals of individuals at the Family Hotel seem to fly in the face of its present structure. For one, employees assume that some department heads don't fill vacancies to save money -- money that could increase the department heads' bonuses. Still another is that Max Evans in maintenance has an informal goal of managing the numerous requests from department heads by responding to whomever yells loudest.

A systematic and in-depth analysis could follow this line of questioning:

a) What does the Family Hotel do? What is its function or task?

b) What type of structure is appropriate for this function? (Form follows function for the entire organization and subparts.)

c) How should the Family Hotel differentiate? By function? By product? By core process? How should this be done?

d) How should the differentiated elements be integrated and coordinated?

e) With regard to the formal structure, what rules and procedures should be established? How will exceptions to rules and procedures be handled? What type of decision making should be done at each level? Who will establish the targets and goals at each level of the organization?

f) Concerning the informal structure, how do the informal rules function to support or hinder the hotel's primary functions? Along what dimensions are individuals informally differentiated (e.g., age, seniority, gender, functional group, etc.) and what is the impact upon the hotel? How do individual goals influence the primary function of the hotel? Are individual and organizational goals in alignment?

g) What behaviors will reinforce or help implement the design? How should these behaviors be rewarded?

D. There are a number of ways to intervene in the Family Hotel, ranging from making complex structural changes to making no changes at all and simply working with the human system. It's important to pay attention to both profit and people. One human system approach would be to have the new operations manager establish a psychological contract with the Schmidt family with the expectation that the family would not countermand managerial decisions.

**Transparency Masters**

20-0 Functional Form of Organization
20-1 Product or Service Form of Organization
20-2 Matrix Form of Organization

**Exam and Review Questions**

1. The boxes and lines on an organizational chart represent
   a. functional relationships
   b. the physical layout of an organization
   *c. functions, authority, and communications network
   d. production flow

2. In a service organizational structure, a social worker in Medical Clinics would report to
   *a. the medical clinics director
   b. the director of social work
   c. the assistant director of social work
   d. the hospital director

3. A matrix organization structure highlights the concept of
   a. management-by-objectives
   b. hierarchy
   *c. dual reporting relationships
   d. stable structures

4. Informal aspects of organizational design refer to
   a. the reward system
   *b. social behavior and relationships
   c. circular versus linear design
   d. organizational sub-systems

5. Contrast mechanistic and organic organizations and provide examples that do not appear in the book. (essay)

6. Which of the following is not a component of organizational structure?
   a. roles
   b. authority
   *c. values
   d. communication

7. What are the five components of a network organization?

Answer: brokers, designers, suppliers, distributors, and producers

8. Compare and contrast closed, one way communication networks with open, two-way communication networks. What are the advantages and disadvantages of each? (essay)

READER QUESTIONS:
**"Managing Innovation: Controlled Chaos" by James Brian Quinn**

9. Which of the following is identified by Quinn as a bureaucratic barrier to innovation?

    a.  tolerance of fanaticism
    b.  appropriate incentives
*c.  time horizons
    d.  top management cooperation

10. According to Quinn, innovative companies try to keep their operating divisions and total units at a maximum of
    a.  100 people
    b.  250 people
    c.  1000 people
*d.  400 people

11. Quinn's notion of incrementalism is characterized by
    a.  well defined goals
    b.  phased program planning
*c.  a narrow framework
    d.  adherence to a specified route

**"Managing 21st Century Network Organizations" by Charles C. Snow, Raymond E. Miles, and Henry J. Coleman, Jr.**

12. Which of the following is <u>not</u> one of the three broker roles in a network organization?
    a.  caretaker
    b.  lead operator
    c.  architect
*d.  coach

13. What environmental driving forces promote network organizations?

<u>Answer</u>:  globalization and technological change

14. Snow et al claim that managers who want their firms to be strong competitors in the 21st century should do <u>all but</u> which of the following
    a.  perform only those functions for which the company has expert skill
*b.  maximize R&D investment
    c.  search globally for opportunities and resources
    d.  outsource those activities that can be performed quicker, more effectively or cheaper by others

**"Restoring American Competitiveness: Looking For New Models of Organization" by Thomas J. Peters**

15. In Peters' new-look organization, the chief role of middle managers is
*a.  horizontally oriented
    b.  functionally oriented
    c.  vertically oriented
    d.  rule oriented

16. Peters believes that the key to unlocking extraordinary productivity and quality improvements lies with
    a. top management
    b. MBA-trained staff
    *c. front-line workers
    d. customers

17. At the top of the list of requirements for Peters' new-look organization is
    *a. an attitude of partnership with outsiders
    b. competition among organizational functions
    c. highly channeled communications
    d. all persons know their place

**Reader Articles**
1. "Managing Innovation: Controlled Chaos" by James Brian Quinn
2. "Managing 21st Century Network Organizations" by Charles C. Snow, Raymond E. Miles, and Henry J. Coleman, Jr.
3. "Restoring American Competitiveness: Looking For New Models of Organization" by Thomas J. Peters

# Chapter 21
# JOB DESIGN AND JOB INVOLVEMENT

**Materials Needed**: None.

**Objectives:** By the end of this chapter, students should be able to:

A. Define and describe the historical roots of work alienation.
B. Describe the impact of technology on job design.
C. Identify characteristics of job situations that motivate people.
D. List and describe six methods for increasing job involvement.

## Sample Design

| | |
|---|---|
| 6:00 - 6:15 | Lecturette on job design and involvement |
| 6:15 - 7:00 | Production of Moon Tents |
| 7:00 - 7:45 | Production of Shallow-Water Cargo Carriers |
| 7:45 - 8:00 | Debriefing |

## Setting the Stage -- Lecturette

In the lecturette we emphasize the relationship between job design and job involvement. Our goal is to teach students how to analyze jobs and to see the effect of various design aspects. We discuss work alienation and Blauner's study. Some instructors have their students fill out the Job Diagnostic Survey on their own jobs, followed by a summary of Hackman et al's theory, using the transparency 21-0, "Job Characteristics Enrichment Model." If you do not use the JDS, you can ask students to do a rough evaluation of their own jobs so they have an opportunity to apply the theory. We also ask students to analyze the job of "student" in terms of this model.

## Issues to Consider in Leading the Experiential Exercise

A. The purpose of this exercise is to contrast different job designs. The Moon Tent exercise is an example of a traditional assembly line design whereas the learning groups have greater autonomy in determining how they design their work in making the Shallow Water Carriers.

B. The major problem for the instructor in this unit is how quickly the class can learn to make Moon Tents so that they may proceed with the exercise. You can assign this as homework or demonstrate the proper procedure yourself. Since in all likelihood you also will be the quality control inspector, it is a good idea for you to be familiar with folding procedure and be able to show the class a prototype of acceptable quality.

C.   Besides the development of a certain manual dexterity, there is more substantive learning potential to be gained from this unit. The first production period (Moon Tents) requires that the teams be organized into an assembly line. The General Manager is in charge of making decisions about work flow and production goals, and the assistant will be in charge of making sure the products are up to specifications before you, the government quality control inspector, get a chance to accept or reject them. The General Manager may consult with the employees about the work flow and production goal decisions, but the decision is not shared. It is made by the GM.

D.   During the second round (Shallow-Water Cargo Carriers), the instructions are not as rigid; the teams are told to organize themselves for production in the way they think best. There may be a variety of organizational forms, from individual piecework to the reinstatement of the assembly line. There are short questionnaires to be filled out after each of the two rounds asking for a numerical response (on a 1-7 scale) on satisfaction and productivity questions and these results should be tabulated for the group on the blackboard for all the class to see at the beginning of the debriefing section. Two other items on the questionnaire call for more qualitative responses and may be used by individuals during the discussion time.

E.   Although the task is of short duration, there should be data available from the questionnaires and the production figures that allow the class to draw some inferences about the design of work to maximize satisfaction and productivity. We point out the lack of correlation between satisfaction and productivity. A key question for the class to ponder is the fourth discussion question, "If you had to continue working in this kind of production, which arrangement of work would you prefer and why?".

F.   This exercise is not intended as a demonstration of the superiority of any particular kind of work arrangement; instead, it is an opportunity for the class to experiment with different approaches to work that are more or less consistent with the task technology and to discover their individual preferences regarding job design. Therefore, it is more important to thoroughly discuss the factors that led to satisfaction and productivity than to attempt to come to a conclusion about the right way to organize. Some instructors present examples of job design differences in auto factories.

G. After the debriefing, we go over the various interventions that aim to improve job design and productivity (job rotation, job enlargement, job enrichment, sociotechnical systems, self-managed work teams, TQM) that are summarized in the Follow-up section.

H. For shorter class sessions, have groups produce the moon tent in session one and the cargo carrier in session two. Another alternative is to have all groups produce the moon tent but assign half of them to use the GM instructions for the cargo carriers (simultaneous comparison). Some instructors devote another session to Total Quality.

**Transparency Masters**

21-0 Job Characteristics Enrichment Model

**Exam and Review Questions**

1. The aspect of alienation where the individual is engaged in activities that are intrinsically unrewarding
   a. social isolation
   *b. self-estrangement
   c. cultural estrangement
   d. meaningless

2. Blauner's classic study on worker alienation indicates that the degree of alienation is determined by
   *a. type of technology
   b. worker skill level
   c. worker attitude
   d. anomie

3. The basic unit of work design for sociotechnical system interventions is
   a. the individual
   *b. the group
   c. the organization
   d. the process

4. Job design that allows the assembly line worker to install the entire turntable rather than only one part of it is
   a. cross training
   b. job rotation
   c. job enlargement
   *d. job enrichment

5. __(Anomie)__ is the term Durkheim coined to describe a social system in which normative standards are weak and people experience a sense of disorientation, anxiety, and isolation.

6. Which of the following is not one of the tenets of Mayo's "rabble hypothesis," whose assumptions formed the basis of economic theory and industrial practice after the industrial revolution?
   a. society consists of unorganized individuals rather than groups
   *b. individual judgment is swayed by emotions and sentiments
   c. individuals act according to calculations of self interest
   d. individuals always think logically

7. According to Seeman, powerlessness is defined as
   a. high expectancies for (or commitment to) socially approved means for the achievement of given goals
   b. the individual's engagement in activities that are not intrinsically rewarding
   c. the sense of the incomprehensibility of personal and social affairs
   *d. the sense of low control over events

8. Identify the causes of work alienation and explain the effect on workers. (essay)

9. What is the relationship between motivation and job design? (essay)

READER QUESTIONS:
**"From Control to Commitment in the Workplace" by Richard E. Walton**

10. According to Walton, which approach is more appropriate in a highly competitive global economy -- control or commitment? Explain your answer.

Answer: The commitment approach is more appropriate because it takes less supervisory effort and workers are more highly motivated to do a good job, when compared with management by control.

11. Compare and contrast the control and commitment approaches to work-force management. Include their pros and cons. (essay)

12. Under the commitment-based approach to work-force management
   a. planning and implementation are separate and distinct
   b. individuals rather than teams are usually accountable for performance
   *c. performance expectations are high
   d. formal position determines influence

135

**"A New Strategy for Job Enrichment" by J. Richard Hackman, Greg Oldham, Robert Janson, and Kenneth Purdy**

13. Job enrichment programs always improve both satisfaction and productivity. ____ True __x__ False    Why?

Answer: Job enrichment programs do not always improve satisfaction and productivity. Other factors, such as faulty program implementation, individual knowledge and skill, need for growth, and satisfaction with contextual factors, determine whether such efforts are successful.

14. A job dimension that elicits the psychological state of experienced meaningfulness is
    a.  autonomy
    b.  feedback
    c.  tenure
    *d. task identity

15. The degree to which the job has a substantial and perceivable impact on the lives of people is known as
    *a. task significance
    b.  skill variety
    c.  impact index
    d.  environmental influence

16. An individual's ability to determine whether or not the outcomes of his or her work are satisfactory is called
    a.  knowledge of ability
    *b. knowledge of results
    c.  experienced meaningfulness
    d.  experienced responsibility

17. __(Vertical loading)__ refers to the unification of the split between planning and controlling and "doing" whereby job functions formerly reserved for high levels of management are added to lower-level jobs.

**"Deming's Redefinition of Management" by Myron Tribus**

18. Given everything we have studied about motivation, why would TQ programs motivate employees? (essay)

19. One managerial practice that is frowned upon by Tribus is
    *a. buying from the lowest bidder
    b.  establishing a "Quality philosophy"
    c.  teaching employees to be problem solvers
    d.  involving employees in system improvement

20. Deming's redefinition of management focuses on the

managerial responsibilities that
   a.   may be delegated
*b.   may not be delegated
   c.   must be well defined in a job description
   d.   are most challenging

21. Why does Tribus recommend replacing mass inspection with a generalized commitment to quality control?

Answer: because everyone should be responsible for and committed to quality, not just a team of inspectors. This eliminates the need for inspectors, reduces wasted effort, and increases both quality and productivity.

22. What are the basic tenets of TQ programs, according to Tribus?

Answer: a) continuity and consistency of purpose; b) widespread understanding of customer wants; c) focus on system and process improvement; d) statistical skill; e) employees as partners in system improvement; f) replace mass inspection with quality control; g) goal of continuous improvement; h) employees and managers as problem solvers; i) adequate training; j) establish a "quality philosophy"

## Reader Articles

1. "From Control to Commitment in the Workplace" by Richard E. Walton
2. "A New Strategy for Job Enrichment" by J. Richard Hackman, Greg Oldham, Robert Janson, and Kenneth Purdy
3. "Deming's Redefinition of Management" by Myron Tribus

# Chapter 22
# MANAGING CHANGE

**Materials Needed**: Most instructors prefer to use **puzzle pieces** made of cardboard (ranging from cut-up folders to stronger cardboard) or some type of plastic. The audio-visual departments in many universities can prepare these materials. You (or the planning teams) can cut out the pieces at the end of the book, but pieces made of stronger material are easier to manipulate. You need one set of **four envelopes** containing a total of 16 pieces for each group of 8-9 students; each envelope should be labeled A, B, C, or D. The implementation teams will need **another classroom** or area in which they can wait.
    **If you are using the puzzle pieces in the workbook, students will need scissors to cut them out. However, students should not look at and work with the pieces until the group exercise begins.**

**Objectives:** By the end of this chapter, students should be able to:

A. Describe the nature of change.
B. Explain the process of planned change.
C. Describe the characteristics of successful change efforts.
D. Understand the manager's role in the change process.
E. Define resistance to change and its function.

## Sample Design

| | |
|---|---|
| 6:00 - 6:20 | Lecturette on managing change |
| 6:20 - 6:30 | Introduction to the Hollow Square exercise |
| 6:30 - 7:00 | Planning period |
| 7:00 - 7:15 | Assembly period |
| 7:15 - 7:30 | Group discussion |
| 7:30 - 8:00 | Debriefing and summary |

## Setting the Stage -- Lecturette

    The purpose of this chapter is to allow students to experience what it is like to plan for others and communicate a change.

    We begin the lecturette by noting the need for managers to understand the change process. Many organizational decisions could be more readily implemented if they were perceived as a change process. We ask students to list what they already know about change and put their responses on the board. If necessary, we add key aspects that are missing. We acknowledge the common roadblocks to change and then present the process of planned change, using the transparency (t22-0).

## Issues to Consider in Leading the Experiential Exercise

A.  The instructor's first consideration is group formation. There is some advantage to having the entire class number off so that students do not work in their regular learning groups. More of the dynamics that occur in organizations will appear in these "stranger" groups than in the learning groups. As the workbook notes, each group of eight students further subdivides into a team of four implementers and four planners (3-5 planners in case of odd numbers of students). Always have four people on the implementation teams.

If you have extra students, they can be observers and assist you with the simulation. Their instructions are to note, without commenting, how the teams behave and react. Observers can also ensure that the teams observe the rules.

B.  Have the groups of eight quickly decide who will be planners and who will be implementers. Tell the implementers to tear out the page containing their instructions or, if they are opposed to textbook desecration, to take their workbooks with them. However, warn them not to read anything in the workbook until the instructor arrives to give them their instructions. If the instructor is doing this, do so after you have instructed the planning teams because they need more time. Another alternative is to have a student instruct the planning team, which involves reading their instructions aloud to them. Make sure the implementers do not read ahead in the workbook and find the instructions with the puzzle key.

C.  Read the planning team's instructions to them. Occasionally students do not understand that they can call in the implementation team whenever they wish during the thirty minutes. If the planners do not call them in, the implementation team will show up automatically five minutes before assembly. Tell the planners not to let the implementers see their instructions and, in particular, the puzzle key on the bottom of the page. Ask them to hide it or turn it over whenever implementers are in the room. Make sure you understand the rules and the logic behind them.

D.  There are always students who do not really hear the instructions, which will become obvious later on in the exercise. The most common rule transgressions are assembling the puzzle, mixing up the pieces (a major headache), writing down instructions for the implementers, marking the puzzle pieces, and coaching the implementers when they should only be observing. As you observe the planning teams at work, make sure they follow the rules but do so without coming off like "the enforcer." Otherwise, you may find your behavior a topic of discussion in the debriefing section. Calmly remind them of the rules ("I'm sorry, but if you check back on the rules, you'll find that the planning team is not allowed to assemble the puzzle or switch pieces because this would be an unfair advantage.")

E. It is tempting for instructors to give the teams hints. For example, students invariably ask if they can write down instructions for the implementation team. The answer, which appears in rule #3, is "no." But there is no need for you to tell them that the implementation team can take notes or make all the drawings they wish; let them figure everything out on their own.

F. Students can learn a great deal from the comparison between planning groups that call their implementation teams in early and those that do not. Therefore, if no planners think of this on their own, some instructors go to the implementers after 15 minutes have passed and "agitate." We tell each implementation team, "You're going to have to do a complex task and if they don't call you in soon, you won't have much time to get all the instructions." Usually someone will go in and ask the planners when they will be called. **You may need to remind the planners at this point to cover up their puzzle keys**. Watch how the planners react. Some immediately call in the implementers while others become downright hostile at being interrupted. Note at what time each planning team calls in their implementers because this could be important in the debriefing section. If the planners never call them in, send in the implementation teams five minutes before assembly.

G. The planners should put the puzzle pieces back into the envelopes in which they came right before the assembly period begins. Make sure the teams are ready and call out a one-minute warning. At the beginning of the assembly period, remind planners <u>not</u> to talk or distract the implementers; there are always students who find this difficult.

H. You can intervene and change the exercise rules to give the implementers greater chance of success if you decide that would be best for the class. We change the rules <u>after</u> the implementation teams that have a good chance of success have already completed the puzzle and <u>if</u> it looks as if the remaining implementation teams have no chance of success (i.e., they were called in late and given confusing instructions, they have zero spatial aptitude, and they appear wildly frustrated). Our rationale is that unsuccessful groups may focus so much on losing that they overlook the other lessons of the exercise. By changing the rules about 9-10 minutes into the assembly period, groups can experience and contrast both frustration and, hopefully, some degree of success.

We announce that there will be a rule change, "For the next minute, everyone should refrain from touching the puzzle pieces; the planners can talk but the implementers may not." Some students will have trouble not touching the pieces at this point.

If there are only 2-3 minutes remaining in the assembly period and some teams are still lost, you can add another rule change. "For the next minute, no one should touch the puzzle pieces, but both planners and implementers may talk." The differences in these rule changes allow the issue of one-way and two-way communication to surface in the debriefing.

I. When teams complete the puzzle, tell them they can silently observe the other teams at work.

J. The purpose of the evaluation forms on both teams, which are filled out by everyone, is to see if there are different perceptions between the two teams. Some teams may be angry with each other, especially if they were unable to complete the puzzle due to inadequate instructions.

K. The lessons that commonly surface during the **debriefing** concern the importance of a common language (shape descriptions), an overall vision of what the team is supposed to construct (hollow square), two-way communication (which necessitates more than a 5-minute instruction period), making sure that the implementers really understand, and thinking about how to transmit the message so implementers can easily understand it.

The debriefing question about what point the planners called in the implementers is significant because the first team to do so usually wins. Implementers have enough time to digest the instructions, ask questions, and feel like part of the team rather than a "pair of hands." Planners can include implementers from the very beginning if they wish, as long as they do not show them their instruction sheet. (A team did this once and their implementers completed the puzzle in less then a minute.) Planners too often get hung up on coming up with the perfect plan and forget all about what is occurring with the implementers. We emphasize (1) the necessity for both a high-quality solution and acceptance of the change and (2) the importance of cohesive teams.

Once the students have exhausted their own lessons, you can direct their attention to Figure 22-2.

L.  After the exercise, we talk about the manager's role in the change process (see the Follow-up section), the role of resistance and how to deal with it.  If the implementer teams exhibited resistance in the exercise, we ask students how this could have been avoided or handled.

**Transparency Masters**

22-0 The Process of Planned Change

**Exam and Review Questions**

1.  Kolb and Frohman's process of planned change emphasizes
    a.   limited participation of people affected by the change
    b.   significant early stages and less significant ending stages
    c.   quick diagnosis
    *d.  change as a sequential process

2.  In Kolb and Frohman's process of planned change, contracting about expectations and contributions is part of
    a.   the scouting phase
    *b.  the entry phase
    c.   the planning phase
    d.   the action phase

3.  C=(abc) > x is a formula for determining readiness for change where "b" stands for
    a.   buy-in from organizational members
    b.   practical first steps toward a desired state
    *c.  clear or understood desired state
    d.   level of dissatisfaction with the status quo

4.  The process of relinquishing old behaviors and testing out new behaviors, values and attitudes is referred to by Lewin as
    a.   unfreezing
    *b.  moving
    c.   freezing
    d.   refreezing

5.  _(Critical mass)_ is defined as the smallest number of people and/or groups who must be committed to a change for it to occur.

6.  What is the positive contribution of resistance to change?

Answer:   Resistance helps us perceive the potential problems of a planned change and is not merely an irrational reaction.

7.  Which of the following is not part of the manager's role in the change process, according to Beer et al?
    a.  foster consensus for the new vision, competence to enact it, and cohesion to move it along
    *b. announce your personal vision for the change
    c.  institutionalize revitalization through formal policies, systems, and structures
    d.  monitor and adjust strategies in response to problems in the revitalization process

8.  Which of the following is not true?
    a.  it is difficult for changes to endure
    b.  changes often upset the political system in organizations
    c.  what works in one part of an organization does not always transfer successfully
    *d. the organizations that most need to change are the ones that do so most easily and successfully

9.  List three tactics for dealing with resistance to change that are most likely to result in commitment to change rather than compliance.

Answer: (1) education and communication, (2) participation and involvement, and (3) facilitation and support.

READER QUESTIONS:
**"Why Change Programs Don't Produce Change" by Michael Beer, Russell A. Eisenstat and Bert Spector**

10. Most change programs don't work because they mistakenly believe that the place to begin is with
    a.  a diagnosis
    b.  behavioral change
    *c. changes in knowledge and attitudes
    d.  changing organizational roles

11. What are the three factors, according to Beer et al, required for corporate revitalization?

Answer: coordination, commitment, competencies

12. Which of the following is not one of Beer et al's six steps to effective change?
    *a. push revitalization from the top
    b.  institutionalize revitalization through formal policies, systems and structures
    c.  monitor and adjust strategies in response to problems in the revitalization process
    d.  mobilize commitment to change through joint diagnosis of business problems

**"Managing the Human Side of Change" by Rosabeth Moss Kanter**

13. According to Kanter, one key to mastering change is
    a. understanding the interdependence of organizations
    *b. the ability to analyze the reasons people resist change
    c. the ability to abandon unsuccessful change efforts
    d. providing monetary incentives to employees

14. Kanter's advice for dealing with "losers" in a change effort
    *a. be honest with them early on
    b. smooth over the effect of the change
    c. notify them about midway through the change
    d. encourage them that things may work out for them

15. Commitment to change is more likely to occur when the change is presented as
    a. as a surprise
    b. at the beginning of the year
    c. as a major shift from routine
    *d. as a continuation of tradition

**"Rules of Thumb for Change Agents" by Herbert A. Shepard**

16. Shepard's rule of thumb for change agents that is known as the Empathy Rule is
    a. keep an optimistic outlook
    b. engage in active listening
    c. stay alive
    *d. start where the system is

17. Shepard appeals for an organic rather than a mechanistic approach to change when he advises change agents to
    a. stay alive
    *b. never work uphill
    c. load experiments for success
    d. follow guidelines

## Reader Articles

1. "Why Change Programs Don't Produce Change" by Michael Beer, Russell A. Eisenstat and Bert Spector
2. "Managing the Human Side of Change" by Rosabeth Moss Kanter
3. "Rules of Thumb for Change Agents" by Herbert A. Shepard

# APPENDIX A
## SAMPLE SHORT-SESSION COURSE DESIGN

UNDERGRADUATE ORGANIZATIONAL BEHAVIOR COURSE
FALL SEMESTER MWF  13:35-14:30

| DATE | TOPIC | ASSIGNMENTS (TO BE COMPLETED PRIOR TO CLASS) |
|---|---|---|
| 1. (F) | MANAGING THE PSYCHOLOGICAL CONTRACT | **Reader:** p. 1-17  **Workbook:** Introduction, p. xix and Ch. 1, pre-meeting preparation, p. 5.  **Homework:** reaction piece on reader article |
| 2. (M) | THE ROLE OF THE MANAGER THEORY X AND Y | **Reader:** p. 30-46, 56-64  **Workbook:** Ch. 2, premeeting preparation, p. 22-27. Don't read Topic Intro yet. |
| 3. (W) | THEORIES OF MANAGEMENT | **Reader:** p. 47-55  **Workbook:** p. 28-40 |
| 4. (F) | LEARNING STYLES | **Reader:** p. 65-75  **Workbook:** Ch. 3, Pre-meeting preparation, p. 45. COMPLETE AND SCORE INVENTORY BEFORE CLASS |
| 5. (F) | LEARNING STYLES (cont.) Formation of learning groups | **Reader:** p. 76-109  **Homework:** HAND IN PERSONAL THEORY OF MANAGEMENT |
| 6. (M) | VALUES | **Reader:** p. 178-192  **Workbook:** Ch. 5, pre-meeting preparation, p.102. |
| 7. (W) | ETHICS Roger Worsham Case | **Reader:** p. 143-167 |
| 8. (F) | MOTIVATION PERSONAL DIAGNOSIS | **Reader:** p. 136-142  **Workbook:** Ch. 4, premeeting preparation, p. 72. **DO THIS FIRST -- WRITE LONG STORIES.** |

9. (W) MOTIVATION THEORY  **Reader**: p. 110-135  
**Workbook**: Follow-up p. 94-98.

10. (F) JOB DESIGN AND INVOLVEMENT  **Reader**: p. 636-653  
**Workbook**: Ch. 21, pre-meeting preparation, p. 546.

11. (M) COMMUNICATION  **Reader**: p. 214-229  
**Workbook**: Ch. 7, pre-meeting preparation, p. 164.

12. (W) ACTIVE LISTENING  **Reader**: p. 203-214  
**Workbook**: p. 179-188

13. (F) PERCEPTION AND ATTRIBUTION  **Reader**: p. 244-250  
**Workbook**: Ch. 8, pre-meeting preparation, p. 194  
**Homework**: COMPLETE GROUP PROCEDURE -- STEPS 1-3, P. 200-1.

14. (M) GROUP DYNAMICS EXERCISE  **Reader**: p. 251-267  
**Workbook**: Ch. 9, pre-meeting preparation, p.216

15. (W) GROUP DYNAMICS TEAM BUILDING  **Reader**: p. 268-289

16. (F) PROBLEM SOLVING  **Reader**: p. 290-316  
**Workbook**: Ch. 10, pre-meeting preparation, p.241.

17. (M) MIDTERM AND MID-COURSE EVALUATION

18. (W) MANAGING CONFLICT SIMULATION  **Reader**: p. 317-332  
**Workbook**: Ch. 11, pre-meeting preparation, p. 281.

19. (F) THE NATURE OF CONFLICT AND NEGOTIATION  **Reader**: p. 332-352  
**Workbook**: p. 295-299

20. (M) EMPOWERMENT AND COACHING  **Reader**: p. 524-534  
**Workbook**: Ch. 17, pre-meeting preparation, p. 430.

| | | |
|---|---|---|
| 21. (W) | PERFORMANCE APPRAISAL THEORY | **Reader**: p. 535-548<br>**Workbook**: Ch. 18, pre-meeting preparation, A-E, p. 477, read Topic Introduction. |
| 22. (F) | PERFORMANCE APPRAISAL PRACTICE | **Reader**: p. 548-561<br>**Workbook**: Ch. 18, read p.482-487.<br>**Homework**: CAREFULLY FILL OUT SELF EVALUATION (#F, p. 477) AND PEER EVALUATION (p. 482-483). |
| 23. (M) | MANAGING DIVERSITY GENDER ISSUES | **Reader**: p. 353-375<br>**Workbook**: Ch. 12, pre-meeting preparation, p. 305. |
| 24. (W) | CROSS CULTURAL DIVERSITY | **Reader**: p. 375-394<br>**Workbook**: p. 314-321. |
| 25. (F) | LEADERSHIP | **Reader**: p. 395-416<br>**Workbook**: Ch. 13, pre-meeting preparation, p. 328. |
| 26. (M) | ORGANIZATIONAL CULTURE | **Reader**: p. 442-452<br>**Workbook**: Ch. 14, pre-meeting preparation, p. 345. AS A LEARNING GROUP COMPLETE UP TO STEP 2, P.358. BRING COMPLETED CHART (P.359) TO CLASS, BUT DON'T READ ANY FURTHER IN THE CHAPTER. |
| 27. (W) | POWER AND INFLUENCE | **Reader**: p. 476-486<br>**Workbook**: Ch. 16, pre-meeting preparation, p. 400. |
| 28. (F) | INFLUENCE ROLE PLAYS | **Reader**: p. 512-511<br>**Workbook**: p. 410-426. |
| 29. (M) | DECISION MAKING THEORY | DO WORKBOOK TASK FIRST.<br>**Workbook**: Ch.15, pre-meeting preparation, p. 374.<br>**Reader**: p. 453-464 |

30. (W) DECISION MAKING          **Reader:** p. 464-475
        PRACTICE --CASES         **Workbook:** p. 386-393

31. (F) ORGANIZATIONAL CHANGE    **Reader:** p. 665-682
                                 **Workbook:** Ch. 22, pre-
                                 meeting preparation, p.
                                 619.

32. (M) CAREER PLANNING          **Reader:** p. 168-178
                                 **Workbook:** Ch.6, pre-
                                 meeting preparation, p.
                                 128.

33. FINAL EXAM (TO BE SCHEDULED)

NOTE: This is a relatively heavy reading load. You may wish to use only one article per session or make half the class responsible for teaching one of the articles to the other half.

## APPENDIX B
## SAMPLE LONG SESSION SYLLABUS

## MBA ORGANIZATIONAL BEHAVIOR COURSE
## TUESDAY  6:30-9:15 P.M.

**WHAT THIS COURSE IS ALL ABOUT**
People often discover at some point in their career that, although they possess the necessary technical skills to do the job, they do not know how to work effectively with others or they lack the interpersonal skills to be a good manager. This course seeks to help you understand human behavior in organizations, starting with your own behavior. By the end of the course, you should know yourself better and have better people skills. The focus of the course is the "micro" level in organizations--issues concerning individual behavior, interpersonal relations, and groups. The topics to be covered are the practical skills all managers should possess; you can immediately begin to apply them at work and home. The specific course objectives are:

1. To help you become more skilled at analyzing behavior in organizations
2. To help you learn what actions are appropriate for different situations
3. To help you acquire a larger repertoire of behaviors or skills.

**CLASS FORMAT**
The most effective method for teaching interpersonal and managerial skills is experiential learning. This means that we will turn the classroom into a laboratory and create conditions for understanding concepts through experience as well as readings. We will use role plays, exercises, and simulations so that you can pull out your own learning points from these experiences. <u>This type of course requires students to take responsibility for their own learning</u>. In order for an experiential course to be successful, students must do all the reading and homework preparation <u>and</u> participate actively in the classroom. Therefore attendance is mandatory because what goes on in class is not a repeat of the readings but the heart of the course. If you have an emergency and cannot attend class, please call me beforehand.

Please do not underestimate the importance of participation in this course. It is an important part of your final grade, not to mention that it gives you an opportunity to practice your communication skills. If you find it difficult to participate in class, please come see me in the beginning of the course so we have time to remedy the situation.

You will receive a packet of self-assessment instruments. The instruments are to help you understand yourself better and are usually filled out prior to class, as indicated on the syllabus. Please fill them out carefully and do the scoring before coming to class. The more honestly you answer these instruments, the more accurate a self-portrait you can construct.

One of the most important skills in today's business world is the ability to work effectively in groups. To give you more practice, you will always work with the same learning group in class and will receive feedback from this group on your performance in the course.

**THE SATURDAY SPECIAL**
The best way to develop teams is through outdoor challenge courses in which people work in groups to solve physical problems. Therefore, we will spend one Saturday (8:00-4:00) in September participating in a team development program. The morning will be spent on an outdoor challenge program or ropes course; the afternoon will consist of indoor team building exercises which are a lot more effective if they are done in the same day. The Saturday Special is the equivalent of two classes, so the course will end two weeks early. Please wear old, comfortable clothes and sneakers; plan to get dirty. The assignments for that day are listed on the last page under "Saturday Special." Attendance is mandatory for this session since it is the equivalent of two classes and is the highlight of the course. The class will decide which Saturday is most convenient.

**EVALUATION**
For 80 of the 100 evaluation points that will determine your grade in the course, you may choose between three evaluation methods: (1) short 5 page essays on topics covered in class called Personal Application Assignments (PAA's); (2) take home mid-terms and finals that are somewhat similar to the PAA's; (3) a learning journal in which you record your thoughts and learning about the entire course. An example of a PAA can be found on page 206-208 in your workbook. You will receive a detailed handout that explains the PAA format and a sample.

Each learning group will be responsible for a group presentation in the last session. The purpose of this assignment is to integrate the course knowledge and give you an opportunity to work on a group project. Your task will be to present the underlying themes of the course in as creative a fashion as possible.

|  | POINTS | DUE DATE |
|---|---|---|
| First PAA | 20 | October 4 |
| Second PAA | 20 | October 25 |
| Third PAA | 20 | November 15 |
| Fourth PAA | 20 | December 1 |

**OR**

| | | |
|---|---|---|
| Midterm | 40 | Take home September 27–Due October 4 |
| Final | 40 | Take home November 22–Due December 1 |

**OR**

| | |
|---|---|
| Learning Journal | Hand in at the end of each month. Final submission date December 1. |

**PLUS (FOR ALL OPTIONS)**

| | |
|---|---|
| Group Presentation | 10 |
| Peer Evaluation | 5 |
| Classroom Contribution | 5 |

<u>NOTE ON PAA CONCEPTS</u>: Use different concepts and theories in your PAA's, i.e., do not use the same concept or theory in more than one PAA.

In all three methods of evaluation (PAA's, exams, journal), you will be asked to follow the adult learning cycle which involves analyzing an aspect of human behavior covered in class, reflecting upon the behavior from a variety of different perspectives, applying and relating the behavioral example to the theories in the readings, and explaining how what you have learned can be applied to your own life and future behavior.

The remaining ten points of the 100 point total will be based upon your contribution to the learning community, 5 points assigned by the instructor and 5 points assigned by your learning group. The instructor's points will be based upon homework and participation. There may be occasional short homework assignments that do not appear on the syllabus. The five points that your learning group could grant you will be based upon your preparation, participation, and contributions to your learning group.

**All work should be typed, double-spaced. Assignments should be handed in on time**, unless you have made previous arrangements with the professor. Make sure you have another copy on diskette in case my dog eats your paper.

**CLASS CONTRIBUTION**
Each student is expected to be an active participant in both the exercises and the debriefing that occurs in class. Your class contribution grade is something to be earned via

consistent contribution to the class discussion and to your learning group. I value quality rather than quantity in terms of comments. Talking for the sake of talking does not improve your grade; I am looking for evidence of good critical thinking on your part. In a course like this, that means getting to the nub of an assigned article, asking thought-provoking questions, tying in outside experiences to what we have learned, coming up with learning points from our experiences in class, and sharing what you have learned about yourself and others during the exercises. Another aspect of participation is how well you help your learning group accomplish the tasks and exercises assigned in class.

The best ways to prepare yourself to contribute in class are:
1) Do whatever is requested in the pre-meeting preparation, which is found in the first few pages of each workbook chapter.
2) Come to class with the key points of the articles you had to read for the day written down. Be prepared to explain the highlights of the article in class.

**PEER EVALUATION**
At the end of the semester, every student will turn in a peer evaluation for their group members plus a written self-evaluation, assessing preparation and contributions to the learning group and the course in general.

**ETHICS**
I want to be sure you get your money's worth out of this course and that you will be able to put what you've learned into practice; that can only happen if you do the work yourself. Any cheating on exams or plagiarizing on papers will automatically result in a failing grade for the course for everyone involved.

**TEXTBOOKS**
1. ORGANIZATIONAL BEHAVIOR: AN EXPERIENTIAL APPROACH by Kolb, Osland, and Rubin. Prentice-Hall.
2. THE ORGANIZATIONAL BEHAVIOR READER by Kolb, Osland, and Rubin, Prentice-Hall.

The workbook consists of content, exercises and tips for managers. **Please bring the workbook to every class**. The reader is a compendium of the best articles in the field, in the authors' opinion. It is a mixture of both classic articles and recent developments, and both theoretical pieces and practical ones. Always read the assigned articles in the reader before coming to class, but it is not necessary to bring the reader with you. I would recommend that you jot down the key points from the articles and bring them to class. Your feedback and comments on the textbooks are always welcome.

# CLASS ASSIGNMENTS

| DATE | TOPIC | ASSIGNMENTS (TO BE COMPLETED PRIOR TO CLASS) |
|---|---|---|
| 1. 8/30 | MANAGING THE PSYCHOLOGICAL CONTRACT | |
| 2. 9/6 | THEORIES OF MANAGING | **Reader**: Ch. 2<br>**Workbook**: Ch. 2, p.24, premeeting preparation<br>**Homework**: Complete the Managerial Leadership Questionnaire. |
| 3. 9/13 | LEARNING STYLES - FORMATION OF LEARNING GROUPS | **Workbook**: Ch. 3, p. 45 Premeeting preparation. **COMPLETE AND SCORE INVENTORY BEFORE CLASS**<br>**Reader**: Ch. 3<br>**Homework**: Hand in your personal theory of management. |
| 4. 9/20 | MOTIVATION | **Workbook**: Ch. 4, p. 72 premeeting preparation. **DO THIS FIRST--WRITE LONG STORIES. Fill out the Job Diagnostic Survey.**<br>**Reader**: Ch. 4 |
| 5. 9/27 | VALUES AND ETHICS | **Reader**: Ch. 5<br>**Workbook**: Ch. 5, p. 102, premeeting preparation. |

## HAND OUT MIDTERM EXAM 9/27 - DUE IN OCT. 4

### FIRST PAA DUE BY OCTOBER 4

| | | |
|---|---|---|
| 6. 10/4 | COMMUNICATION | Reader: Ch. 7<br>Workbook: Ch. 7, p. 164 premeeting preparation. |
| 7. 10/11 | PERCEPTION AND PERFORMANCE APPRAISAL | **Reader**: Ch. 8 and 18<br>**Workbook**: Ch. 8, p. 194, pre meeting preparation. Ch. 18, p. 477, pre-meeting preparation. **CAREFULLY FILL OUT SELF EVALUATION ( #F, p. 477.** |

8. 10/18 MANAGING CONFLICT AND NEGOTIATION
**Reader**: Ch. 11
**Workbook**: Ch. 11, p. 281.

9. 10/25 MANAGING DIVERSITY
**Reader**: Ch. 12
**Workbook**: Ch. 12, p. 305, premeeting preparation.

10. 11/1 LEADERSHIP AND ORGANIZATIONAL CULTURE
**Reader**: Ch. 13 and 14
**Workbook**: Ch. 13, p. 328 and Ch. 14, p. 345, pre-meeting preparation.

11. 11/8 POWER AND INFLUENCE
**Reader**: Ch. 16
**Workbook**: Ch. 16, p. 400 premeeting preparation.

12. 11/15 DECISION MAKING
**DO WORKBOOK TASK FIRST**, **Workbook**: Ch. 15, p. 374, premeeting preparation., **Reader**: Ch. 15

13. 11/22 ORGANIZATIONAL CHANGE
**Reader**: Ch. 22
**Workbook**: Ch. 22, p. 619, premeeting preparation.

**HANDOUT FINAL EXAM 11/22 - DUE IN 12/1**
**HAND IN THIRD PAA BY 11/15 AND FOURTH PAA BY 12/1**

<u>**SATURDAY SPECIAL**</u>(8:00-4:00 - OLD CLOTHES & SNEAKERS)

A. TEAM BUILDING EXERCISES

B. GROUP DYNAMICS SIMULATION
**Reader**: p. 246-269
**Workbook**: Ch. 9, p. 216 pre-meeting preparation.

C. PROBLEM SOLVING
**Reader**: p. 270-303

D. CARDIOTRONICS CASE
**Workbook**: Ch. 10, p. 241, premeeting preparation.

# APPENDIX C

## PEER EVALUATION FORM

Name _____     Group #   1

As you know, five points of your final grade are allotted by your study group. Please take this grading responsibility seriously (it's a chance to think like a manager and evaluate group performance), and do not give everyone the entire five points unless you can justify that everyone really earned it. As with any performance evaluation, your personal feelings about the person should not enter into your decision; be as objective as possible.

**CLASS CONTRIBUTION.** Assign 0 to 5 points in both column A and B. (These will be averaged later.) In-class contribution refers to participation within your learning group rather than total class discussions.

| GROUP #1 MEMBERS | CLASS PREPARATION (Reading & Homework) | IN-CLASS CONTRIBUTION (Group Partipation) |
|---|---|---|
| Tammy MacDonald | _____ | _____ |
| Danielle Xitco | _____ | _____ |
| Luke Loomis | _____ | _____ |
| Peter Strickland | _____ | _____ |
| Steve Hawkins | _____ | _____ |
| Eve Powell | _____ | _____ |

**GROUP PROJECTS.** Assign 0 to 10 points in both column A and B. Base your evaluation on how much of a contribution each person made to each project. What percentage of the group grade does each member deserve for these projects?

| GROUP #1 MEMBERS | GROUP PAA | GROUP PROJECT |
|---|---|---|
| Tammy MacDonald | _____ | _____ |
| Danielle Xitco | _____ | _____ |
| Luke Loomis | _____ | _____ |
| Peter Strickland | _____ | _____ |
| Steve Hawkins | _____ | _____ |
| Eve Powell | _____ | _____ |

**NOTE TO PROFESSORS:** Figuring out these grades is quicker if student names are typed in ahead of time. We use different colors for each learning group to keep them separated.

# Annotated Bibliography Of Cooperative/Collaborative Learning Research and Practice (Primarily) at the Collegiate Level*

## James Cooper and Randall Mueck
### California State University Dominguez Hills

**PRIMARILY APPLIED WORKS** (e.g. setting up classrooms for Collaborative or Cooperative Learning)

Abercrombie, M. I. J. (1974). Aims and techniques of group teaching. London: Society for Research into Higher Education Ltd.
A short book describing a variety of small group techniques, including syndicate learning, peer tutoring and associative group discussions. Emphasis is on work conducted in Britain. Abercrombie's work on Collaborative Learning with medical students at the University of London is considered by Kenneth Bruffee and others as seminal.

Billson, J. M. (1986). The college classroom as a small group: Some implications for teaching and learning. Teaching Sociology, 14, 143-151.
A discussion of 15 principles concerning effective implementation of Collaborative Learning in the college classroom. Literature on group processes and development brought to bear on the subject in a very practical way.

Bishop, W. (1988). Helping peer writing groups succeed. Teaching English in the Two Year College, 15. 120-125.
A short, practical paper detailing issues to be considered in setting up peer writing groups in college composition classes. Useful for anyone setting up Collaborative Learning in any discipline.

Bohlmeyer, E. M., & Burke, J. P. (1987). Selecting cooperative learning techniques: A consultative strategy guide. School Psychology Review, 16. 36-49.
Although focusing on K-12 applications, this article is highly recommended for teachers at the collegiate level as well. A number of Cooperative Learning techniques are described and assessed in terms of a variety of categories, including type of knowledge to be fostered, ease of implementation and method of assigning students to learning teams.

Bouton, C., & Garth, R. (Eds.). (1983). Learning in groups. San Francisco: Josey-Bass.
A text in which a number of different chapter authors describe research and practice in Collaborative Learning. A good overview concerning how

*Published in The Journal of Staff, Program & Organization Development, (1989), 7, 143-148.

Collaborative Learning can be applied in a variety of college disciplines. Recommended for the new practitioner and those already implementing collaborative techniques.

Bruffee, K. A. (1985). <u>A short course in writing</u>. Boston: Little, Brown.
   A very applied short text on using Collaborative Learning in the teaching of college writing. Useful for faculty teaching writing and for college faculty in other disciplines as well. Highly recommended.

Collier, G. (ed.). (1983). <u>The management of peer-group learning: Syndicate methods in higher education</u>. Guildford, Surrey: Society for Research into Higher Education Ltd.
   A collection of chapters written by authors from postsecondary institutions and focusing on small group instruction at the college level.

Cooper, J. L., Sanchez, P., Prescott, S., & Lawrence, T. (1988, April). <u>Cooperative learning and college instruction: Part II</u>. Paper presented at the meeting of the Western Psychological Association, San Francisco, CA.
   A set of handouts which describe the characteristics of Cooperative Learning, positive outcomes associated with the use of the technique and a description of three applications of the technique by professors in different content areas. Also contains a summary of student perceptions (N=400+) concerning the efficacy of the technique, indicating that students feel that Cooperative Learning improves higher level thinking skill, general academic achievement and quality and frequency of student-student interactions when compared with traditional forms of college instruction.

DiPardo, A., Warshauer-Freedman, S. (1988). Peer response groups in the writing classroom: Theoretic foundations and new directions. <u>Review of Educational Research, 58</u>, 119-149.
   As noted in their abstract, this article "examines the pedagogical literature on response groups, places the literature in the context of current theories of teaching and learning of writing, and then examines the small number of studies of peer response groups." Suggests moving away from teacher-controlled response groups to student-centered peer talk during the writing process.

Feichtner, S. B., & Davis, E. A. (1984-5). Why some groups fail: A survey of students' experiences with learning groups. <u>The Organizational Behavior Teaching Review, 9</u>(4), 58-71.
   A description of good and bad Collaborative Learning procedures in college settings. Very practical.

Feichtner, S. B., & Michaelsen, L. K. (1984). Giving students a part in the process: An innovative approach to team learning. <u>College Student Journal, 18</u>, 335-344.

A general description of team learning using heterogeneous groups of six or seven.

Gere, A. R. (1987). <u>Writing groups: History, theory, and implications</u>. Carbondale: Southern Illinois University Press.
A short book containing good chapters concerning theories of Collaborative Learning and theories of language development. The language development chapter includes a good comparison of Piaget and Vygotsky's approaches to language acquisition and cognitive development. (Vygotsky is a pivotal figure in the history of Collaborative/Cooperative Learning). Excellent bibliography with brief commentaries on citations.

Hanson, P. G. (1981). <u>Learning through groups: A trainer's basic guide</u>. San Diego, CA: University Associates.
A general overview of group learning techniques from the standpoint of a human relations trainer.

Hawkins, T. (1976). <u>Group inquiry techniques for teaching writing</u>. Urbana, IL: ERIC Clearinghouse on Reading and Communication Skills and National Council of Teachers of English. (ERIC Document Reproduction Service No. ED 128 813)
A monograph describing a team learning approach to the teaching of collegiate writing. Author cites the experiential learning principles of Carl Rogers extensively, as well as the earlier work of Kenneth Bruffee in Collaborative Learning. Quite practical.

Johnson, D. W., & Johnson, R. T. (1987). <u>Learning together and alone: Cooperative, competitive, and individualistic learning</u> (2nd ed.). Englewood Cliffs, New Jersey: Prentice-Hall.
A good overview of Cooperative Learning from researcher/practitioners who have done much of the landmark work in Cooperative Learning. Focus is on practical applications at the precollegiate (K-12) level, but ample discussion of generic principles applicable at all levels. Recommended for all practitioners seeking an overview of research and practice in Cooperative Learning.

Johnson, D. W., Maruyama, G., Johnson, R. T., Nelson, D., & Skon, L. (1981). Effect of cooperative, competitive and individualistic goal structures on achievement: A meta-analysis. <u>Psychological Bulletin, 89</u>, 47-62.
Classic meta-analysis in the Cooperative Learning literature. A review of 122 studies (largely K-12) which compared the effect of cooperative, competitive and individualistic goal structures in promoting student achievement and productivity. Results of the meta-analysis indicated that cooperation was considerably more effective than competitive or individualistic goal structures. Potential mediating variables accounting for the results were described.

Johnson, D. W., Johnson, R. T., & Smith, K. A. (1986). Academic conflict among students: Controversy and learning. In R. S. Feldman (Ed.). <u>The social psychology of education: Current research and theory</u> (pp. 199-231). Cambridge: Cambridge University Press.
A textbook chapter which describes a specific form of Cooperative Learning known as structured controversy. In structured controversy, different members of the same learning team assume different positions concerning an issue in an attempt to ultimately maximize learning for all team members through discussion and research relating to the differing positions. Authors conclude that this technique sparks conceptual conflict within students, creates epistemological curiosity and promotes higher-level thinking skills.

Johnson, R. T., Johnson, D. W., & Smith, K. A. (1988). <u>Underline learning: An active learning strategy for the college classroom</u>. Unpublished manuscript. University of Minnesota.
A brief description of several Cooperative Learning techniques which may be used in college settings, apparently based on applications in the authors' own classes. Problems with traditional lecture procedures are described. Recommended.

Krayer, K. J. (1986). Implementing team learning through participative methods in the classroom. <u>College Student Journal, 20</u>, 157-161.
This article describes five evaluation procedures which may be used in classes using team learning. A rather complicated set of procedures which may be difficult to implement.

McEnerney, K. (in press). Cooperative learning as a strategy in clinical laboratory science education. <u>Clinical Laboratory Science</u>.
Describes the features of Cooperative Learning and how CL can be applied in a college classroom. Although Clinical Science is the course content used in this paper, the information presented can be generalized to a variety of academic disciplines. Very practical. Recommended.

Michaelsen, L., Watson, W. E. & Sharder, C. B. (1984-5). Informative testing-a practical approach for tutoring with groups. <u>The Organizational Behavior Teaching Review, 9</u>(4), 18-33.
A description of a collegiate Collaborative Learning technique, using organizational behavior as a framework. Focus is on the use of criterion-referenced testing to diagnosis and remediate students' learning.

Radebaugh, M. R. & Kazemek, F. E. (1989). Cooperative learning in college reading and study skills classes. <u>Journal of Reading, 32</u>, 414-418.
This short article describes how Cooperative Learning can be implemented in a college study skills class. Focus is on literacy as a social construct. The Cooperative Learning techniques described may be applied to many academic disciplines and courses.

Slavin, R., Sharan, S., Kagan, S., Hertz-Lazarawitz, R. Webb, C., & Schmuck, R. (Eds.). (1985). <u>Learning to cooperate, cooperating to learn</u>. new York: Plenum Press.

A compilation of chapters dealing with research and practice in Cooperative Learning. Chapter authors are some of the leading researchers/practitioners in the field. Focus is on precollegiate level. Chapters within the text are based on presentation made at the second meeting of the International Association for the Study of Cooperation in Education. Text can as easily be listed under the "Primarily Research" category of this bibliography, as with several other citations in this section.

Smith, K. A. (1984). Structured controversies. <u>Engineering Education, 74</u>, 306-309.

A brief paper outlining the use of structured controversy within a Cooperative Learning context. Focus is on collegiate engineering courses, but applications can be made across many disciplines. Recommended.

Smith, K. A., Johnson, D. W., & Johnson, R. T. (1981). Structuring learning goals to meet the goals of engineering education. <u>Engineering Education, 72</u>, 221-226.

An application of Cooperative Learning techniques to collegiate engineering courses. Of interest to those teaching at the collegiate level in any discipline. Recommended.

Treisman, U. (1985). A study of the mathematics performance of black students at the University of California, Berkeley (Doctoral dissertation, University of California, Berkeley, 1986). <u>Dissertation Abstracts International, 47</u>, 1641-A.

A description of Treisman's important research concerning Collaborative Learning with minority math and science students at Berkeley. Black students enrolled in his enrichment program received significantly higher grade point averages in freshman calculus, graduated in math-based majors four times more often, and had significantly lower attrition rates than comparable black students not enrolled in the program. Treisman's model now used at a number of colleges in math, science and engineering programs, with minority and other students. Call or write Treisman for materials or sites near you using the technique.

Wales, C. E. & Stager, R. A. (1977). <u>Guided design</u>. Morgantown, WV: University Center for Guided Design.

A good general introduction to Guided Design, a technique for teaching problem solving. Typically, teams of students are led to the solution of complicated problems through a series of structured steps, designed by the teacher.

Wiener, H. S. (1986). Collaborative learning in the classroom: A guide to

evaluation. College English, 48, 52-61.
A description of the teacher's role in setting up college courses using Collaborative Learning. Recommended.

Whipple, W. (1987). Collaborative learning: Recognizing it when we see it. American Association for Higher Education, 40(2), 3-7.
A short overview paper offering characteristics of Collaborative Learning from Bill Whipple, who chairs AAHE's Collaborative Learning Action Community (CUE).

# APPENDIX E
# MID-COURSE EVALUATION: IN SEARCH OF PINCHES

Please evaluate the exercises or assignments in terms of how much you learned from them.

1- Learned a great deal
2- Learned a fair amount
3- Learned a little
4- Waste of time
5- Absent physically or mentally that day = no comment

```
_____    Forming the Psychological Contract with professor
_____    Values video
_____    Theories of Management module (lecture, your
             speeches and theories, theory X and Y
             instrument)
_____    The Learning Style Inventory and forming the grid
_____    The TAT test (story writing) to determine your
             motives
_____    The Roger Worsham Case
_____    Active Listening exercise on a controversial
             issue
_____    Sharing your perceptions of group members (who's
             a pizza, etc.)
_____    Practicing performance evaluations on classmates
_____    The outdoor ropes course exercises
_____    The Inner-Outer Exercise (Group Dynamics)
_____    Cardiotronics Case (Problem solving)
_____    Nadir Case  (Conflict and Negotiation)
```

Comments/Suggestions:




In general, how would you rate the articles in the reader?

_____ 1 - really helpful, interesting articles --
           excellent
_____ 2 - good ideas but not reader friendly
_____ 3 - fair -- some good, some not
_____ 4 - not worth assigning (author should be taken out
           and shot)
_____ 5 - never read them (student should be taken out
           and shot)

Comments/Suggestions regarding specific articles:

Is the course meeting your expectations so far?

_____Yes          _____No          _____Sometimes

Why?




What is occurring during the course that helps your learning?




Is anything occurring that hinders your learning?




If you could give the professor one suggestion about how to be a better instructor, what would it be?




Other comments/suggestions:




Thanks for your feedback!

## THE PERSONAL APPLICATION ASSIGNMENT (PAA)

A variety of texts and articles over the past few years have argued for the use of an alternative approach to teaching organizational behavior, one that emphasizes experiential learning. This approach "emphasizes an existential, emergent view for learning organizational behavior" (McMullen, 1979), where the role of the instructor is that of learning facilitator, responsible for designing experiences for students to base learning upon, rather than as teacher, responsible for lecturing on theory and concepts. While gaining wide acceptance, this approach has nevertheless created problems in the assessment of students' performance. Significant learnings in this model of teaching occur not only from the development of concepts, but also from the experiences themselves. McMullen (as well as others) has proposed the use of a personal application assignment to help solve the problem of performance assessment. This assignment is based upon the experiential learning model formulated by Kolb (1971).

Kolb's model argues that learning occurs through a process which might begin with a <u>concrete experience</u>, which leads to <u>reflective observation</u> about the experience. <u>Abstract conceptualization</u> follows in which models, paradigms, strategies, and metaphors are applied to the results of the experience. <u>Active experimentation</u> concludes the cycle as the concepts are then put into practice, thus generating new concrete experience. Figure 1 shows the model more clearly.

Figure 1: Experiential Learning Model (Kolb)

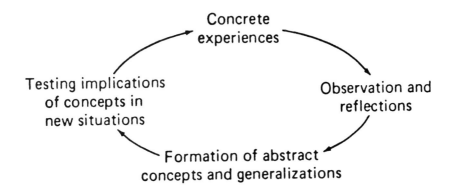

In one sense, persons able to learn using all modes of the model will be better able to take away learning from the variety of contexts in which they interact. We feel that the Personal Application Assignment is a useful tool for both evaluation of a student's work in courses taught using an experiential approach; and further, that the Personal Application Assignment can serve as a way to help students learn to learn. The PAA is both an evaluation and a teaching technique.

Our past history of teaching using this method has shown that the PAA, in order to be most useful, must include clear guidelines for the student. To that end we have undertaken to set forth the guidelines below to help students to understand the requirements for effective PAAs.

General Comments

First of all, we believe that a zero-based grading system is important. In this system, 20 points are given for the total PAA. Four points are awarded for each of the four elements in the learning style model and four points are awarded for the integration and synthesis and general quality of the PAA. Students start with zero points and are given specific points for each area, depending on their having met the criteria listed in the following section. For the instructor's part, we believe that instructors need to provide specific feedback as quickly as possible to students on why they were awarded points in each area and, more importantly, what they need to do to achieve the maximum points in each area.

Choosing a good topic is essential. Select an experience that relates to the assigned course topics. It should be an experience that you would like to understand better, (e.g., there was something about it that you do not totally understand, that intrigues you, that made you realize that you lacked certain managerial skills, or that was problematical or significant for you.) When students are excited about learning more about the incident, their papers are lively and interesting. The topic must be meaty enough to take it through the entire learning cycle. The incident does not have to be work related; an incident in any setting (sports teams, school, family, club, church, etc.) that relates to the course topics is acceptable.

Elements of the PAA

1. Concrete Experience (CE)

In this part of the paper, students briefly describe what happens in the experience. A simple description of the events which occurred is not sufficient. The feelings experienced by the student as well as his or her thoughts and perceptions during the experience are relevant to this discussion.

Another way of looking at CE would be that it possesses an objective and a subjective component. The objective part presents the facts of the experience, like a newspaper account, without an attempt to analyze the content. The subjective part is the "here-and-now" personal experience of the event. This experience is composed of feelings, perceptions and thoughts.

Helpful hints: (1) It often helps students to replay the experience in their mind. After reviewing the experience, students should write a report of what they saw, heard, felt, thought, and heard and saw others doing. (2) Students should avoid presenting the detailed mechanics of the experience unless these are critical to the remainder of the paper. This section of the paper should be no longer than 1 - 1.5 pages long. (3) Students should avoid reporting the feelings and thoughts experienced <u>after</u> the experience being described. This retrospection is more appropriate in the reflective observation section.

Example:
> We all sat at the table together. Not a sound came from any of us. Finally, after what felt like an hour to me, I simply had to say something. "Why are all of you taking this course?" I asked. One person, a small foreign looking man said, "I needed this course to complete my MBA." Others laughed. Another person, a nicely dressed woman, said, "I'd like to get an easy 'A.'" I thought to myself: What a bummer! I didn't want to be in a group with people who didn't take the subject matter seriously. When the meeting ended, my perceptions of the group had somehow changed. Maybe this was a good group to be in after all. Some of the members had similar interests to mine, and most of them were nice people that I could see getting along with. I felt

somehow hopeful that this semester wouldn't be so bad after all.

2. <u>Reflective Observation (RO)</u>

The student should ask him/herself: What did I observe in the experience and what possible meanings could these observations have? The key task here is to gather as many observations as possible by observing the experience from different points of view. The main skill to work on is <u>perspective taking</u> or what some people call "re-framing." Try to look at this experience and describe it from different perspectives. For example, how did other participants view the situation and what did it mean to them? What would a neutral ("objective") observer have seen and heard? Now that you are older do you see the situation differently? What perspective did your parents have, if any? Look beneath the surface and try to explain why the people involved behaved the way they did. <u>Reflect</u> on these <u>observations</u> to discover the personal meaning that the situation had for you.

Helpful hints: (1) Discuss the experience with others to gain their views and clarify your perceptions. (2) "Unhook" yourself from the experience and meditate about it in a relaxed atmosphere. Mull over your observations until their personal meaning comes clear to you. Try to figure out <u>why</u> people, <u>and you in particular</u>, behaved as they did. What can you learn about yourself, looking back on the experience? If you write about a conflict or interaction, be sure to analyze both sides and put yourself in the shoes of the other people involved.

Examples:

In thinking back on the meeting, I began to see how the group might have taken my comments. They were, after all, somewhat aggressive. Some might even call them belligerent. Had I said these things before this class, or at work, I must confess that I would have surprised even myself.

But it seemed there was more going on here than met my eye at the time. Sarah and Bob at first didn't seem to be the kind of people to combine forces on this job, so why was I arguing against them this time? Then it dawned on me: Their departments were about to be combined into the same division! Why hadn't I remembered that during the meeting?

Many thoughts raced through my head. Was the cause of last night's "high" that we won the game? Was it the first time we had worked together as a group? Maybe the fact that member X wasn't there that night helped! But I still had a nagging hunch that my involvement, downplayed as it was from previous meetings, helped.

3. Abstract Conceptualization (AC)

By relating assigned readings and lectures to what you experienced, you are demonstrating your ability to understand conceptually abstract material through your experiences. This process will help you refine your model of people and organizations. While some assigned readings and lectures will have varying degrees of relevance to your experience, it is important that you make several references and not limit your conceptualizing to just one source. Use at least two concepts or theories from the course readings. Provide the source for each reference in the following manner: (workbook, p. 31) or (reader, p. 97). This is also the place to insert your own personally developed theories and/or models if they assist you in making sense of the experience.

By reviewing theoretical material, you should be able to identify several specific concepts or theories that relate to your experience. First, briefly define the concept or theory as you would for someone who was not familiar with it. Next, apply the concept <u>thoroughly</u> to your experience. The tie-in should include the specific details of how the theory relates to and provides insight into your experience. Does the experience support or refute the theory? Avoid merely providing a book report of what you have read -- you should discuss in some detail how you see concepts and theories relating to your experiences.

Helpful hints: (1) It is sometimes useful to identify theoretical concepts first and then search out and elaborate on an experience that relates to these concepts. (2) A slightly more difficult approach is to reverse the above procedure and search out those concepts that apply to your "raw" experience.

<u>Example</u>: Below is an example of <u>one</u> of the concepts defined and applied in a student PAA.

> <u>Abstract Conceptualization</u>
> There are several organizational behavior concepts that help me understand this experience. One is the Thomas-Kilman theory of conflict (workbook, p. 284-285) which is based upon two axes, either the concern for one's own interests or the concern for the interests of the other party. The five styles reflect a low or high position on these two axes and are labeled competition, compromise, avoidance, accommodation, and collaboration. In the incident I described, my coach began with a collaborative style, high concern for both his own interests and the interests of the other party. He tried to work out a solution that would satisfy both of us but I neither saw nor heard his point of view. I just wanted to get my own way and practice in the same way I had on my previous team. I see now that the conflict style I used was the competitive style, high concern for my own interests and low concern for the

interests of the other party. Looking back, this is the style I have used most often throughout my life; I usually got away with it before because I was such a good athlete. However, my experience with the coach supports the workbook's description (p. 285) of the losses that may result from using this style. I lost everything when I was kicked off the team and I certainly alienated the coach and the other players and discouraged them from wanting to work with me.

4. <u>Active Experimentation (AE)</u>

This section of the paper should summarize the practical lessons you have learned and the action steps you will take to make you more effective in the future. How can you test out your concepts developed in the preceding phase? These ideas can be stated in the form of rules of thumb or action resolutions. (Future actions must be based on the experience reported in Concrete Experience.) You should elaborate <u>in detail</u> how you see your action ideas being carried out. Be <u>specific</u> and <u>thorough</u>. Don't just repeat tips from the workbook. Include at least one action resolution that is based upon new knowledge that you have gained about yourself as a result of writing the paper. Depending on the complexity of your ideas, you should present at least four things that you learned and a well-thought out description of how you will apply them in the future. If you were to relive your experience, what would you do differently? If you were the manager in the story, what would you do differently? Based on the insight you've gained about yourself and others, how would you handle a similar situation in the future?

Helpful hints: (1) Project a future experience in which you envision the implementation of your ideas and then elaborate on that experience as a way of demonstrating how your actions will be carried out. (2) Where does this model exist in your life (home, work, school)? Do you need a support system to make it happen? Someone to "contract" with? (3) Try to imagine the final results of your experimentation. What will it be like if you accomplish what you want to do?

Example:

> How then can I best utilize and improve my achievement motivation? First, I must arrange for some accomplishment feedback. This will be done by designing or perceiving tasks so that I succeed bit-by-bit, gaining a reward each time and thus strengthening my desire to achieve more. Also, I must look to "models of achievement." If people around me succeed, it will further stimulate me. Third, I should modify my self-image to include my desire for personal challenges and responsibilities and my requirement of continual feedback. (As a first step, I imagine myself as a person who <u>requires</u> or <u>must have</u> success, responsibility, challenge and variety.) Fourth, I must learn to control my reveries. Just beyond the borderline of awareness, many of us are constantly talking to ourselves... Finally, although I would never admit so, I agree that salary is a potential "dissatisfier" for me. Therefore, I must insist on what I perceive as a "fair return" for my performance. Wish me luck!

5. Integration and Synthesis

The well written PAA has a focal issue and a story line with themes that are carried throughout each of the four sections. The idea of synergy applies here: "The whole is greater than the sum of the parts." If integration is present, then the reader can attend to the content without distraction; if integration is absent, barriers prevent the reader from gaining a full appreciation of the content.

Other barriers that prevent the reader from fully appreciating the paper's content are spelling and grammatical errors. Since good writing skills are so important in the business world, <u>there should be no errors in your paper</u>. Use the spell check on your computer and have others read your paper before you hand it in.

Helpful hints: (1) This factor is largely a matter of good writing skills. (Strunk and Whites's <u>Elements of Style</u> is a good refresher for those unsure of their skills.) (2) The student should keep in mind the following points:

    (a) Decide what one or two main points you wish to convey and make sure that you do.

    (b) Label each section: Concrete Experience, Reflective Observation, etc.

    (c) Transitions are important (between sentences, paragraphs, and sections) and make the paper flow.

    (d) The four sections should be equally well-developed and fairly similar in length.

<u>Example</u>:

The attached SAMPLE PAA, written by an MBA student, is well integrated.

SAMPLE PAA

Concrete Experience

I worked for one year in the marketing group in the Chicago office of a large public accounting firm. The internal service departments were organized into profit centers and operated like little fiefdoms. We worked very closely with the graphics department. We provided the majority of their work but that did not mean the two departments got along well. In fact, we spent more time battling each other than collaborating. A constant bone of contention for both groups was missed deadlines. Most of the time, a marketing person was the contact with the client, usually a partner in the firm. We set up a production schedule, to which the client would agree, and made every effort to stick to it. But 99 times out of 100, something would happen on the partner's end that would cause a delay. However, the original deadline was never modified to take these setbacks into account because we were not allowed to tell the partners their requests were unreasonable. This put terrific pressure on <u>both</u> departments, but graphics personnel continually accused us of purposely holding onto information or dragging our feet in order to make their jobs more difficult.

It was very frustrating for me to get my projects completed. From the very beginning, I felt they thought I was an incompetent jerk who was just trying to make their job more difficult. It wasn't long before I adopted the perception of the rest of my department - graphics was a bunch of uncooperative whiners. I never expected to get good service from them and I didn't. I dreaded going into their office with changes and kept my communications with them to a minimum. Occasionally, I'd have a confrontation with an artist which would escalate into an argument with two or three other graphics people. Then I was angry for the rest of the day. I had no idea how to remedy the situation and I was under such pressure to get my work done that I had no time to repair the relationships, even if I had known how to do it.

Reflective Observation

Looking back, I think that if I had not been so caught up in the intergroup fighting, I would have recognized that the graphics personnel were under as much pressure as I was. At the time it always seemed like "once again graphics was being uncooperative." But I never stopped to ask myself why they were being so hostile to me and I never put myself in their shoes. One of the things this taught me was that I can be somewhat self-centered and ignore the problems of others when they are a barrier to getting my work done. When graphics stereotyped me, I let myself be influenced by my co-workers rather than making the effort to develop a positive relationship with graphics and get beyond the stereotypes. I felt like one of the gang when we all shared our horror stories about the latest thing graphics had done.

For their part, graphics was probably struggling to keep up with their work and deadlines. Just when they thought they had things under control, we would appear with new changes and requests. Perhaps a lot of their resentment stemmed from feeling that, because of us, they could not control their own work flow. We didn't want to lose the partners' business by asking for extended deadlines since they could have hired an outside firm, but graphics had no investment in our service to the partners. Instead, they were worried about satisfying their own clients. And our last-minute changes got in the way of serving their other clients.

There was another person in a different department who was very positive about the graphics department. At the time I remember thinking, "Oh, he must not deal with them on a regular basis like I do or they wouldn't be so cooperative with him." It never occurred to me that this person was doing something different than I was and, as a result, had a better relationship with the graphics personnel. And it certainly never occurred to me to ask him what he did to have such a great rapport with the group.

Since other people and groups managed to have good relations with graphics, we could hardly be justified in thinking that they were totally in the wrong. But both groups had stereotyped the other and were unwilling to change their opinions. Even though both our managers knew about the problem, they did not intervene, perhaps because the work always got done somehow. These managers were more focused upon tasks than people so they never worried about the personal cost of the conflict, and probably did not know how to resolve the problem.

Abstract Conceptualization

Conflict, defined as "a form of interaction among parties that differ in interests, perceptions, and preferences" (reader, p. 305) is the concept that best helps me understand my experience. Our two departments had different interests in serving our customers and different perceptions about each other and our work demands.

The situation between marketing and graphics was an example of when too much conflict occurs. The following passage could have been written about us. "The combination of negative stereotypes, distrust, internal militance, and aggressive action creates a vicious cycle: 'defensive' aggression by one group validates suspicion and 'defensive' counter aggression by the other, and the conflict escalates (Deutsch, 1973) unless it is counteracted by external factors" (reader, p. 307). Graphics never believed that we weren't holding back information or dragging our feet on purpose. And we never trusted them to do our work well without giving us a hard time. We both complained bitterly about each other and never lost an opportunity to slander the "enemy" to others in the organization, which is a form of aggression. Brown (reader, p. 306) states that managers must intervene when conflict reaches a dysfunctional level but our managers never did. They probably did not want to "rock the boat" as long as things were getting done. But it makes me wonder how much more effective we could have been, had we been able to work through our differences. Someone should have helped the two groups diagnose the conflict and its underlying causes (competing for the scarce resource of time, struggling with uncontrollable last minute demands and iron deadlines, and allegiance to our department rather than the company as a whole).

Another concept that applies to this incident is perception, the process by which we read meaning into stimuli (workbook, p. 204). Marketing and graphics personnel constructed barriers to communication between each group by using the techniques of selective exposure, selective attention, distrusted source and erroneous translation. We saw, heard and paid attention to what we wanted to, not necessarily the behaviors that may have been actually occurring. Our stereotypes were consistently reinforced by the perceptions we chose to respond to.

Active Experimentation

If I were in situation like this again, I would first try to do a better job of managing myself. I would remember that it takes two sides to make a conflict and I need to be as objective as possible and not go along with the group in criticizing "them" so that I feel more a part of the group. Second, had I made the effort, I might have been able to establish at least one positive relationship with someone in graphics. I should have asked my positive colleague how he managed to develop such a good relationship with them. I suspect his advice would have been to spend more time with them, treat them with greater respect, refrain from blaming them when things go wrong, and be more empathetic.

Third, I would talk to my manager or supervisor about the problem. By making my feelings known and telling him or her that

I wanted to do my part in conflict management maybe he or she would be more willing to take action. If not, at least I tried. At the bottom line, my negative actions only made my job more difficult. I now realize that was not a very smart or effective way to conduct myself.

The positive thing about having negative experiences is that hopefully I learn from them. I do not have control over other people but if I act appropriately, I will have a much better chance of getting the cooperation I desire. This experience taught me about the dangers of going along with the group. I know that the next time I am in this situation I will behave differently.

# APPENDIX G

# WHAT WE LOOK FOR WHEN GRADING PERSONAL APPLICATION ASSIGNMENTS

Please bear these grading criteria in mind as you are writing your paper and doing your final revision.

## CONCRETE EXPERIENCE - 4 points

_____ Does the paper contain a clear, objective description of facts in your personal experience? (up to 2 points)

_____ Does it contain a subjective description of FEELINGS, perceptions, and thoughts that occurred during (not after) the experience? (up to 2 points)

_____ Does this section provide enough information so the reader will understand the rest of the paper but not too much irrelevant detail? Remember that **this section should not be longer than 1-1.5 pages.** (Delete 1 point)

## REFLECTIVE OBSERVATION - 4 points

_____ Did you look at the experience from the different points of view of all the major actors? (up to 2 points)

_____ Did you make an attempt to figure out why the people involved, **and you in particular,** behaved as they did? (up to 1 point)

_____ Did the different perspectives and behavioral analyses add significant meaning to the situation? (up to 1 point)

## ABSTRACT CONCEPTUALIZATION - 4 points

_____ Did you briefly define and explain at least two different concepts or theories from the assigned readings that relate to your experience and did you reference them properly? (up to 2 points)

_____ Did you thoroughly apply the concepts/theories to your experience? (up to 2 points)

## ACTIVE EXPERIMENTATION - 4 points

_____ Did you summarize the practical learnings you derived from writing this paper on your experience? (1 point)

_____ Did you describe <u>thoroughly</u> at least four actions you will take in the <u>future</u> so you can be more effective? For example, "If I am confronted with a similar situation, I will...", "If I had to relive this experience, I would...", or "When I am the boss..". Are these actions described in the form of guidelines or action resolutions? (up to 2 points)

NOTE: Did you remember to check back through the previous sections and make sure you came up with learnings and/or action steps that respond to <u>all</u> the major themes found in the paper?

_____ Did you identify and include at least one action step that is based upon what you learned about **yourself** as a result of writing the paper? (1 point)

_____ Did you merely copy action steps from the workbook or reader without adding any of your original thinking? (delete 1 point)

## INTEGRATION, SYNTHESIS AND WRITING - 4 points

_____ Does the PAA have major themes that are carried throughout each section of the paper and are the sections well-integrated and fairly equally developed? (1 point)

_____ Is the paper clear and well-written? (1 point)

_____ Is the paper free of spelling errors? (1 point) Did you use the spell-check on your computer or a good human editor?

_____ Is the paper free of grammar errors? (1 point)


NOTE: Did you consult the writing assistant about your paper?

_____ TOTAL GRADE

## Appendix H
### EXAMPLE PERSONAL APPLICATION ASSIGNMENTS

### Socialization Unit--Example PAA

No one was telling me what I was supposed to learn from this first class after three hours of meeting, discussing, questioning, etc. In fact, the whole three hours seemed totally useless. "I haven't gotten anything out of this," I said to myself.

"Are there any more questions?" the professor asked.

I raised my hand. "What was the central purpose of this first class?"

"What is the statement behind that question?" was the essence of the response.

In later thinking about my question, the response, and the process of analysis which the response initiated within me, I began to understand what those three hours were all about.

What were my learning objectives for this course? Was I willing to participate actively in the setting of those objectives and in their attainment? No course I had ever taken had asked me these questions. I have since realized that is what the first three hours were all about. Though in retrospect these questions seem very important, I was wholly unprepared to answer them; in fact, as queries they made no sense to me. I was so conditioned by my previous experiences of entering into organizations wherein on the first day I would listen to and accept objectives so that when I was asked during those three hours to participate actively in objective setting, I was unprepared to respond in any meaningful way.

My question at the end of class was a reflection of my unwillingness to accept an _active_ role in objective setting. The statement behind my question was, of course, that these three hours seemed purposeless. Rather than face that statement squarely and examine it in light of what had transpired (an active process), I converted the statement into a question, thus attempting to retain a _passive_ role while putting the professor in the position of having to set objectives for those three hours. Through later analysis of this interaction, I began to understand what the active learning process was.

Out of the confusion of those first three hours, two very important elements of a psychological contract between myself and the organization (the course including professors and learning groups) emerged. The elements directly concerned the learning process in which I would engage in this course.

First, this is to be an active learning experience. This sounds almost trivial but it is the basis of the psychological contract between myself and the group and, furthermore, is fundamental to learning within the course. It means that I will learn about interpersonal interactions in organizational behavior by actively experiencing those interactions. I must scrutinize the functioning of the group of which I am a member, observe important interactions, make hypotheses about these interactions, and actively test these hypotheses within the group in order to learn.

Second, I am to be responsible for setting the learning objectives of this experience. (This almost directly follows from the first element.) These objectives are not given and thus cannot constrain or limit in any way the scope of learning which can be obtained.

The ramifications for the learning process of these two elements taken together are enormous. The most significant of these is the fact that now the scope of learning has no bounds other than those set by the student. This situation compares very favorably with the more traditional passive learning process where course objectives essentially place certain bounds on the learning process. Furthermore, when the student sets his own objectives, he has a vested interest, so to speak, in accomplishing them since they are his objectives and are not externally imposed. In the very process of setting these objectives, the student becomes committed to their attainment.

In combination, these two elements thus lead to a higher motivation to learn and make a broader scope of learning possible. In point of fact, both my attitude toward learning and my behavior in learning have begun to reflect these effects. I am more inquisitive, more committed to learning and, in short, more involved in the learning process than I have ever been. It is my judgment that this involvement will ultimately result in large rewards.

It is interesting to note that I have made little or no mention of grades as they affect the learning process. It has become apparent to me that grades can and do interfere with the learning process. Grades represent another form of constraining objectives set by the professor (organization) in the traditional (passive) learning process. Grades represent an artificial and artificially allocated reward system which comes to replace learning. The objective of study is the attainment of the greatest artificial reward rather than the greatest participation and involvement in the learning process. Attempting to gain the greatest reward generally interferes directly with the process of participation in a learning experience.

As an example of this interference, I have just finished a short paper for another course. Looking back at my efforts I can see that one of my prime concerns was whether or not the conclusions which I was drawing would be in direct conflict with those that the professor might have drawn and thus, whether or not I was doomed to getting a failing grade on the paper because of my extreme stance. This concern definitely affected and otherwise interfered with what should have been my prime concern, i.e., expressing and supporting my views and research findings on the topic.

This type of interference has not hindered me in the process of writing this paper since in writing it I am accomplishing real learning objectives which I have set for myself. In writing this paper I have made explicit, via verbalization, some of the things which I learned during the first session of this course and some of the things I would like to learn in future sessions. By making them explicit, they have become much clearer and more reasonable to me. Writing this paper has thus been an essential part of the learning process initiated in the first session.

It is interesting to note that the writing of this paper is an active process. For the first time in my academic career, writing a paper has been a pleasure.

## Communications Unit--Example PAA

### Introduction

After reading pages and pages of literature for this course, I finally found an article that seems to have great relevance to my behavior, and, thusly, I feel compelled to write about it. Gibb's paper on "Defensive Communication" outlines almost precisely the way I behaved in small task-oriented groups a few years ago. This paper will attempt to outline my behavior in these groups, compare it to Gibb's analysis, explore why I acted this way, examine the results of this course of action, and draw some conclusions.

### Background

As the reader may recall from previous PAAs, a year or so ago I was president of numerous things. In this period, with special relevance to my position as president of a fraternity, I was often faced with small groups whose purpose was to accomplish some sort of task.

### Behavior

In general, when decisions had to be made, or when ideas had to be generated, I handled this in a very small group: one person, me. When I approached a TOG (task-oriented group), I had the solution in mind and saw my role in the group as simply to get them to accept the same idea and to get to work on it in a minimum of time. (We'll explore this attitude more later.) With this attitude, my communication in the group was very defensive:

1. My statements were full of value judgements, and I always used the trick of asking people questions, the answers to which I knew, to put them on the spot and prove a point (evaluation).

2. My entire orientation was based on control--to change attitudes or influence behavior (control).

3. My statements and reactions were never spontaneous. I carefully planned how I reacted, what I said, etc. (strategy).

4. I never even tried to empathize with other persons' ideas because this seemed irrelevant to my goals. Clearly when using this method one does not even really hear what others are saying, since one is always planning the next move instead of listening (as clearly pointed out in the "repeat what the other person said" game) (neutrality).

5. When it was needed, I used my position of superiority in official rank to aid my goals in the discussion. The great white father bit works very well on some people (superiority).

6. It follows that I was not there to investigate new ideas, so I tried to make it clear that I did know all the answers (certainty).

Before we go on, one thing should be noted. After reading the previous text, one may wonder how this approach could accomplish anything besides getting the person shot by the group. As it turns out, if this approach is used carefully, and with skill, it can give the appearance of being very successful.

Two things need to be examined now: (1) why did I use this approach since I don't always communicate this way, and I haven't done it lately, and (2) what are the results of this approach versus a non-defensive one as described by Gibb or Roethlisberger.

Why

The approach that I used seems to be based upon a number of assumptions that I made: (1) purely egotistical--I am much better able to generate ideas and make decisions than anyone else, (2) the time involved in letting the group generate anything is too great, (3) my relationships with these people is not being hurt by this approach.

It is very easy once one is in a position of power to assume a paternal king attitude. My numerous positions allowed me to discuss and find out ideas about fraternities from other fraternity leaders, from MIT administration people, and from national fraternity leaders. This can lead one to assume that he should go home and provide all of this needed change to his house. I also believed that the group would probably be unable to generate these ideas by themselves.

This leads us to the second assumption. The fastest way to accomplish this, if one is less than a military dictator, is by defensive communication tactics. The time element here is important as outlined in PAA No. 4. I was getting a great deal of motive satisfaction by working in certain areas, and time that detracted from these areas caused great pain (loss of motive satisfaction) so I avoided wasting the slightest bit of time.

The third assumption, which can also be seen in the light of satisfaction of motives, was based upon my relative insensitivity to relationships. As long as people gave me a certain amount of proper respect (that I could see), said hello when passing, and did most of what I wanted them to do, I felt they were close enough friends. I was completely unaware of the distrust and dislike that my behavior was causing. This leads us to the next section on the results of this approach.

### Results

The results of my approach have only become obvious to me recently. I think that they can be broken down into three categories. First of all there is a deep resentment of me among some of the people still in the fraternity. I'm sure that it would have become more and more difficult to continue this approach if I were president for more than one year, since much of its effectiveness was due to the fact that I was respected, but that was slipping. So its success is somewhat based upon its short period of use. Also, the present resentment would not have bothered me too much once upon a time, but now it hurts.

Second, some of the changes and innovations that came last year are slowly dying. This stems from the fact that the people never understood these foreign ideas, and it is only reasonable that they will relieve the frustrations that they had by discarding them. Finally, due to the fact that people became accustomed to not applying their creativity to the house, a less creative leadership is looking to the members and getting a slow response. People indeed got used to my approach and are having trouble changing it. These last two points are hurting the fraternity this year.

### Conclusions

1. The approach that I used is not the best way to achieve things in either the short or the long run, although it can be somewhat successful in the short run.

2. The reasons for this approach are related to my motive satisfaction in that period, my lack of awareness concerning interpersonal relations, and my general lack of understanding of the previous conclusions.

# APPENDIX I

## COURSE OBJECTIVES

- FOSTER AN UNDERSTANDING OF BASIC SOCIAL PROCESSES IN ORGANIZATIONS

- PROMOTE SELF-AWARENESS IN PARTICIPANTS

- HELP PARTICIPANTS:

    1. BECOME MORE SKILLED AT ANALYZING BEHAVIOR IN ORGANIZATIONS

    2. LEARN WHAT ACTIONS ARE APPROPRIATE FOR DIFFERENT SITUATIONS

    3. ACQUIRE A REPERTOIRE OF USEFUL BEHAVIORS AND SKILLS

## APPENDIX J
## NAME BINGO

1. Approach another person in the class (preferably someone you don't know) and guess which category might fit him or her. If your guess is incorrect, you may make one and only one more guess about another category. If your second guess is also incorrect, let your partner make a guess about you and then move on to someone else.

2. If your guess <u>is</u> correct, write the person's name in the appropriate box.

3. The object of the exercise is to fill in names for as many boxes as possible. A person's name may not appear more than once.

| Has never played a video game | Hates Pizza | Wanted to be a rock star | Has 7 brothers & sisters | Speaks 3 languages fluently |
|---|---|---|---|---|
| Writes poetry | Plays 3 musical instruments | A rabid _____ fan | Ran cross country | Has 4 or more kids |
| Gourmet cook | Painted outside of a house | Dislikes beer | Vegetarian | Parachuted from an airplane |
| Never watched a soap opera | Played in a marching band | Poker demon | Flew over the Pacific | Worked in last presidential campaign |
| Born in another country | Owns a bowling ball | Reads philosophy in spare time | Does not own a credit card | Drives a car over 10 yrs. old |

## APPENDIX K
## HOW TO SUCCEED IN ORGANIZATIONAL BEHAVIOR BY REALLY TRYING

**PRIOR TO CLASS**

- Think back on an experience related to the subject to be studied for the next class session. (For example, before the group dynamics session, think about a group to which you belonged. What made it effective or ineffective?) Do you have any theories or models about the subject and, if so, what are they?

- What do you want to learn about the subject? (Returning to the group dynamics example, when should managers use their staff to make decisions and when should they make them alone? How could I learn to conduct better staff meetings? Why do some people act so differently in groups than they do outside them? What are groups good for?)

- What are the significant learning points in the readings? Write them down; you'll have an opportunity to contribute them in class. Did you find some answers to what you want to learn about this subject in the readings?

- How can you apply what you've learned from the readings at work or in other areas of your life?

- Are there any particular behavioral skills you want to practice during the experiential exercise that will take place in class?

**DURING CLASS**

- Tell your learning group when there is a particular skill you want to practice during class so you can get feedback from them.

- Did you find some answers to what you wanted to learn about the subject during the class session? If not, raise your questions with your learning group or the instructor.

- Figure out how you can apply the learning from the class exercise to your work or other areas of life.

- Contribute your theories about the subject, your experiences, and what you've gleaned from the readings and the exercise to class discussions.

**AFTER CLASS**

- Take time to reflect on what happened in class and read the learning points at the end of the chapter. Review what you learned and try it out.

# APPENDIX L
## Procedure for Group Meeting:
## Performance Appraisal Role Plays by Carolyn Jensen

Time Allotted: One hour and 30 minutes for both role plays (45 minutes a piece)

*This exercise provides students with the opportunity to participate in, as well as observe, an appraisal interview. The class should be divided into groups of three. This exercise consists of two role plays. One takes place in a manufacturing environment, while the other occurs in a white collar setting. Each role play simulates a performance appraisal interview between two group members; one acts as employee or rater, while the other acts as the supervisor or rater. The third group member acts as observer. If time allows for both role plays to be conducted, roles should be rotated so each group member has the opportunity to perform two of the three roles. The performance to be evaluated in each role play is outlined in the "script" of each individual role play.*

STEP 1. Decide who will act as rater, employee, and observer.

STEP 2. Take 10 to 15 minutes for each group member to read his or her section of the role play.

   A. The student acting as rater should read only the section of the exercise with RATER at the top.

   B. The student acting as employee should read only the section of the exercise with EMPLOYEE at the top.

   C. The student acting as observer should read both the RATER and EMPLOYEE section.

STEP 3. During the interview the rater should ask the employee for his or her self-appraisal on each of the five criteria. The employee should present his or her self-appraisal on each criterion individually, followed by his or her reasoning for such a rating. At this time the rater should present his or her rating of the employee on these criteria, as well as the reasoning behind it. The rater has the opportunity at this time to adjust his or her rating of the employee on the blank scale provided. If the ratings are adjusted, the rater should explain why they were changed. If they were not changed, the rater should also explain why he or she feels such ratings are justified.

STEP 4. After each individual criterion is discussed the rater has the opportunity to improvise a bit, selecting one or several of the issues below for discussion.

The rater can guide the interview toward:

A. The employee's opinions regarding their problems, performance, motivations, and career goals.
B. Problem solving with an individual or organization focus.
C. Training needs of the organization.
D. The employee's view of the organization's performance and related problems.

STEP 5. Discuss and determine the training and development need of the employee.

STEP 6. The rater should properly conclude the interview. Included in this step the rater should share the final rating with the employee.

STEP 7. After the performance appraisal interview is completed, the rater and employee should answer the questions at the end of their sections, and the observer should answer the observer questions at the very end of the role play.

**Rater**
**Role Play 1**

**In today's exercise....**

You are Pat Cole, and Chris Smith is one of your employees on day shift.

**Background...**

You are a line supervisor at Sweetlane Candy, Pennsylvania's largest candy manufacturer. It is time for you to conduct your annual performance appraisals of the 55 employees you supervise on your shift. You are not looking forward to conducting the appraisals. A memo from management has stated that not only must you evaluate these employees, but you must also submit a list of employee training and development needs (something you have never done before). Due to an open bid system that started this year, you have only supervised 18 of your employees for nine months. You are uncomfortable because you don't know them or their work as well as you'd like.

**Next Appraisal to be Conducted....**

You have already conducted 11 appraisals, all with employees you have worked with for 3 or more years. This next appraisal is with Chris Smith, who has been working for you only 9 months. Adding to your apprehension over the appraisal are two factors: 1) Sweetlane's new policy of asking employees to conduct a self-appraisal prior to your meeting, and 2) the lack of knowledge you have about the machines in your department since it has updated eleven of the forty-five production lines. Although you rose to a management position from these same ranks, you have not been "one of them" in 9 years.

**How you see it....**

You have evaluated Chris' performance below, knowing you can change it if you wish after your meeting.

*Work Quantity -*

Defined as the amount or volume of the work produced. Your line expects employees to move 20 units a minute, or 1200 units an hour. With two ten minute breaks, and a forty minute lunch, 8400 units should be produced a day by an employee. A counter appears at the end of each line which cannot be seen by the employee without moving approximately 12 feet from where he or she needs to stand on the line. Chris' production has averaged 8259 units a day.

*Work Quality -*

Defined as the reliability and accuracy of the work produced. Employees are expected to produce 8400 units a

                                            Rater
                                            Role Play 1

day with a 98% accuracy rate. Thus only 2% or 168 units out of the 8400 average daily production should fail quality standards. Chris' average over the nine months of units failing the quality test is 1.9%.

**Work Quantity and Quality schedule for Chris**

| Month | Average Units a Day | Average % Per Day Failing Quality Test |
|---|---|---|
| 1 | 8290 | 1.8% |
| 2 | 8300 | 1.9% |
| 3 | 8390 | 1.9% |
| 4 | 8400 | 1.9% |
| 5 | 8400 | 1.9% |
| 6 | 8500 | 1.8% |
| 7 | 7900 | 2.0% |
| 8 | 8000 | 2.0% |
| 9 | 8150 | 1.9% |
| **Average Over Nine Months** | 8259 | 1.9% |

*Absentee Rate -*
Employees are allowed 5 days (or forty hours paid absences a year for illness without a doctor's excuse, and an additional 4 days (or 32 hours) paid absences with a doctor's excuse. They are allowed 2 personal days (16 hours). Employees are docked for late time up to one hour, on 9 occasions. After that, disciplinary action is determined by the immediate supervisor. One option is to dock sick time on an hourly basis. Chris has been from 25 minutes to 40 minutes late 4 times. The fourth time Chris' sick time was docked 30 minutes. In addition, Chris has missed 2 days or 16 hours sick time in this 9 month period.

*Cooperation -*
Defined as the willingness of an employee to accept supervision and adapt to various situations. As the supervisor, you have noticed Chris has been unresponsive to your help lately. Chris seems to have changed in the last three months, rejecting the help of other employees as well.

*Compatibility -*
Defined as the ability of the employee to get along with others including supervisory personnel, peers, and

Rater
Role Play 1

subordinates. Chris seems to get along well with fellow employees on breaks and in any situation where advice is not being given. Chris seems to like doing his job without the input of others.

Here are the ratings you have come up with:

```
Work Quantity    I----------X-----------I----------I---------I
                 Poor       Below       Average    Above     Excellent
                            Average                Average

Work Quality     I----------I-----------I----------X---------I
                 Poor       Below       Average    Above     Excellent
                            Average                Average

Attendance       I----------X-----------I----------I---------I
                 Poor       Below       Average    Above     Excellent
                            Average                Average

Cooperation      I----------X-----------I----------I---------I
                 Poor       Below       Average    Above     Excellent
                            Average                Average

Compatibility    I----------I-----------X----------I---------I
                 Poor       Below       Average    Above     Excellent
                            Average                Average
```

**Note:** Before deciding on Chris' ratings you just rated Sidney, one of your best employees. You and Sidney both bowl on Saturday's at the same alley.

Final ratings after your meeting with Chris...

**Note:** You do not have to change the previous ratings. Only do so if you feel your previous ratings were incorrect.

```
Work Quantity    I----------I-----------I----------I---------I
                 Poor       Below       Average    Above     Excellent
                            Average                Average


Work Quality     I----------I-----------I----------I---------I
                 Poor       Below       Average    Above     Excellent
                            Average                Average
```

```
                                                          Rater
                                                          Role Play 1
```

Attendance     I-----------I-----------I----------I---------I
               Poor        Below       Average    Above     Excellent
                           Average                Average

Cooperation    I-----------I-----------I----------I---------I
               Poor        Below       Average    Above     Excellent
                           Average                Average

Compatibility  I-----------I-----------I----------I---------I
               Poor        Below       Average    Above     Excellent
                           Average                Average

After the meeting...

1) Did your ratings of Chris change after the meeting? If so, how and why?

2) What have you determined to be Chris' training and development needs (if any)?

3) What form of bias did you exhibit?

4) How could your company's performance appraisal system be improved?

5) What active listening skills did you use?

6) In retrospect, what would you do differently if you were to act as rater again?

Employee
Role Play 1

**In today's exercise...**
You are Chris Smith, and your supervisor on day shift is Pat Cole.

**Background...**
You are an employee at Sweetlane Candy, Pennsylvania's largest candy manufacturer. It is time for your annual performance appraisal. You are not looking forward to this particular appraisal. You are uncomfortable with the fact that due to an open bid system, you are one of 18 new employees on day shift whose performance appraisal will be conducted by a supervisor who has only known you for nine months. Most of the other employees on this shift have been in this department for at least 3 years.

**Your performance appraisal...**
Adding to your apprehension over the appraisal are two factors: 1) Sweetlane's new policy of asking employees to conduct a self-appraisal prior to their meeting with their supervisor, and 2) the lack of familiarity you feel in your department since it has updated eleven of the forty-five production lines. It updated these lines in the seventh month of your employment in this department.

**How you see it...**
You have evaluated your performance below, knowing it's probably not seen in the same light by your supervisor, Pat Cole.

*Work Quantity -*
Defined as the amount or volume of the work produced. Your line expects employees to move 20 units a minute, or 200 units an hour. With two ten minute breaks, and a forty minute lunch, 8400 units should be produced a day by an employee. A counter appears at the end of each line which cannot be seen by the employee without moving approximately 12 feet from where he or she needs to stand on the line. Your production has averaged 8259 units a day. When you first started here it took you two to three months to get up to speed. On your sixth month here you hit a high daily average of 8500 units per day. After that they switched you to one of the new production lines without any hands-on training, and only a half hour verbal introduction to the line in a classroom environment. You know your production has dropped, but you only know just how slow your going at

Employee
Role Play 1

break time and at lunch when you can check the counter at the end of he line. You feel you can't learn from others there. No one on the new lines, from what you can see, is doing well.

*Work Quality -*
Defined as the reliability and accuracy of the work produced. Employees are expected to produce 8400 units daily with a 98% accuracy rate. Thus only 2% or 168 units out of the 8400 a day average production should fail quality standards. Your average percentage of failed units over the nine months is 1.9%. You feel this is excellent considering you are in a new department, and on a new line.

**Work Quantity and Quality schedule for Chris**

| Month | Average Units a Day | Average % Per Day Failing Quality Test |
|---|---|---|
| 1 | 8290 | 1.8% |
| 2 | 8300 | 1.9% |
| 3 | 8390 | 1.9% |
| 4 | 8400 | 1.9% |
| 5 | 8400 | 1.9% |
| 6 | 8500 | 1.8% |
| 7 | 7900 | 2.0% |
| 8 | 8000 | 2.0% |
| 9 | <u>8150</u> | <u>1.9%</u> |
| **Average Over Nine Months** | 8259 | 1.9% |

*Absentee Rate -*
Employees are allowed 5 days (or forty hours) paid absences a year for illness without a doctor's excuse, and an additional 4 days (or 32 hours) paid absences with a doctor's excuse. They are allowed 2 personal days (16 hours). Employees are docked for late time up to one hour, on 3 occasions. After that disciplinary action may be determined by the immediate supervisor in the case. One option is to dock sick time on an hourly basis. You have been from 25 minutes to 40 minutes late 4 times. The fourth time your sick time was docked 30 minutes. In addition you have missed 2 days or 16 hours sick time in this 9 month period. You are a single parent and your child is in first grade. The school bus picks him up quite a ways from your

Employee
Role Play 1

house. You can't let him wait alone in this day and age, so when the bus is late you're late. That's just how it is as you see it. After all, your child comes first.

*Cooperation -*
Defined as the willingness of an employee to accept supervision and adapt to various situations. You have always been able to accept help and criticism very well, but with these new machines you reject the help of others because, quite frankly, they do not know any better than you how to operate this new line. You are frustrated because no hands-on training was offered.

*Compatibility -*
Defined as the ability of the employee to get along with others including supervisory personnel, peers, and subordinates. You get along well with fellow employees on breaks and in any situation where advice is not being given about those damn new machines. You just want to learn this new job so you can bring up those numbers that are so important to Sweetlane management.

Here are the results of your self-appraisal:

Work Quantity   I-----------I-----------I---------**X**---------I
                Poor        Below       Average    Above       Excellent
                            Average                Average

Work Quality    I-----------I-----------I-----------I---------**X**
                Poor        Below       Average    Above       Excellent
                            Average                Average

Attendance      I-----------I-----------**X**---------I---------I
                Poor        Below       Average    Above       Excellent
                            Average                Average

Cooperation     I-----------I-----------I---------**X**---------I
                Poor        Below       Average    Above       Excellent
                            Average                Average

Compatibility   I-----------I-----------I-----------I---------**X**
                Poor        Below       Average    Above       Excellent
                            Average                Average

**Employee
Role Play 1**

**Note:** Before your performance appraisal interview, you see Pat talking to Sidney, and you wonder whether Sidney had his performance appraisal conducted this morning. You know Pat and Sidney are tight.

**After the meeting...**

1) Do you think Pat's original ratings were accurate?

2) Did the original rating change after your interview? Were Pat's final ratings of you fair?

3) Do you think they (the ratings) changed because of your self-appraisal?

4) What form of bias do you think Pat may have exhibited?

5) What active listening skills did Pat exhibit?

6) How could the appraisal have been more effective and useful?

Observer
Role Play 1

**Observer Questions**

On another piece of paper answer the following questions.

1)  Did the supervisor give the employee sufficient time to present his or her self-appraisal?

2)  Did the supervisor use active listening skills, or did he or she do most of the talking?

3)  Did the supervisor create a nondefensive climate and refrain from becoming defensive himself or herself?

4)  Did the supervisor discuss training needs with the employee?

5)  What mistakes, if any, were made by either the supervisor or employee?

6)  What forms of bias should the supervisor be aware of when rating Chris?

7)  Were the supervisor's final ratings of Chris fair?

8)  Other comments:

Rater
Role Play 2

**In today's exercise...**
You are Cary Dunn, and Bernie Tate is one the employees in the department you oversee.

**Background...**
You are one of eight Vice Presidents at Wayne Gaskets, the largest producer of gaskets in the United States and the second largest producer of gaskets in the world. It is time for you to conduct your annual performance appraisals of the 22 employees in your department. You are Vice President of the Total Quality Department, which consists of 16 Quality Specialists and 6 support people. You are not looking forward to conducting the appraisals. You find it difficult to rate the specialists because: 1) many have become your friends over the years, and 2) the performance appraisal system at Wayne seems to ask you to wear too many hats at once. You feel pulled between acting as a coach and judge. After all, you are forced to suggest training and development needs, suggest raises, and evaluate performance all at once. A memo from management last month emphasized the importance of raters going over the employees' self-appraisal with them. In previous appraisals you have only devoted a minute or so to this, and are now uncomfortable with the thought of using it to any great extent. All you have wanted in the past is to assign employees ratings that make all parties happy.

**Next Appraisal to be Conducted...**
You have only conducted 5 appraisals so far. All of them have been with Quality Specialists. Your next appraisal is with Bernie Tate. You have known Bernie for seven years. You were there for only 2 and a half years when Bernie was hired. You worked side by side with Bernie as a Specialist for 4 years before you were promoted to Vice President. Bernie has an engineering degree from the same university as you. You are apprehensive about evaluating Bernie due to the new emphasis you must place on self-appraisal and because of your friendship with Bernie. Another concern you have is with the lack of definite guidelines for assessing a high score to an employee on a particular criterion versus a low one. Last but not least, you have to draw up those training and development needs.

**How you see it...**
You have evaluated Bernie's performance, knowing you can change the evaluation if you wish after your meeting.

Rater
Role Play 2

*Work Quantity* -

Defined as the amount or volume of the work produced in terms of project starts, project completions, consulting services performed, and committee work. Bernie has started two new projects this year, one of which is to develop a computerized expertise index of company personnel. This project's estimated completion time was 8 months. It is now into the eleventh month, and it is still not completed. The second project was to improve the current inventory system. It was projected to take 6 months. Bernie and another specialist completed it in 5 months. You as V.P. do not have the feedback on how the system is doing. Bernie consulted on 12 occasions in the last year.

*Work Quality* -

Defined as the reliability and accuracy of the work produced. You have no feedback on the inventory system project. On the consulting work Bernie performed, the company has received seven excellent reviews, two good reviews, two average reviews, and one below average review. Both the below average and average reviews cited Bernie's difficulty in communicating strategies and ideas as the main weakness of the consulting work.

*Absentee Rate* -

Employees are allowed 7 days paid absences a year for illness without a doctor's excuse, and an additional 9 days paid absences with a doctor's excuse. They are allowed 2 personal days per year. Bernie has two weeks vacation a year. One week (five day period) must be taken together. The second may be taken only one or two days at a time. Employees here work on a flextime schedule allowing them to arrive from 7 AM to 9 AM and leave from 4 PM to 6 PM. Bernie has missed six days this year. Bernie used all available vacation in July and August. You hardly saw Bernie in those two months. These two months were part of the eleven in which the expertise project was a priority. You also noticed Bernie's absence at both 8:45 AM and 5:45 PM. You have begun to wonder what flextime schedule Bernie selected. Flextime to you means you select a schedule (a time to come in and one to leave) and stick to it. You must ask Bernie at the performance appraisal interview about this issue.

**Rater**
**Role Play 2**

*Cooperation* -
    Defined as the willingness of an employee to accept supervision and adapt to various situations. Bernie is open to constructive criticism from what you can see, and has always accepted supervision well. Often Bernie invites you, as well as the specialists in the quality department, to get involved with a project that has been delegated to Bernie.

*Compatibility* -
    Defined as the ability of the employee to get along with others including supervisory personnel, peers, and subordinates. Bernie's a team player from what you can see. Bernie invites the participation of others often and usually gets it. Bernie's easy going and laid back almost to a fault. Sometimes Bernie lacks motivation on different projects.

Here are the ratings you have come up with:

```
Work Quantity   I-----------I-----------I---------X---------I
                Poor        Below       Average   Above      Excellent
                            Average               Average


Work Quality    I-----------I-----------I-----------I---------X
                Poor        Below       Average   Above      Excellent
                            Average               Average


Attendance      I-----------I-----------I----------X---------I
                Poor        Below       Average   Above      Excellent
                            Average               Average


Cooperation     I-----------I-----------I-----------I---------X
                Poor        Below       Average   Above      Excellent
                            Average               Average


Compatibility   I-----------I-----------I-----------I---------X
                Poor        Below       Average   Above      Excellent
                            Average               Average
```

Rater
Role Play 2

**Note:** You just finished rating Alex, the worst employee in the department, before deciding on Bernie's ratings. No one can figure out how Alex managed to get hired in the first place. As you began jotting down Bernie's ratings, another V.P. dropped by to complain about the conflict she was facing from employees who disagreed with their low ratings. You thought to yourself, "I don't need that hassle."

Final ratings for Bernie from you...

**Note:** You are not required to change the ratings from the previous page. Only do so if you feel the previous ratings were incorrect.

```
Work Quantity    I-----------I-----------I----------I---------I
                 Poor        Below       Average    Above     Excellent
                             Average                Average


Work Quality     I-----------I-----------I----------I---------I
                 Poor        Below       Average    Above     Excellent
                             Average                Average

Attendance       I-----------I-----------I----------I---------I
                 Poor        Below       Average    Above     Excellent
                             Average                Average

Cooperation      I-----------I-----------I----------I---------I
                 Poor        Below       Average    Above     Excellent
                             Average                Average

Compatibility    I-----------I-----------I----------I---------I
                 Poor        Below       Average    Above     Excellent
                             Average                Average
```

**After the meeting...**

1) Did your ratings of Bernie's performance change after the meeting? If so, how and why?

2) What have you determined to be Bernie's training and development needs, if any? Your company's needs?

3) What form of bias did you exhibit?

**Rater**
**Role Play 2**

4) How could your company's performance appraisal system be improved?

5) What active listening skills did you use?

6) In retrospect, what would you do differently if you were to act as rater again?

Employee
Role Play 2

**In today's exercise...**

You are Bernie Tate, and Cary Dunn is the Vice President of the department in which you work.

**Background...**

You are Quality Specialist at Wayne Gaskets, the largest producer of gaskets in the United States and the second largest producer of them in the world. It is time for your annual performance appraisal. As a Specialist in the Total Quality Department, which consists of 16 Quality Specialists and 6 support people, you are not looking forward to your appraisal. You are uncomfortable with the idea of drawing up a self-appraisal this year, more than ever before. You feel burnt out at your job, though you do feel lucky to have it in this changing economy. You could have been more productive this year and you know it. But back to this appraisal, if you rate yourself completely honestly you'll be embarrassed first, and maybe out of a job second. After all, management doesn't want to hear excuses for slacking. Not even Cary Dunn, who is your friend and your boss, will be able to help you then. A memo from management last month emphasized the importance of employees developing an honest self-appraisal and sharing it with the rater.

**Your appraisal...**

You are apprehensive about this appraisal, and the fact that you and Cary are friends only makes it worse. You have known Cary for 7 years. Cary had been there for only 2 and a half years when you were hired. You worked side by side with Cary as a Specialist for 4 years before Cary was promoted to Vice President. Cary has an engineering degree from the same university as you. You are worried about inflating your performance to Cary for two reasons: 1) you are friends, and 2) since Cary was at one time a Specialist, chances are this V.P. will be able to see through the desperate act of over-estimating your own performance.

**How you see it...**

You have evaluated your own performance below, knowing Cary Dunn, your supervisor, probably has a different view.

*Work Quantity -*
Defined as the amount or volume of the work produced in terms of project starts, project completions, consulting services performed, and committee work. You have started two new projects this year. One project focuses on

**Employee
Role Play 2**

developing a computerized expertise index of company personnel. This project's estimated completion time was 8 months. It is now into the eleventh month and it is still not completed. The second project was to improve the current inventory system. It was projected to take 6 months. You and another specialist completed it in 5 months. You consulted on 12 occasions in the last year.

*Work Quality -*

Defined as the reliability and accuracy of the work produced. On the consulting work you performed, the company received seven excellent reviews, two good reviews, two average reviews, and one below average review. You know your department receives feedback on these consulting jobs, but all you receive is a memo telling you how you were rated. No additional feedback is passed on to you. Just a few days ago you heard that the new inventory system you designed reduced stock outs by 12%, and cut inventory carrying costs by 20%. Your goal was to reduce stock outs by 18%, and cut carrying costs by 15%. The expertise project is still not finished. You lost your motivation working on it yourself. You finally see a trend in your performance. You perform better in a team environment.

*Absentee Rate -*

Employees are allowed 7 days paid absences a year for illness without a doctor's excuse, and an additional 3 days paid absences with a doctor's excuse. They are allowed 2 personal days per year. You have two weeks vacation a year. One week (five day period) must be taken together. The second may be taken only one or two days at a time. Employees here work a flextime schedule allowing them to arrive from 7 AM to 9 AM and leave from 4 PM to 6 PM. You have missed six days this year. You used all your vacation during the summer months. You avoided the office these months because it had just become too depressing. Same old job, same old people, same old everything. The expertise project just became a real downer to face every day. The flextime program was a lifesaver for you. On nice days you would start early and leave early. On ugly days, you started late and left late. After all, that's what flextime is for.

*Cooperation -*

Defined as the willingness of an employee to accept supervision and adapt to various situations. You always

**Employee Role Play 2**

felt you were open to criticism and supervision, but you know you have a tendency to attempt to get others to "share the load" in work situations so to speak.

*Compatibility -*
Defined as the ability of the employee to get along with others including supervisory personnel, peers, and subordinates. You've always been a team player at the office. You invite the participation of others often and usually get it. You are easy going and laid back almost always.

Here are the ratings you have come up with:

```
Work Quantity     I------------I-----------X-----------I---------I
                  Poor         Below        Average     Above      Excellent
                               Average                  Average

Work Quality      I------------I------------I----------X---------I
                  Poor         Below        Average     Above      Excellent
                               Average                  Average

Attendance        I------------I-----------X-----------I---------I
                  Poor         Below        Average     Above      Excellent
                               Average                  Average

Cooperation       I------------I------------I----------X---------I
                  Poor         Below        Average     Above      Excellent
                               Average                  Average

Compatibility     I------------I------------I----------X---------I
                  Poor         Below        Average     Above      Excellent
                               Average                  Average
```

**Note:** Before deciding on your self-appraisal, you speak to another specialist in your department who has already been rated. You feel his performance is below yours, and his ratings were high. So you decide to go ahead and rate yourself somewhat better than you feel you deserve, but not as high as you were going to at first. Damn that conscience!

**After the meeting...**
1) Did you think Cary's original ratings were accurate?

**Employee
Role Play 2**

2) Did the original rating change after your interview? Were Cary's final ratings of you fair?

3) Do you think they (the ratings) changed because of your self-appraisal?

4) What form of bias did Cary exhibit?

5) What active listening skills did Cary exhibit?

6) How could the appraisal have been more effective and useful?

Observer
Role Play 2

**Observer Questions**

On another piece of paper answer the following questions.

1) Did the supervisor give the employee sufficient time to present his or her self-appraisal?

2) Did the supervisor use active listening skills, or did he or she do most of the talking?

3) Did the supervisor create a nondefensive climate and refrain from becoming defensive himself or herself?

4) Did the supervisor discuss training needs with the employee?

5) What mistakes, if any, were made by either the supervisor or employee?

6) What forms of bias should the supervisor be aware of when rating Bernie?

7) Were the supervisor's final ratings of Bernie fair?

8) Other comments:

# T1-0 CHARACTERISTICS OF ORGANIZATIONAL BEHAVIOR

- MULTIDISCIPLINARY NATURE
- THREE LEVELS OF ANALYSIS; INDIVIDUAL, GROUP AND ORGANIZATIONAL
- ACKNOWLEDGEMENT OF ENVIRONMENTAL FORCES
- GROUPED IN THE SCIENTIFIC METHOD
- PERFORMANCE ORIENTATION
- APPLIED ORIENTATION
- CHANGE ORIENTATION

# T1-1  MODEL FOR MANAGING PSYCHOLOGICAL CONTRACTS

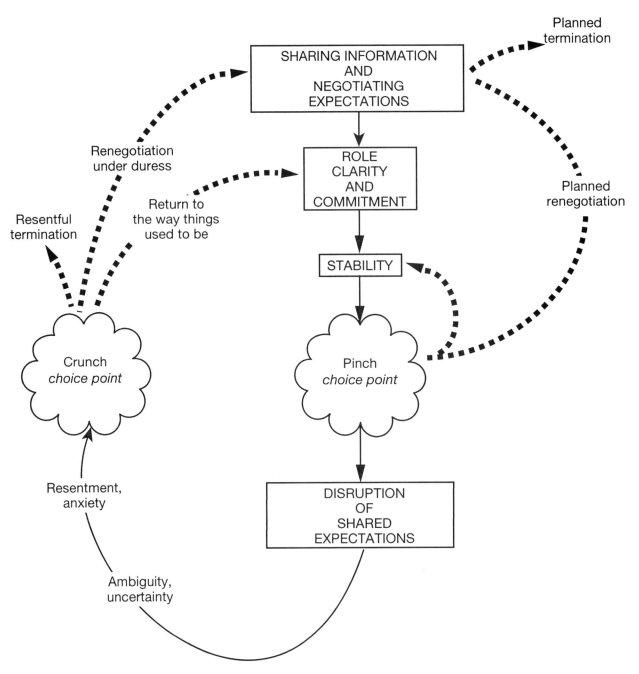

(From J.J. Sherwood and J.C. Glidewell. Used with permission.)

Organizational Behavior: An Experiential Approach 6/E
David A. Kolb, Joyce S. Osland and Irwin M. Rubin

# T2-0 YOUNG LADY

# T2-1 OLD LADY

Organizational Behavior: An Experiential Approach 6/E
David A. Kolb, Joyce S. Osland and Irwin M. Rubin

© 1995 by Prentice-Hall, Inc.
A Simon & Schuster Company
Englewood Cliffs, New Jersey 07632

# T2-2 OLD LADY / YOUNG LADY

Organizational Behavior: An Experiential Approach 6/E
David A. Kolb, Joyce S. Osland and Irwin M. Rubin

© 1995 by Prentice-Hall, Inc.
A Simon & Schuster Company
Englewood Cliffs, New Jersey 07632

# T2-3 ROBERT QUINN'S COMPETING VALUES MODEL OF LEADERSHIP

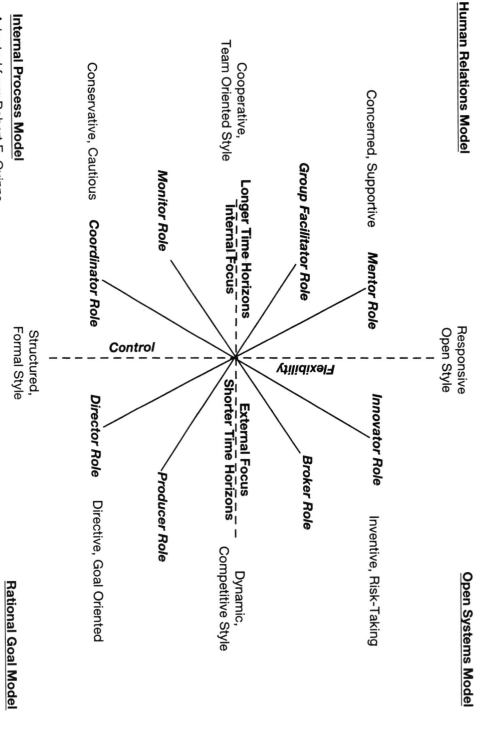

Organizational Behavior: An Experiential Approach 6/E
David A. Kolb, Joyce S. Osland and Irwin M. Rubin

© 1995 by Prentice-Hall, Inc.
A Simon & Schuster Company
Englewood Cliffs, New Jersey 07632

# T2-4 THE POSITIVE AND NEGATIVE ZONES

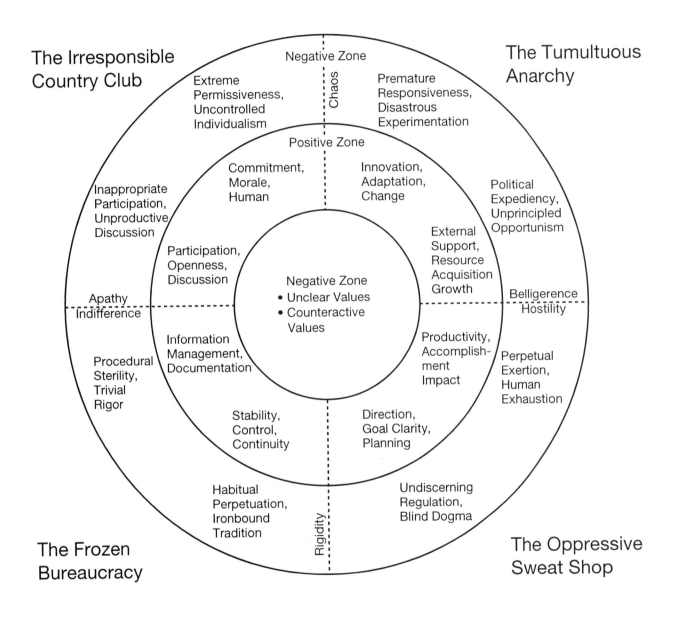

Organizational Behavior: An Experiential Approach 6/E
David A. Kolb, Joyce S. Osland and Irwin M. Rubin

© 1995 by Prentice-Hall, Inc.
A Simon & Schuster Company
Englewood Cliffs, New Jersey 07632

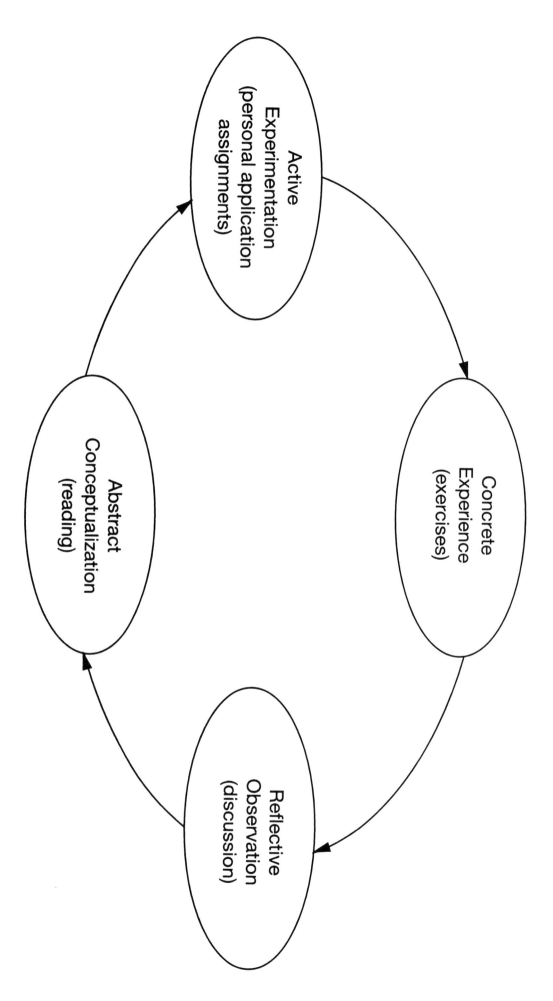

# T3-1 LEARNING STYLE TYPE GRID

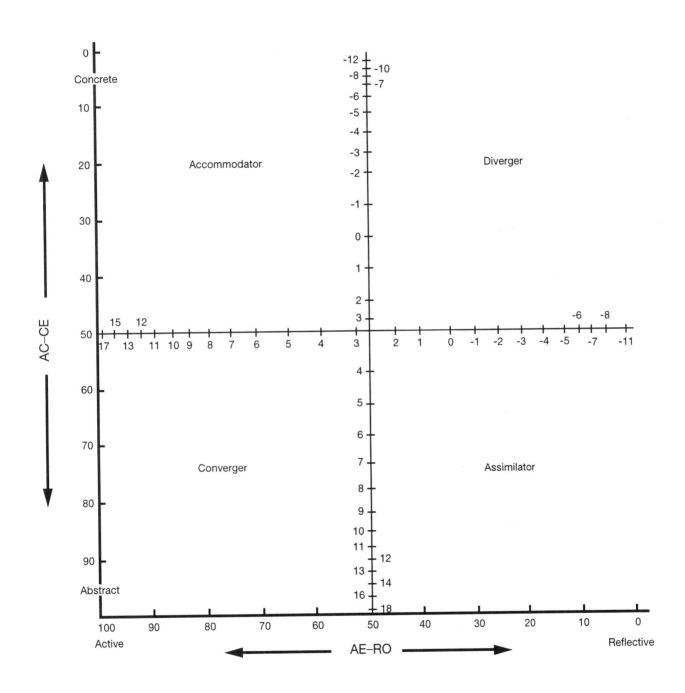

Organizational Behavior: An Experiential Approach 6/E
David A. Kolb, Joyce S. Osland and Irwin M. Rubin

© 1995 by Prentice-Hall, Inc.
A Simon & Schuster Company
Englewood Cliffs, New Jersey 07632

# T4-0 DAVID MCCLELLAND'S MAJOR MOTIVES

| Motive | Need | Typical Behavior | Typical Leader/Manager Level |
|---|---|---|---|
| (n-Ach) Need for Achievement | To improve, do better<br>• Achieve personal and others' standard of excellence<br>• Unique accomplishment<br>• Long-term career involvement | • Set goals and measures outcome<br>• Takes calculated (moderate) risks<br>• Likes immediate, concrete feedback<br>• Takes responsibility for own success or failures<br>• Likes to work alone | Entrepreneurs |
| (n-Aff) Need for Affiliation | To have warm, close relationships:<br>• Have friends<br>• Establish friendship<br>• Sustain relationships<br>• Avoid conflict | • Prefers to work with others<br>• Holds meetings<br>• Participates in friendly activities<br>• Writes letters, sends cards, and calls | Supervisors |
| (n-Pow) Need for Power | To impact others:<br>• Influence others<br>• Impress others<br>• Lead others<br>• Control others | • Seeks leadership<br>• Seeks prestige for self and organization<br>• Gives unsolicited help and advice<br>• Displays strong, forceful behavior<br>• Competitive | Middle-Upper-Level Managers |

## T4-1 EXPECTANCY THEORY

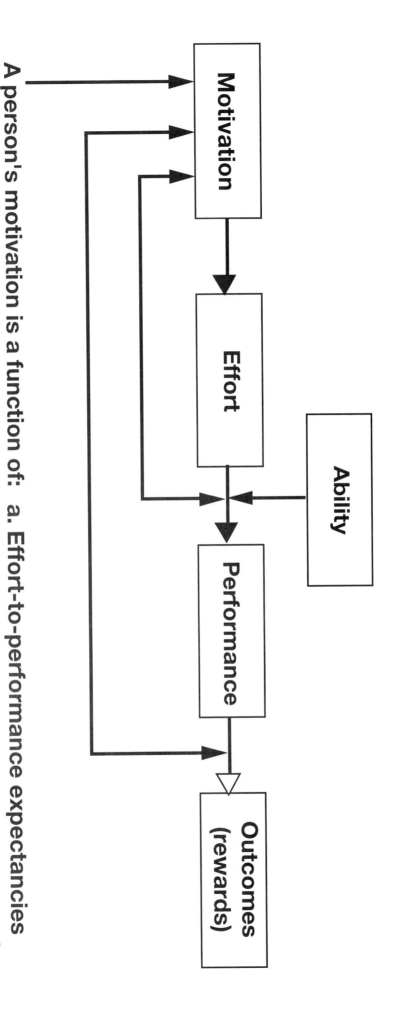

A person's motivation is a function of:
a. Effort-to-performance expectancies
b. Performance-to-outcome expectancies
c. Perceived valence of outcomes

# T5-0 THREE LEVELS OF MORAL DEVELOPMENT ACCORDING TO KOHLBERG

| Stage | What is considered to be right |
|---|---|
| **Level One-Self-centered (Preconventional)** | |
| Stage One—obedience and Punishment Orientation | Sticking to rules to avoid physical punishment. Obedience for its own sake. |
| Stage Two-Instrumental Purpose and Exchange | Following rules only when it is in one's immediate interest. Right is an equal exchange, a fair deal. |
| **Level Two-Conformity (Conventional)** | |
| Stage Three-Interpersonal Accord, Conformity, Mutual Expectations | Stereotypical "good" behavior. Living up to what is expected by peers and people close to you. |
| Stage Four-Social Accord and System Maintenance | Fulfilling duties and obligations of social system. Upholding laws except in extreme cases where they conflict with fixed social duties. Contributing to the society, group. |
| **Level Three-Principled (Postconventioal)** | |
| Stage Five-Social Contract Individual Rights | Being aware that people hold a variety of values; that rules are relative to the group upholding rules becouse they are the social contact. Upholding nonrelative values and rights regardless of majority opinion. |
| Stage Six-Universal Ethical Principles | Following self-chosen ethical principles of justice and rights. When laws violate principles, act in accord with principles. |

Source: Adapted from Kohlberg by Linda K Trevino, " A Cultural Perspective on Changing and Developing Organizational Ethics," in Research in Organizationa Change and Development (Eds.) W.A. Pasmore and R.W. Woodman, (Greenwich, CT: JAI Press, 1990) p.198.

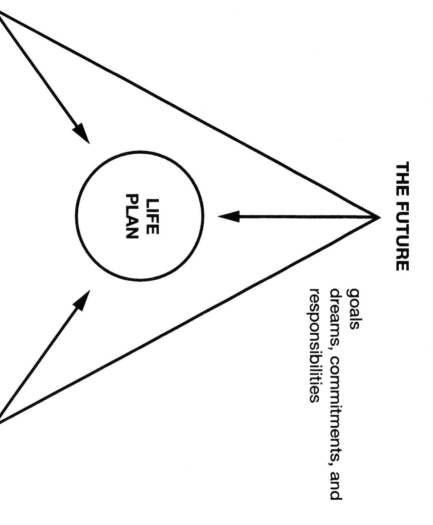

# T6-0 TRIPOD OF LIFE PLAN PERSPECTIVES

**THE PAST**
experiences, skills, and achievements

**THE FUTURE**
goals dreams, commitments, and responsibilities

**THE PRESENT**
current satisfactions/frustrations, present life situations, and time commitments

LIFE PLAN

# T6-1 TRANSACTIONAL MODEL OF CAREER STRESS

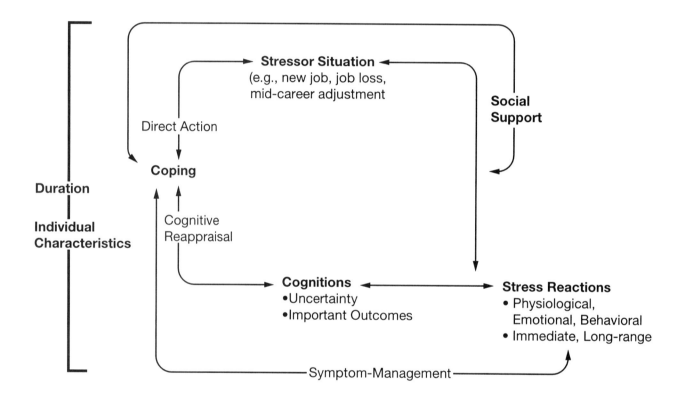

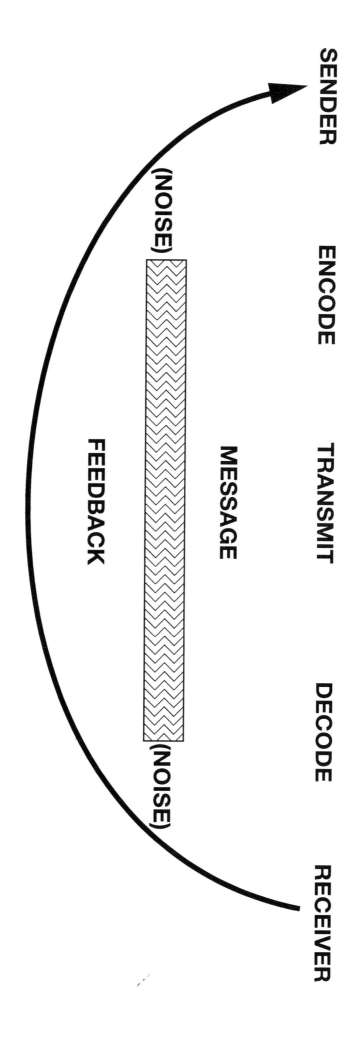

# T7-1 ARC OF DISTORTION

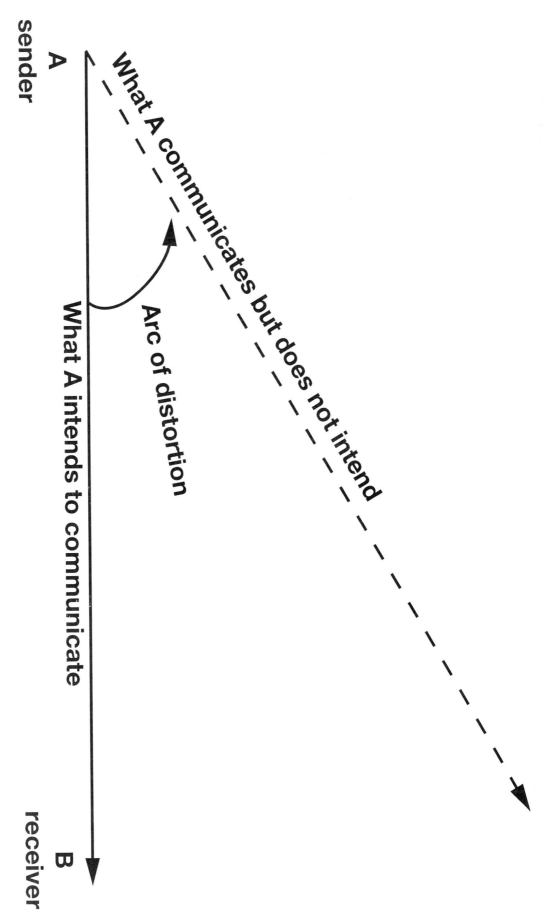

**T7-2. Categories of Behavior Characteristic of Supportive and Defensive Climates in Small Groups**

| Defensive Climates | Supportive Climates |
|---|---|
| 1. Evaluation | 1. Description |
| 2. Control | 2. Problem orientation |
| 3. Strategy | 3. Spontaneity |
| 4. Neutrality | 4. Empathy |
| 5. Superiority | 5. Equality |
| 6. Certainty | 6. Provisionalism |

# T8-0 JOHARI WINDOW

|  | Known to Self | Not Known to Self |
|---|---|---|
| **Known to Others** | Arena | Blindspot |
| **Not Known to Others** | Facade | Unknown |

Organizational Behavior: An Experiential Approach 6/E
David A. Kolb, Joyce S. Osland and Irwin M. Rubin

© 1995 by Prentice-Hall, Inc.
A Simon & Schuster Company
Englewood Cliffs, New Jersey 07632

# T8-1 COUNT THE SQUARES

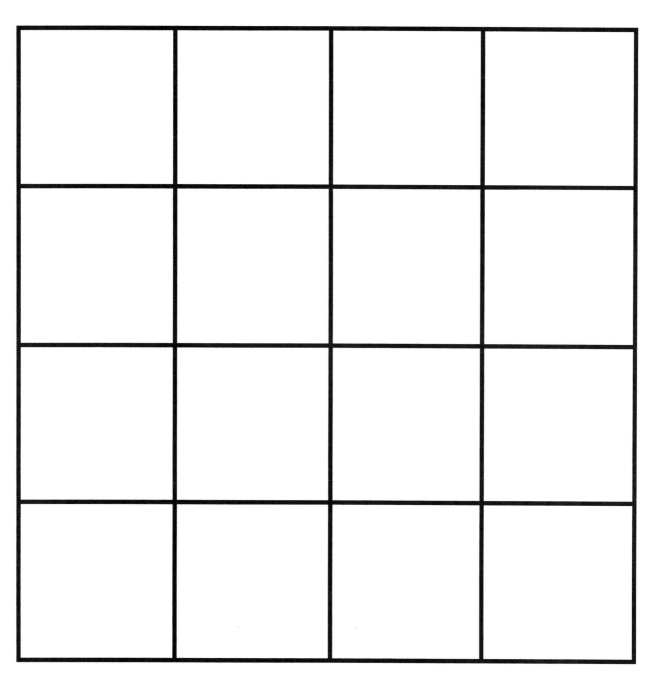

How many squares do you see

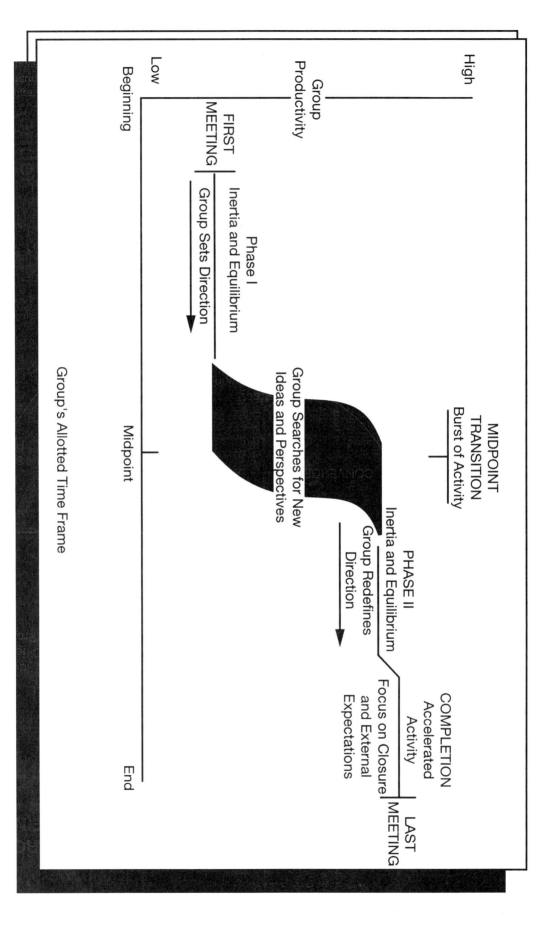

**T9-1 "PURE TYPES" OF EMOTIONAL BEHAVIOR IN ORGANIZATIONS**

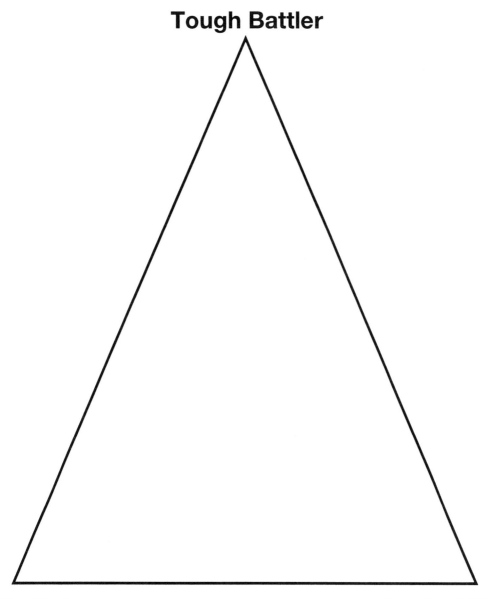

# T9-2 SYMPTOMS OF GROUPTHINK

- ILLUSION OF INVULNERABILITY
- ILLUSION OF MORALITY
- RATIONALIZATION
- STEREOTYPING
- SELF-CENSORSHIP
- ILLUSION OF UNANIMITY
- DIRECT PRESSURE ON DISSIDENTS
- RELIANCE ON SELF-APPOINTED MINDGUARDS

# T9-3 REMEDIES FOR GROUPTHINK

LEADER ASSIGNS ROLE OF CRITICAL EVALUATOR TO EACH MEMBER AND ACCEPTS CRITICISM

TOP MANAGEMENT ADOPTS AN IMPARTIAL STANCE TOWARDS POLICY PLANNING MISSIONS CARRIED OUT BY SUBORDINATES

UTILIZATION OF SEVERAL OUTSIDE POLICY-PLANNING AND EVALUATION GROUPS TO WORK ON THE SAME POLICY QUESTIONS, EACH DELIBERATING UNDER A DIFFERENT LEADER

AT INTERVALS EACH MEMBER DISCUSSES THE GROUP'S DELIBERATIONS WITH ASSOCIATES IN THEIR OWN UNITS AND REPORTS THEIR REACTIONS BACK TO THE GROUP

THE GROUP INVITES OUTSIDE EXPERTS TO MEETINGS AND ENCOURAGES THE EXPERTS TO CHALLENGE THE VIEWS OF CORE MEMBERS

ASSIGN A DEVIL'S ADVOCATE TO CHALLENGE THOSE WHO ADVOCATE THE MAJORITY POSITION

EXAMINE ALTERNATIVES FOR FEASIBILITY AND EFFECTIVENESS IN SUBGROUPS WITH DIFFERENT LEADERS

HAVE A "SECOND-CHANCE" MEETING AT WHICH EVERYONE EXPRESSES ALL HIS OR HER RESIDUAL DOUBTS ABOUT A PRELIMINARY CONSENSUS BEFORE MAKING A DEFINITIVE CHOICE

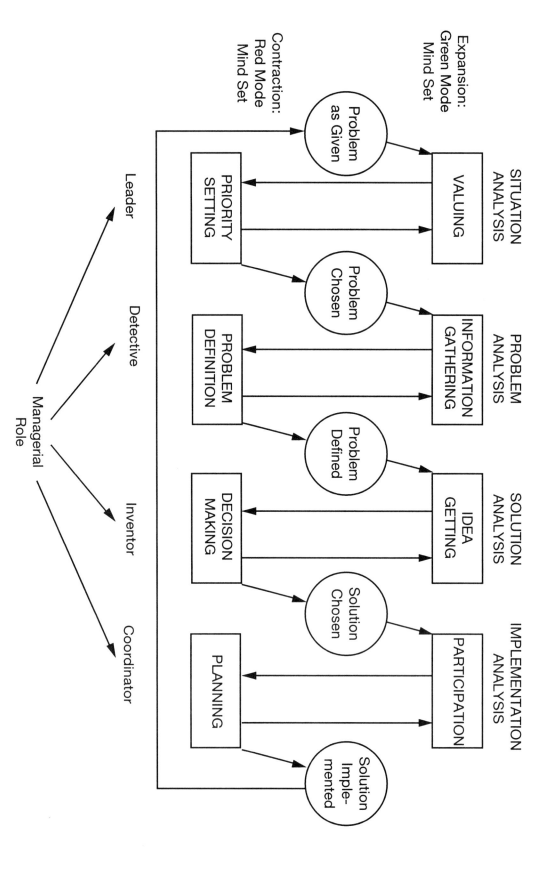

# T10-1 THE LEARNING MODEL AND THE PROBLEM-SOLVING PROCESS

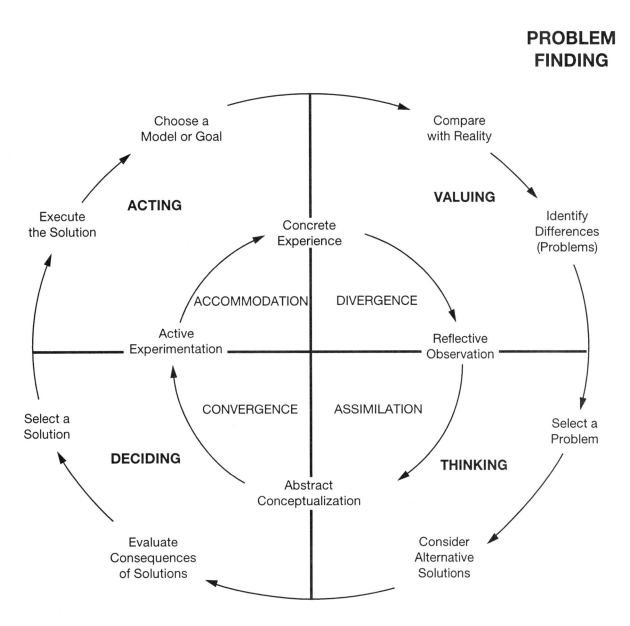

Organizational Behavior: An Experiential Approach 6/E
David A. Kolb, Joyce S. Osland and Irwin M. Rubin

## T11-0 FIVE CONFLICT-HANDLING ORIENTATIONS

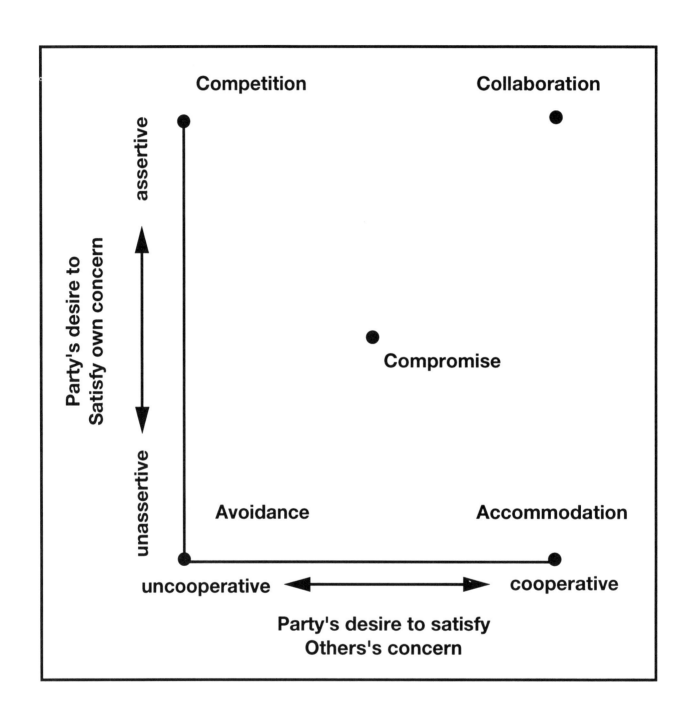

Organizational Behavior: An Experiential Approach 6/E
David A. Kolb, Joyce S. Osland and Irwin M. Rubin

© 1995 by Prentice-Hall, Inc.
A Simon & Schuster Company
Englewood Cliffs, New Jersey 07632

# T12-0 GEERT HOFSTEDE'S FOUR VALUE DIMENSIONS OF NATIONAL CULTURE

### A. Power Distance Dimension

### B. Uncertainty Avoidance Dimension

### C. Individualism Dimension

### D. Masculinity Dimension

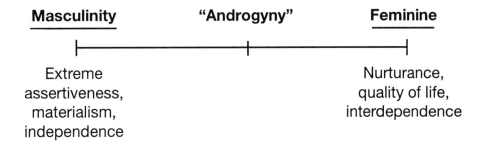

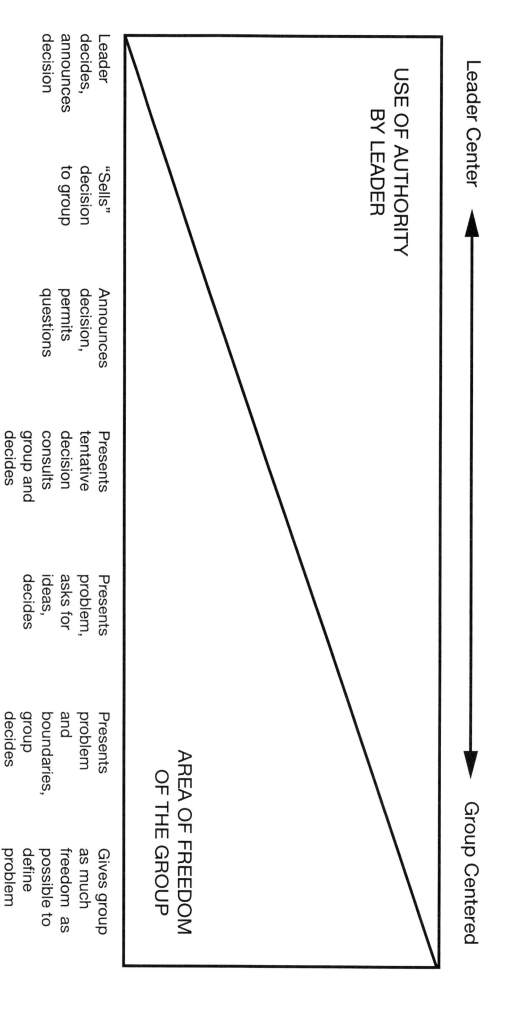

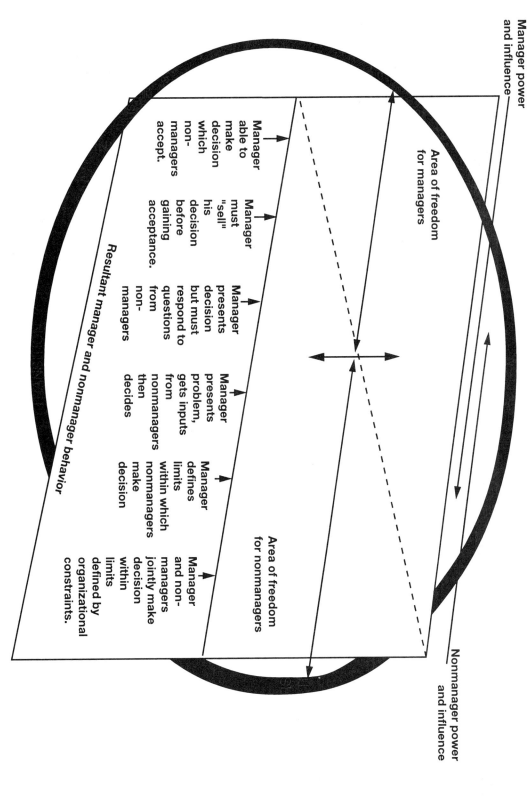

T13-1 CONTINUUM OF MANAGER/NON-MANAGER BEHAVIOR

Organizational Behavior: An Experiential Approach 6/E
David A. Kolb, Joyce S. Osland and Irwin M. Rubin

© 1995 by Prentice-Hall, Inc.
A Simon & Schuster Company
Englewood Cliffs, New Jersey 07632

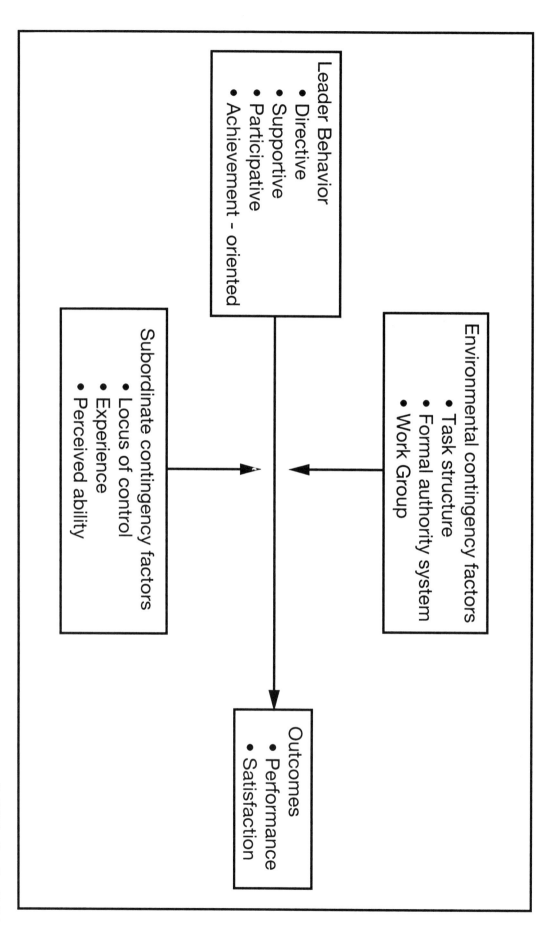

T13-2 THE PATH GOAL THEORY

# T14-0 THE FIVE PHASES OF GROWTH

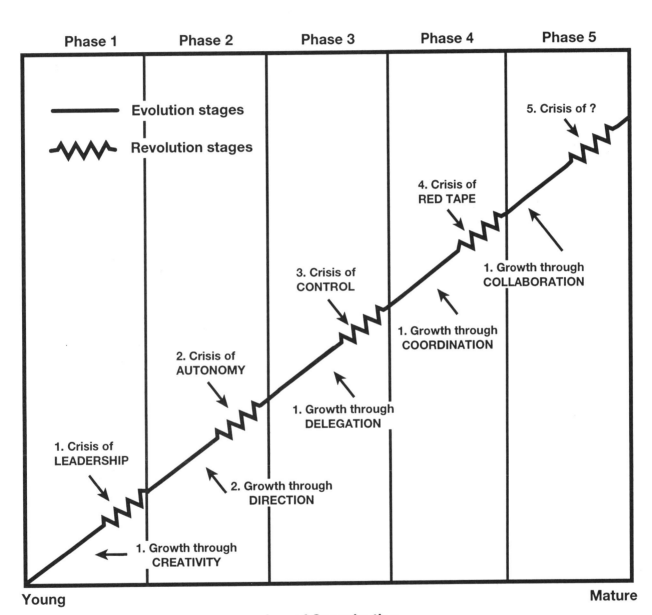

Organizational Behavior: An Experiential Approach 6/E
David A. Kolb, Joyce S. Osland and Irwin M. Rubin

# T15-0 DECISION PROCESS FLOW CHART

| | | |
|---|---|---|
| QR | Quality Requirment | Is there a quality requirement such that one solution is likely to be more rational than another? Does it really matter which solution is chosen? |
| LI | Leader's information | Do I have sufficient info to make a high-quality decision? |
| ST | Problem structure | Is the problem structured? |
| AR | Acceptance Requirement | Is subordinate commitment to the decision critical to effective implementation? |
| AP | Acceptance Probability | If I were to make the decision by myself, is it reasonably certain that my subordinates would be committed to the decision? |
| GC | Goal Congruence | Do subordinates share the organizational goals to be obtained in solving the problem? |
| CO | Subordinate Conflict | Is conflict among subordinates likely in preferred solutions? (This is irrelevant to individual problems.) |
| SI | Subordinate Information | Do subordinates have sufficient info to make a high quality decision? (This applies only to the indiividual problems.) |

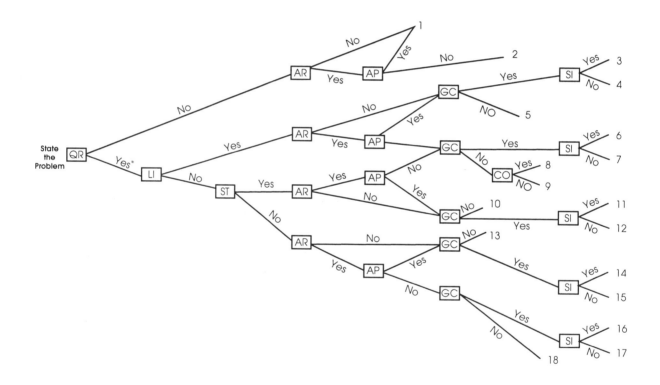

Organizational Behavior: An Experiential Approach 6/E
David A. Kolb, Joyce S. Osland and Irwin M. Rubin

© 1995 by Prentice-Hall, Inc.
A Simon & Schuster Company
Englewood Cliffs, New Jersey 07632

# T16-0 DEFINITION OF INFLUENCE TACTICS

| | |
|---|---|
| Rational Persuasion: | The agent uses logical arguments and factual evidence to persuade the target that a proposal or request is viable and likely to result in the attainment of task objectives. |
| Inspirational Appeals: | The agent makes a request or proposal that arouses target enthusiasm by appealing to target values, ideals, and aspirations, or by increasing target self-confidence. |
| Consultation: | The agent seeks target participation in planning a strategy, activity, or change for which target support and assistance are desired, or is willing to modify a proposal to deal with target concerns and suggestions. |
| Ingratiation: | The agent uses praise, flattery, friendly behavior, or helpful behavior to get the target in a good mood or to think favorably of him or her before asking for something. |
| Personal Appeals: | The agent appeals to target feelings of loyalty and friendship toward him or her when asking for something. |
| Exchange: | The agent offers an exchange of favors, indicates willing-ness to reciprocate at a later time, or promises a share of the benefits if the target helps accomplish a task. |
| Coalition Tactics: | The agent seeks the aid of others to persuade the target to do something, or uses the support of others as a reason for the target to agree also. |
| Legitimating Tactics: | The agent seeks to establish the legitimacy of a request by claiming the authority or right to make it, or by verifying that it is consistent with organizational policies, rules, practices, or traditions. |
| Pressure: | The agent uses demands, threats, frequent checking, or persistent reminders to influence the target to do what he or she wants. |

Source: Adapted from Gary Yukl, Leadership in Organizations (Englewood Cliffs, NJ: Prentice Hall, 1994) p. 225.

# T16-1 INFLUENCE STYLES

**PUSH STYLES:**

### ASSERTIVE PERSUASION (INTELLECT)

BEHAVIORS: REASONING, DEBATING, PRESENTING IDEAS PROPOSALS, AND SUGGESTIONS THAT INVOLVE FACTS AND LOGIC

LANGUAGE: I SUGGEST WE ADOPT THE SECOND PROPOSAL FOR THE FOLLOWING THREE REASONS.

### REWARD AND PUNISHMENT (WILL)

BEHAVIORS: STATING EXPECTATIONS, USING INCENTIVES AND PRESSURES, EVALUATING, DEMANDING, BARGAINING

LANGUAGE: I EXPECT YOU TO BE AT WORK ON TIME. IF YOU ARE LATE, I WILL HAVE TO DOCK YOUR PAY.

**PULL STYLES:**

### PARTICIPATION AND TRUST (TRUST)

BEHAVIORS: UNDERSTANDING, INVOLVING AND SUPPORTING OTHERS, PERSONAL DISCLOSURE, ACTIVE LISTENING

LANGUAGE: WHAT DO THE REST OF YOU THINK WE SHOULD DO?

### COMMON VISION (HOPE)

BEHAVIORS: INSPIRING, VISIONING, FINDING COMMON GROUND, ALIGNING

LANGUAGE: IMAGINE WHAT WE COULD ACCOMPLISH IF WE WORKED TOGETHER.

Organizational Behavior: An Experiential Approach 6/E
David A. Kolb, Joyce S. Osland and Irwin M. Rubin

© 1995 by Prentice-Hall, Inc.
A Simon & Schuster Company
Englewood Cliffs, New Jersey 07632

# T17-0 EFFECTIVE AND INEFFECTIVE FEEDBACK

| EFFECTIVE | INEFFECTIVE |
|---|---|
| DESCRIPTIVE | EVALUATIVE |
| SPECIFIC AND DATA BASED | GENERAL |
| DIRECTED TOWARD CONTROLLABLE BEHAVIORS | PERSONALITY TRAITS |
| SOLICITED | IMPOSED |
| CLOSE TO THE EVENT | DELAYED |
| OCCURS WHEN RECEIVER IS READY TO ACCEPT IT | OCCURS AT CONVENIENCE OF SENDER |
| SUGGESTS | PRESCRIBES |
| IS INTENDED TO HELP | IS INTENDED TO PUNISH |

Organizational Behavior: An Experiential Approach 6/E
David A. Kolb, Joyce S. Osland and Irwin M. Rubin

© 1995 by Prentice-Hall, Inc.
A Simon & Schuster Company
Englewood Cliffs, New Jersey 07632

# T18-0 GENERAL BELIEFS ABOUT PERFORMANCE APPRAISAL

| | | Disagree | Neutral | Agree |
|---|---|---|---|---|
| 1. PA should be done only for the subordinate's personal development | appraisers<br>subordinates | 78<br>71 | 7<br>9 | 15<br>20 |
| 2. Salary and promotion decisions should be based on PA results | appraisers<br>subordinates | 5<br>12 | 3<br>3 | 92<br>85 |
| 3. Salary and promotion decisions are based on PA results | appraisers<br>subordinates | 24<br>41 | 8<br>10 | 68<br>49 |
| 4. PA practices provide accurate feedback of the subordinates and superiors and subordinates agree on what constitutes good and poor performance | appraisers<br>subordinates | 22<br>36 | 6<br>8 | 72<br>55 |
| 5. PA makes a difference. It motivates employees, leads to more productive behavior, and increases understanding about the subordinate's role. | appraisers<br>subordinates | 17<br>25 | 9<br>13 | 74<br>62 |
| 6. Superiors and subordinates carry out PA activities only because the organization requires it | appraisers<br>subordinates | 35<br>28 | 8<br>9 | 57<br>63 |
| 7. Subordinate's PA should be based on goals previously agreed to by the superior and subordinate. | appraisers<br>subordinates | 4<br>8 | 3<br>5 | 93<br>87 |
| 8. A subordinate's self-appraisal should be an important part of PA. | appraisers<br>subordinates | 6<br>8 | 4<br>6 | 90<br>86 |

Adapted from "Performance Appraisal Revised" by E. Lawler III; A. Mochman, Jr.; S. Resnick. Used with permission.

Organizational Behavior: An Experiential Approach 6/E
David A. Kolb, Joyce S. Osland and Irwin M. Rubin

© 1995 by Prentice-Hall, Inc.
A Simon & Schuster Company
Englewood Cliffs, New Jersey 07632

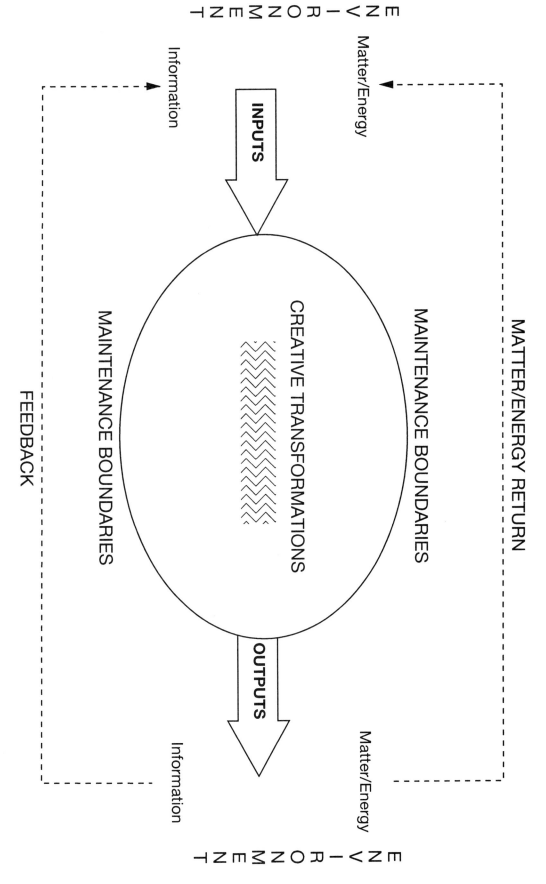

# T19-1 THE OPEN SYSTEM VIEW OF ORGANIZATIONS

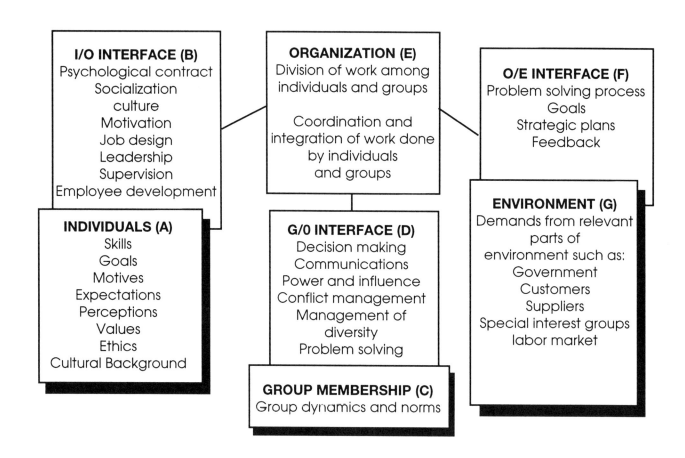

Organizational Behavior: An Experiential Approach 6/E
David A. Kolb, Joyce S. Osland and Irwin M. Rubin

© 1995 by Prentice-Hall, Inc.
A Simon & Schuster Company
Englewood Cliffs, New Jersey 07632

# T20-0 FUNCTIONAL FORM OF ORGANIZATION

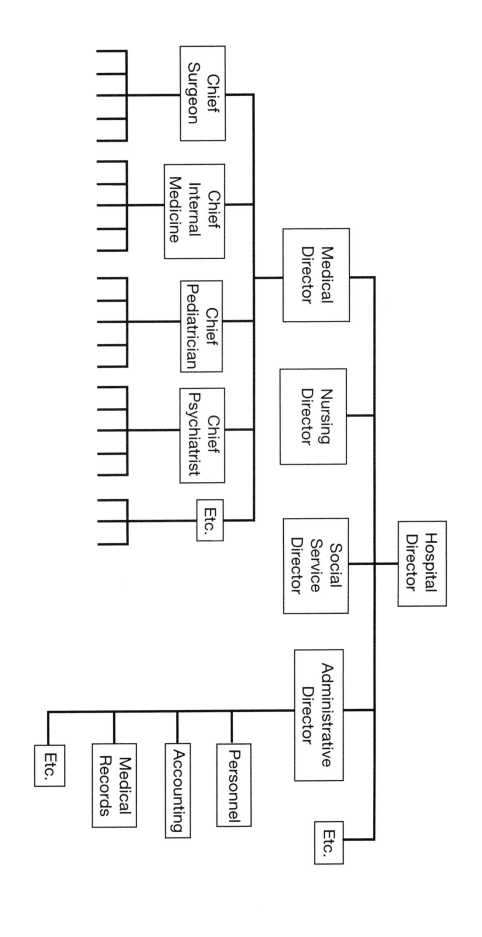

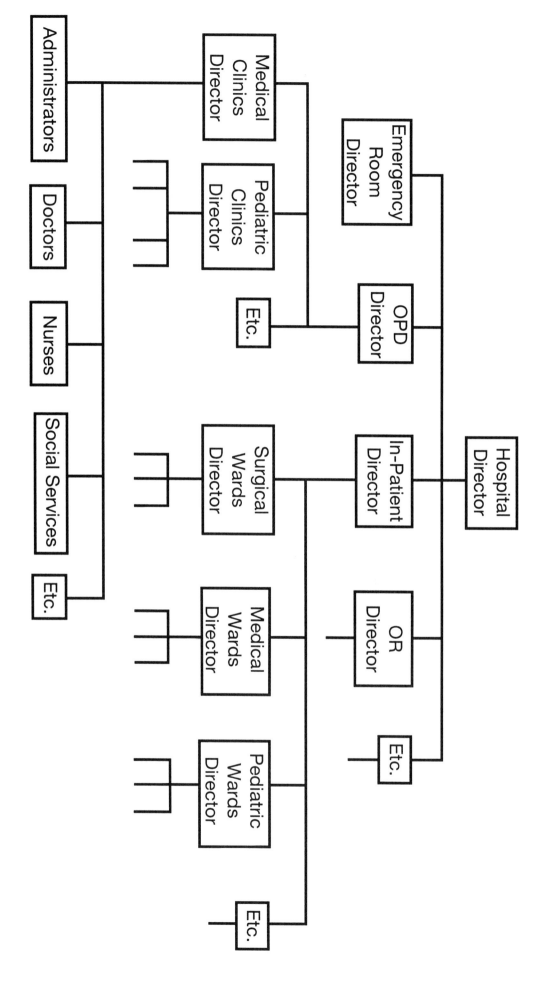

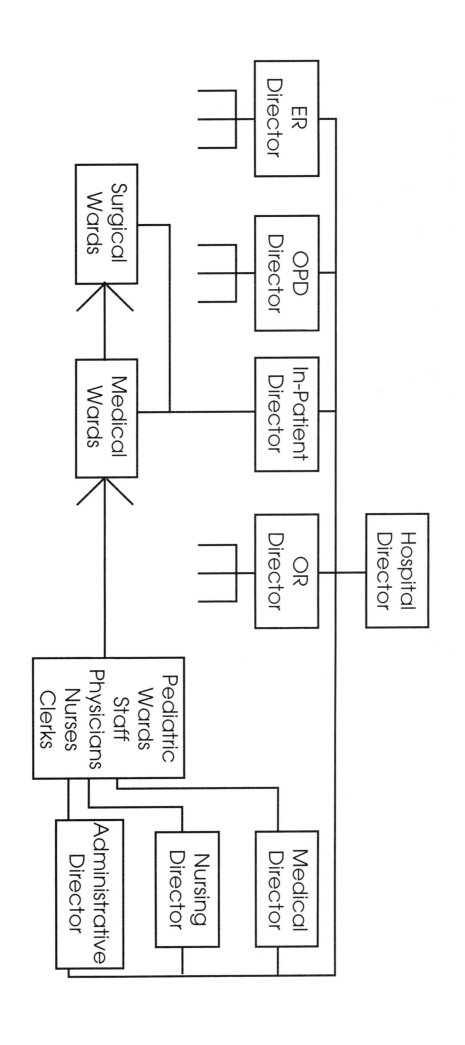

T20-2 MATRIX FORM OF ORGANIZATION

# T20-2 MATRIX FORM OF ORGANIZATION

```
                          Hospital
                          Director
                              |
    ┌─────────────┬───────────┼───────────┬─────────────┐
    |             |           |           |             |
   ER           OPD       In-Patient     OR
 Director    Director     Director    Director
                              |
              ┌───────────────┼───────────────┐
              |               |               |
          Surgical         Medical        Pediatric
           Wards            Wards           Wards
                                              |
                              ┌───────┬───────┼───────┐
                              |       |       |       |
                          Medical  Nursing  Administrative  Etc.
                          Director Director   Director
```

Organizational Behavior: An Experiential Approach 6/E
David A. Kolb, Joyce S. Osland and Irwin M. Rubin

© 1995 by Prentice-Hall, Inc.
A Simon & Schuster Company
Englewood Cliffs, New Jersey 07632

# T21-0 JOB CHARACTERISTICS ENRICHMENT MODEL

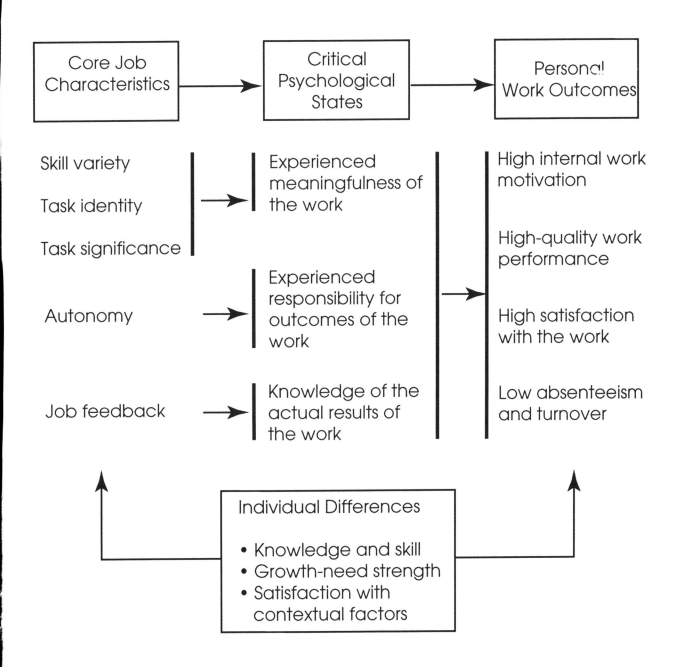

Organizational Behavior: An Experiential Approach 6/E
David A. Kolb, Joyce S. Osland and Irwin M. Rubin

© 1995 by Prentice-Hall, Inc.
A Simon & Schuster Company
Englewood Cliffs, New Jersey 07632

# T22-0 THE PROCESS OF PLANNED CHANGE

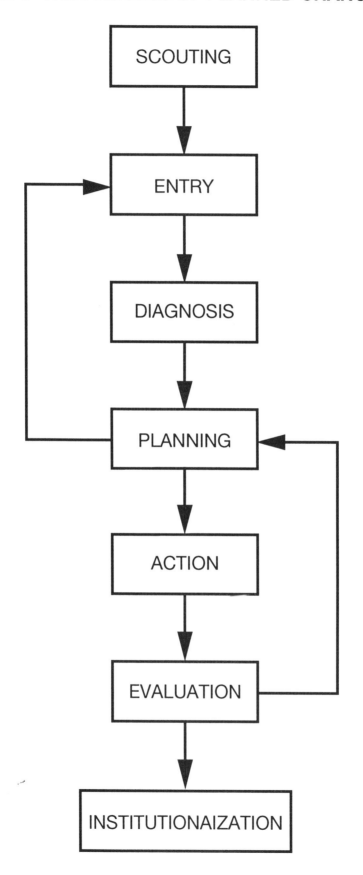

Organizational Behavior: An Experiential Approach 6/E
David A. Kolb, Joyce S. Osland and Irwin M. Rubin

© 1995 by Prentice-Hall, Inc.
A Simon & Schuster Company
Englewood Cliffs, New Jersey 07632